The Nuclear We
Theological and ~~Ethical Issues~~

The
NUCLEAR WEAPONS DEBATE

Theological and Ethical Issues

EDITED BY

Richard J. Bauckham

AND

R. John Elford

SCM PRESS

British Library Cataloguing in Publication Data

The nuclear weapons debate.
1. Nuclear warfare – Christian viewpoint
I. Bauckham, Richard   II. Elford, R. John
261.8'73

ISBN 0-334-01140-X

First published 1989
by SCM Press Ltd
26–30 Tottenham Road, London N1 4BZ

Phototypeset by Input Typesetting Ltd, London
and printed in Great Britain by
The Camelot Press Ltd, Southampton

Contents

The Contributors

Dr Sydney D. Bailey is a Quaker active in the Ecumenical Movement regarding international affairs

Dr Richard Bauckham is Reader in the History of Christian Thought, Department of Theological Studies, University of Manchester

General Sir Hugh Beach is Director, The Council for Arms Control, and was previously Warden, St George's House, Windsor Castle

Revd Keith W. Clements is Senior Tutor, Bristol Baptist College

Professor Anthony Dyson is Samuel Ferguson Professor of Social and Pastoral Theology, University of Manchester

Dr R. John Elford is Pro-Rector, Head of College, St Katharine's College, Liverpool Institute of Higher Education

Dr John J. Haldane is Lecturer in Moral Philosophy and Director of the Centre for Philosophy and Public Affairs, University of St Andrews

Professor Donald M. MacKinnon was formerly Norris-Hulse Professor of Divinity, University of Cambridge

Professor Simon S. Maimela is Chair, Department of Systematic Theology, University of South Africa, Pretoria

Professor Ronald H. Preston is Emeritus Professor of Social and Pastoral Theology, University of Manchester, and Canon Emeritus of Manchester Cathedral

Dr Geoffrey L. Price is Lecturer, Department of Theological Studies, University of Manchester

Revd J. K. Riches is Senior Lecturer in Biblical Studies, University of Glasgow

Professor Gillian White is Professor of International Law and Dean of the Faculty of Law, University of Manchester

Professor Rowan D. Williams is Lady Margaret Professor of Divinity, University of Oxford

The editors gratefully acknowledge that the preparation of this volume was assisted by a research grant from the University of Manchester

Introduction

JOHN ELFORD

The history of attempts to control the possession and use of the weapons of warfare is as old as Western civilization, but it has assumed an urgent imperative in the modern world. The reason for this is the nature, size, proliferation, and increasing accuracy of modern weapons systems in general and of nuclear ones in particular. All this is compounded by the uses to which nuclear weapons have been put in the military strategies of their possessors. They have become, in the space of fifty years, an integral part of international relations, defence and diplomacy, at least among the super powers. Their possessors all claim that they are deployed for defensive purposes alone, but this seeming passivity is exacerbated by the fact that they are designed and deployed for use, the credibility of which is an essential feature of their alleged deterrent capacity. The potential nature of such uses is ever-changing with the appearance of new technologies and this is a major cause of the endemic arms races.

There have always been those who, even if not opposed to the use of force in general, have nonetheless been specifically opposed to the possession, deployment and possible use of nuclear weapons. The burden of this, until very recently, has been to create a polarization of opinion between those so opposed to them and those who, even if reluctantly, accept their necessity. These latter, however, have acknowledged the need for their control, but have invariably insisted that this should only be contemplated if possessors act multilaterally, thereby maintaining the balances on which the effectiveness of the deployments as deterrents is claimed to depend. Hence participation in the debate about nuclear weapons has been polarized between those opposed to them in principle (unilateralists) and those not so (multilateralists). Such a conceptual polarization is no longer adequate and can be misleading. There are a number of reasons for this.

Chief among them is the growing realization by all that the security of nations and their alliances cannot depend indefinitely on unchecked nuclear deployments, along with a steadily growing awareness that such deployments may well themselves impede the creation of the degrees of international trust and co-operation which are a necessary pre-condition of arms control agreements. In practice, we do not know if trust and peace are a pre-condition of disarmament in general, or whether they are the consequences of it. Which is why we have to work assiduously for both at all times. Whereas until very recently, there was only deadlock and even despair in the face of the task, we now thankfully have the INF Treaty Agreement of May 1988 and the more recent USSR commitments to unilateral reductions in its conventional forces and some of its tactical nuclear weapons in Eastern Europe. This has brought a renewed determination generally to seek other more far-reaching agreements which will bring even more extensive reductions in nuclear deployments. We should now hope for a combination of multi- and uni-lateral agreements and with that the erosion of the formerly held supposition that these approaches are exclusively alternative ones. These achievements and the degree of optimism they raise provide no reason for complacency. Quite the reverse. They call for a renewal, also, of every form of activity which can build on, consolidate, and make possible a future in which the present overwhelming extent of the deployments is reduced to at least manageable levels. Whilst these may never be zero ones, that is no reason for despair.

For reasons which are essayed in this volume throughout, Western Christianity has long been engaged in the quest for the control of force in general and of military force in particular. That engagement has, furthermore, been particularly evident since the dawn of the nuclear age in 1945 and has been especially so in the last decade. Whilst much of this engagement has been by individual labour, the greater part of it has come about as a result of official working parties appointed by the World Council of Churches, the British Council of Churches and churches individually.

In 1945 the BCC published *The Era of Atomic Power* and the debate which followed in the General Assembly of the Church of England called for more information. That, in turn, led to the publication of *The Church and the Atom* in 1948. Whilst recognizing that the indiscriminate and disproportionate use of nuclear weapons could never be tolerated morally, the Report did contemplate the moral acceptability of their limited use against specifically identified targets. It must be remembered that this Report was written in the shadow of Hiroshima and Nagasaki and, also, in the then prevailing general ignorance about the harmful effects of radiation, short and long-term. Nor could the Report have been expected to anticipate the unimaginable increase in the size and proliferation of nuclear weapons. *The Church and the Atom* can now, rightly, be seen as a period piece, but the nature of its arguments and general manner of its approach can be said to have set a standard by which subsequent discussions of its type were to be judged.

Since 1948 there have been a number of such reports. The BCC produced *The British Nuclear Deterrent* in 1963 and the Church of England addressed itself briefly to the subject in *International Morality; an Agenda for the Churches* in 1969. This was followed by *Force in the Modern World* from the Board for Social Responsibility of the Church of England in 1974 and *Christians in a Violent World* in 1979.[1]

The present decade has seen renewed efforts of this kind. Four major church reports have appeared. The first *The Church and the Bomb* (1982) attempts three things; to describe the technological, military and political nature of the problem: to outline the theological resources with which it can be approached; and to argue why these resources pointed towards specific policy options for peace, as well as noting others. These specific options were variously received but were not approved by the General Synod of the Church of England when it debated them in 1983, although the Synod did pass a resolution opposing the first use of nuclear weapons. *The Church and the Bomb* did help, however, to provoke considerable debate and a number of volumes accordingly appeared.[2]

Simultaneously with research leading to *The Church and the Bomb*, the WCC requested its Sub-units on Church and Society and the Commission of the Churches on International Affairs 'to arrange jointly an international public hearing on the current threat to world peace with special focus on the increased danger of nuclear war.'[3] The report, *Before it's too Late* appeared in 1983. Its extensive multidisciplinary discussions remain an important contribution to the debate, principally because, rather than press for specific conclusions to it, they critically essayed the relevant issues and options.

In North America the United States National Conference of Bishops published the Pastoral letter, *The Challenge of Peace: God's Promise and our Response* in 1983. All three of these reports are critically discussed in Chapter 7. More recently, the Board for Social Responsibility of the Church of England has published *Peacemaking in a Nuclear Age*, 1988. Here there is less urgency to identify specific policy options for peace, a feature made possible, no doubt, by the fact that unlike the earlier three reports it was written in the knowledge of the changed, or about to change situation in the arms deadlock. This report is more inclined to accept the necessity of nuclear deterrence strategies, than some others have been and it does not subject this to the rigour of examination to be found in the earlier works mentioned.

All four of these reports, appearing as they have done in the short space of five to six years, provide abundant material for the serious discussion of the nuclear weapons problem from a Christian point of view. But, of course, they far from exhaust the topic. With the possible exception of *Before it's too Late*, their discussion of theological and ethical themes raised many issues which were desiring of longer treatment. This need was partly and well met by a volume published in 1986, *Ethics and Defence* by the Religion and Technology Project of the Church of Scotland under the editorship of Howard Davis. Although the contributors to this volume, generally, accepted the need for a radical change in nuclear weapons defence strategies, the central concern was to attempt the demystification of the arguments which would have to be won for that to occur.

The present volume is offered as a similar contribution to the on-going debate. Its content is primarily, but not exclusively, theological. In addition, there are contributions on ethics, politics and international law. There is no intended systematic relation between the chapters with the result that each contribution stands in its own right, although there has been as much consultation and collaboration between the authors as time and circumstances have allowed. For this reason, no attempt has been made to direct or conform the arguments. Each was individually written from an initial brief. The selection of the topics may be considered idiosyncratic, but they have all been identified as arriving from the previous discussions mentioned. Comparatively little treatment is given to the INF Agreement of May 1988, since the writing largely occurred prior to that date. This is, itself, an indication of the need for constant contributions of this kind as happenings are subjected to on-going analysis.

The flourishing of academic attention to the problem in the Christian churches since 1945, and especially in the present decade, witnesses to the conviction that Christian theological resources have a great deal to contribute to it. More, doubtless, than has yet been essayed. This flourishing, it may be hoped, shows Christian theology at its most earnest. Here it is bereft of its often domesticated innocence, as it addresses nothing less than a central question which bears on the total well-being of the human race. An underlying assumption here draws' deep on Christian convictions. It is the assumption that the Christian view of creation is a cosmic one and one, moreover, which is capable of contemplating a pluralist world of many religions and secular ideologies. One in which the imperative of peace is theologically prior to formally conceived imperatives of Christian world domination. As a religion with specific claims to ultimate truth about the human lot, Christianity has sadly, if understandably, been seen as a religion which lends itself to secular imperialist pretentions. All that is here left aside, as it properly should be. This, in itself, elicits a trust and grace in God's greater purposes for his creation, as the central truths of Christianity are brought to bear with a humility which seeks, in a world of conflict, to make progress in the now crucial quest for peaceful co-existence. In this, older pretentions have to be checked and seen, perhaps, as the cloaked expressions of sinfulness they were. The debate to which this volume is a contribution needs constantly to address 'the two most fundamental questions confronting twentieth-century man, the one social, the other personal, both involve religion: how to turn our nascent world society into a world community, on a group level: and on a personal level, how to find meaning in modern life.'[4]

1

On Comprehending the Threat

DONALD MACKINNON

What is there in the nuclear threat that is new? To answer this question, we may best begin by asking what analogies may be extracted from history, both remote and relatively recent.

1. A comparison has been drawn with the Black Death in the fourteenth century. Certainly its shadow lay dark over 'Merrie England'; men and women knew what it was for their hearts to fail them for fear. But the analogy breaks down because the Black Death was a natural catastrophe; because of the deficiencies of high mediaeval bacteriology, virology and parasitology, its impact could not be met. Immunization and effective treatment were alike inconceivable. Yet there is this in common between the two threats; they are both alike uncontrollable in impact and consequences, even if we say that the nuclear threat is one that we have brought, and are bringing on ourselves. There is an element, more than an element, of the sheerly unknown, even if it is an unknown into which we wilfully precipitate ourselves.

2. More recently there is the Jewish Shoah (or holocaust). Again we must be careful. Those who are prepared e.g. to take the risk of escalation by the use of tactical nuclear weapons are not guilty (at least in intention) of the malevolently planned and carefully executed genocide that we associate with the Nazis. What we should rather consider is the mood of acquiescence which rendered even Churchill powerless to put a spoke in the wheels of the trains that ran to Auschwitz: (and here the testimony of his biographer, Martin Gilbert, is massively impressive). Further we must never forget the complicity of many public servants, doing their duty in that state of life to which it had pleased God to call them, who made possible the smooth running of those ghastly transports in time of global war. Further, as Professor George Steiner has remarked, there were others who were listening to a Kant lecture in Weimar or a Mozart recital in Munich

even as, a few miles away, the freight trucks with their human load were driven on to their terminus.

We have allowed ourselves to take the rubbishing of entire communities as an inevitable feature of life in the twentieth (and twenty-first) centuries. It is as if the scale of the iniquity has become so great that we regard it as a built-in feature of our human environment: or else the very enormity of what has been done somehow atrophies our initial mood of protest, as if we confronted a demonic force that eludes any sort of check or control.

Yet the very consequences of the Shoah (and here we need do no more than remind ourselves of what is presently happening in the 'Gaza Strip') should remind us that here we were faced with a radical deficiency of political will. If 'crisis-management' in the Middle East today is exceptionally difficult for those who would seek to contain the perilous escalation of its conflicts, these difficulties find their source in part at least, in the unparalleled sufferings of European Jewry. We are paying today for the failure of many generations to do other than pass by on the other side in presence of continuing Gentile Christian disdain for the ancient people of God, a disdain which reached its climax of bland disregard in face of the Nazi policy of extermination. Whereas with the Black Death, we have to reckon with something outwith human control, with the Shoah we touch what is a matter of human devising, of sustained and elaborate planning and execution.

Part of the novelty of the nuclear threat lies in our apparent readiness to risk a leap into the unknown which is, to some extent, quite deliberate. The fourteenth-century peasant feared the Black Death as a threat altogether outside his control. It spoke to him of a deity whose ways were inscrutable, whose fiat was absolute. He lived in a spiritual world, which was too often one of darkness, calling for the consolation offered for instance in Mother Julian's *Revelations of Divine Love,* if it was to be remotely bearable. It is not a world into which those who have benefited from the work of the Enlightenment (the target of much ill-informed criticism by contemporary Christian sillies) can easily enter by exercise of their imagination. We are, I suppose, protected from such religious pessimism by our sense that, frightening though the prospect of nuclear escalation undoubtedly is, a remedy may be found to protect us from its terrors, provided that we avoid enervation of political will. If in the fourteenth century the mystical vision of Mother Julian offered light in darkness, the contemporary counterpart would seem to lie in what J. B. Metz, in a very telling phrase, has called 'a hermeneutic of danger'.

Such a hermeneutic must necessarily be many-sided in its reach. It will in part be concerned with cosmological, even metaphysical issues; but it will also be concerned with very mundane political realities. Thus it must take note of the 'economy with the truth' so diligently practised in this area of human concern by our political masters. Hence the revelation in 1988 (under the thirty years rule governing access to public records) of the way in which, thirty years ago, deliberate lies were told concerning the scale of the Windscale-Sellafield accident is highly alarming. The anxiety is intensified when we take note (as daily reports in the press remind us) of our present government's obsession with preserving maximum secrecy, prepared for continual recourse to the courts at home and overseas, in the interest of so-called confidentiality, quick to charge one of its own supporters in the House of Commons with gross impertinence in moving a private member's bill to amend the Official Secrets' Act. It is a paradox that an administration whose spokesmen and spokeswomen praise the virtues of independent initiative, is at the same time relentless in its determination to curtail effective individual scrutiny of its own policies. A 'hermeneutic of danger' must be quick to respond to the spiritual perils involved in this widespread resolve of central government to render its operations immune from any sort of informed interrogation: and this always in the name of state security. Such justification inevitably brands the critic as somehow irresponsible, trifling with the safety of the state in the interests of his own curiosity, or ill-informed personal, moral prejudice.

Yet it is not only the revelations concerning the Windscale-Sellafield affair that should give us pause in this regard, highly significant though such disclosures are for the central concern of this chapter. The secret history of the Suez war of the autumn of 1956 is a disreputable tale of collusion, conspiracy and deceit. Yet in the weeks of the crisis those who, with very good ground, suspected what lay behind the façade, were severely criticized for their irresponsibility, more particularly their seeming indifference to the dangers to which members of the armed forces, committed to the operation, were exposed. Yet the protesters were abundantly justified by the reality; their action was not a flight from historical actuality, but a most perceptive and pertinent comment on it.

A contemporary 'hermeneutic of danger' must be interrogative in mood. Since Socrates the questioner has always found himself or herself at loggerheads with the cherished complacencies of the society to which he or she belongs. The constraints to silence are particularly strong when the range of issues is as complex as those raised by nuclear weaponry; for inevitably these issues reach beyond the immediately political to include those touching 'our posture as human beings under the sun'. The comprehension of the threat must include judgment concerning the future of human existence on this planet; it must involve reference, for instance, to the questions raised by Dr Jonathan Schell in his book: *The Fate of the Earth*,[1] whose remarkable lucidity makes his warnings easily intelligible to any layman.

It is perhaps the layman's first duty at this time to refuse to be deflected from interrogation, as informed as disciplined study can make it. The obstacles in the way of such questioning have already been illustrated; we live in a society in which the rewards are manifestly greater for those who eschew disturbance of its standards, in which indeed the present assault on the intellectual independence of the Universities is further evidence of its obsessive desire to promote uncritical conformity with those standards and policies.

To write in this way is to emphasize the more immediate considerations that may deter anyone from undertaking any sort of 'hermeneutic of danger'. But at the same time it has been possible to encourage the hesitant by recalling instances of quite unscrupulous misrepresentation of significant fact, aimed at muzzling, or rendering ineffective, the expression of serious disquiet. Yet the sheer technicality of the nuclear issue, whether one concentrates attention on the theoretical arcana of nuclear physics, or on the ramifications of a continually developing nuclear technology, is an inevitable deterrent, particularly to the cautious academic, anxious at all costs not to make a fool of himself. Inevitably peaceful and war-like uses of nuclear power are intertwined in such a way that the promotion of the one advances the development of the other, and similarly any curtailment of the one inevitably occasions damage to the other. The apologist for the nuclear industry in particular is quick to point to the hurt likely to be done to future prosperity if any sort of fear of the destructive power of nuclear weaponry is allowed to stand in the way of an increasing reliance on nuclear energy as a source, for instance, of cheaper and more readily available electrical power. It is judged irresponsible to play ducks and drakes with our industrial future by opposing the proliferation of nuclear power stations at a time when other energy resources e.g. coal, and other fossil fuels are seemingly beginning to run out. It is foolish to suppose that one can separate reliance on nuclear power for industrial production from a measure of reliance on the same resource, for means of defence.

Yet there have been informed protesters against these developments: I think in particular of the late Professor Sir Martin Ryle, FRS, the Astronomer Royal, aware in his own way of that threat to the earth of which Dr Schell has written. In his last years he devoted his energies to a sustained critique of over-all nuclear commitment, aware of its grave perils, sensitive to the reality of risks which arguably, human beings have no right to take with the future of the race to which they belong. It is indeed at this point that we touch the metaphysical issue which cannot be dodged in a serious effort to comprehend the threat: the attempt to define, as far as possible, the extent to which this threat goes beyond anything we have hitherto encountered.

Thus it was no accident of personal choice that compelled attention at the outset of this essay to extreme instances in our historical experience, mediaeval and recent. We are dealing with questions that go beyond the familiar argument concerning allegedly legitimate as over against illegitimate matters of warfare. Certainly (as we shall see) that argument overlaps the matter of our primary concern. We have to reckon with the fact that in a nuclear age, the long disputed claims of a reflective Christian pacifism have acquired a new confirmation. Nor do we forget that the bomber offensive of the last world war helped dull the conscience of men and women to the point of accepting as a necessary evil, the enormity of Hiroshima and Nagasaki. But the threat with which this chapter is concerned is one perceived to hang over the future of the world as we know it. We are committed in the name of deterrence, to policies that dismiss as insignificant the likelihood of irretrievable damage to our genetic inheritance. We announce ourselves as prepared to take this risk: of course, glossing our commitment by claiming that the announcement is made in order to ensure that it shall never be implemented. But do deceive ourselves into supposing that this publicly announced willingness has the force of a magic charm that will somehow ensure that we never have to fulfil our undertaking? Or have we not rather taken the first step on the dangerous path of a posturing heroism, ending when we see ourselves as justified in a leap into the abyss, precipitating hardly conceivable consequences not for ourselves but for mankind? Do we not fear a little, the spell upon our imagination, of the vision of ourselves cast by intractable circumstance, for the role of those who will achieve the coming of the unknown? We have, after all, in this century paid a terrible price to those who were entranced by conviction of their own heroic destiny. It is less the temper of the Enlightenment than that of the romantic pessimism too often set against it as embodying a greater, tragic realism that we need to fear. The Christian in particular requires the discipline of a sane eschatology to preserve him from the spell of a self-indulgent apocalyptic. Certainly there is every need of a renewal of vision, and where the visionary component in apocalyptic is concerned, the reference to the *Revelations* of Mother Julian earlier in this chapter will have suggested appreciation of its relevance. But we must beware of a readiness to curtail a many-sided effort by appeal to an allegedly unavoidable catastrophe.

And here the theological influence of the work of Jürgen Moltmann[2] must surely prove of great significance. His readiness to combine evangelical emphasis on the mystery of the crucified Son of God with renewed appreciation of the significance of hope in the Christian scheme is extremely valuable even to those who feel the need to emend the detail of his argument. His source of hope is visionary in quality; but he has disciplined his awareness by putting himself to school with the great German Marxist Ernst Bloch, whose wide-ranging *Das Prinzip Hoffnung*,[3] open though it often is to criticism in matters of detail, achieves by the boldness of its explanatory range, a paradigm of the sort of many-sided response that alone can deserve to be called comprehension of the nuclear threat. We need an interpenetration of religious and metaphysical judgment with moral sensitivity and political awareness that is novel, and almost certain to prove at once too untidy and too definite for the average academic mind.

Thus we need to ask ourselves whether we are not inclined to allow sense of catastrophe to be endured to inhibit effective diplomatic response to immediate international needs. We must never forget in these islands how preoccupation with the Suez adventure in October/November 1956 distracted attention from what was then happening in Hungary as the Nagy government reached its moment of crisis, and the Western powers were too absorbed by the consequences of the Anglo-French-Israeli attempt to destroy Nasser to consider any sort of intervention aimed at averting the tragedy in Budapest.

It is surely no accident that members of the general public as well as professional students of European history turn constantly to consider and reconsider the weeks of crisis that divided the assassination of the grand-duke Ferdinand and his consort in Sarajevo from the outbreak of general war in August 1914. It is not only the controversial reassessment of events by German historians, e.g. Fischer, that has provoked this almost feverish revival of interest; it is the dim, but insistent perception that where the contemporary scene is concerned, we are nearer the sort of situation that arose in the summer of 1914 than to that confronting Europe in 1939. And such a situation, if it is to be managed aright (and inevitably one thinks of the complexities of the Middle East) calls for an emotional dedication and expenditure of effort, a long way removed from the boastful 'keeping up with the Joneses' suggested by the UK's vast expenditure on Trident. It is not the least element in the threat we are concerned to evaluate that its over-arching presence may prove destructive of sane political effort.

We are constantly reminded by apologists for the policy of nuclear deterrence that the threat of mutual destruction has maintained or at least helped to secure a relatively stable peace in Europe for over forty years. Within this framework we have seen in the West the laying at least of the foundations of the European Economic Community, and in the growth of the clearly related European movement, the promise of something much greater to come. Further, more recently we have seen in the countries of the Warsaw Pact, and in particular in the USSR itself, the advent of *Glasnost*, and *Perestroika*, the latter conveying as a necessary part of its successful achievement, the negotiations that led to the conclusion of the INF agreement.

Yet those who claim that it is only under the 'balance of terror' that these steps have been taken, are also quick to advocate the case for the so-called 'independent nuclear deterrent', as if at one level they acknowledge the vesting of strategic nuclear armament in the arsenal of the two super-powers as insufficient security for their own national interests. It is hard not to be disturbed by those who seem to argue at once for the constructive significance of the monopolization of nuclear force by the super-powers, and for the need, at least where their own nation is concerned, for a measure of proliferation. So in the UK we are committed to Trident, emphatic that that item of our equipment shall not be included in any estimate of the nuclear resources at the disposal of NATO over against those commanded by the powers of the Warsaw Pact. And by our commitment we render ourselves unable to criticize the initiation of similar development in Israel or South Africa, in India or Pakistan, in areas sufficiently volatile for any sane man or woman to fear such extension in their military potential. Where Israel is concerned, the whole story of Vanunu's abduction and trial provides alarming confirmation of the fear that that country has equipped itself already with a nuclear device that it is prepared, in certain circumstances, to use.

Further, no one can recall the still unfinished history of the American intervention in Vietnam without a measure of very genuine alarm. True, no use was made in those years of tactical, let alone strategic nuclear weapons. But the widespread use of chemical weapons, e.g. defoliants, is alarming evidence of the readiness of a great power to adventure any expedient, however dangerous, provided, of course, that the remoteness of the terrain renders the boomerang effect of the use, in this case, of chemical weapons, negligible. Again the 'fate of the earth' is written off as a consideration counselling restraint. But it is highly relevant, reminding us that it is not simply fear, nor even simply a proper prudence, but a reverence for life which enjoins hesitation, which insists that we do not lull ourselves to sleep, in a mood compacted of false optimism, and false realism in which we say that 'it can never happen'. There is sufficient evidence to remind us that in an unstable world a kind of madness may indeed overtake us before we fully realize what we are doing.

Further, it is hard as already suggested not to be aware of a kind of conspiracy of silence that surrounds the whole world of nuclear testing. The secrecy is not simply that which is pleaded for, what is regarded as matter of state security: it is a kind of wilful refusal to investigate the extent of the human and ecological damage that such testing makes hardly avoidable. We are afraid to accept the reality of what we are risking, and quick to write off the growing need of ecological protest as self-indulgent posturing. Yet such protest is expressive of human awareness of what Bertrand Russell in a striking phrase called 'cosmic impiety'. And it is to the more precise identification of this impiety that I now turn.

Are there, or are there not limits set to what human beings may do to their environment, where that environment is not narrowly conceived, but imaginatively enlarged to include the total context within which human life, indeed life itself, is possible? Russell is well-known as an agnostic, veering at times towards atheism: and much of his vast philosophical *oeuvre*[4] has been concerned not simply with the foundations of mathematics, and related logical issues, but with the epistemological implications of the modern scientific enterprise. His writings on these issues show many changes in his outlook and judgment: but his sense of the magnitude of this human achievement has never wavered. His attitude has never been clouded by any sort of romantic attachment to a lost primitive simplicity of vision any more than he has bowed before a theologically grounded conception of an ultimate order. Therefore his use of language as overtly religious as 'cosmic impiety' is significant, indicating, as it does, a sense that there are issues not, in the last resort, in human hands, that irreparable violation of the scheme of things is something to be avoided at all costs. If the language hardly escapes the charge of borrowing a frankly religious idiom, it may be excused on the ground that only in such a lexicon can resources of metaphor be found adequately to articulate the scale of the risk contemplated.

There is something frivolous in the eager endorsement of the need by the United Kingdom for an independent nuclear deterrent (and that means inevitably the Trident system and/or its successor) as something not much more than a 'status symbol'. We are bidden to envisage situations in which we would be lost without such a resource, even to fear what is called 'de-nuclearization' as if it were a folly to which the United States might be tempted in the interest of a presidential candidate's chance in a race for the presidency, gambling the future of the West on the supposed reality and continuance of Soviet good will. That there is human validity in the hope, even the Utopian dream, of a 'nuclear-free world' (leaving on one side the question of the future use of nuclear energy as a necessary resource) is brushed impatiently aside, as if matters of *Real-politik* had sovereignty over concerns that are, in the last resort, residually metaphysical.

And here it might be wise to emphasize again the important fact that the continuous and costly witness of the pacifist tradition in the

Christian churches, to the possible use of the means whereby evil is to be resisted and overcome, is assuming in the present a new significance. It is not enough to dismiss CND and cognate movements of protest as if they were no more than the by-products of trends and attitudes typical of those soon to be 'seen off' by the excitements of a saner 'enterprise culture'. Within the Christian churches these movements were indebted to the steadfast witness of those men and women who were never prepared to let the question of means go by default. It should never be forgotten that they included adherents of great theological distinction; such men as Herbert Farmer[5] and Percy Hartill[6] were very far from being undisciplined 'trendies', but men whose judgment sprang from their deepest reflection on the nature of the gospel. And when we turn to their writings today, we find that their insights suddenly assume a new, global significance. They are (for all their tragic implications) expressive of the postures becoming us 'under the sun'. The risk they involve is less a melodramatic indulgence than acceptance of a new and living way, leading into the unknown, but the unknown of affirmation rather than posturing folly.

In the philosophy of science in the 1940s and 1950s there was an interesting controversy between Professor Michael Polanyi and the brilliant Marxist Professor J. D. Bernal, whose book – *The Social Function of Science*[7] – published shortly before the war exercised a considerable influence. Polanyi in a series of books and articles culminating in his Gifford Lectures – *Personal Knowledge*[8] – published in 1958, attacked Bernal's claim that a science harnessed to the purposes of technology could prove an effective instrument of enlarged human opportunity. To Polanyi, himself a Marxist converted to liberalism, such subordination of the properly autonomous world of the sciences to an externally imposed programme was bound to prove intellectually destructive, and in his published work he sought to lay bare the traditional context in which alone he supposed it possible to push back the frontiers of human knowledge. If he failed to do justice to Bernal's massive achievement as an historian of the sciences, he succeeded in calling attention to the elusive foundation of metaphysical assumption on which research rested, even if that foundation needed a much more thorough definition than he succeeded in offering, even in his Gifford Lectures.

Today there is much to remind us of the significance of that controversy, even if Bernal's mantle is worn today less by members of the Communist Party of Great Britain than by champions of the advancing materialism, characteristic of present right-wing educational policies (and indeed of the values endorsed by the Thatcher government). Disinterestedness is regarded by advocates of those policies as irresponsible and destructive, and the spirit of interrogative wonder, issuing in speculative enterprise, something to be suppressed as an unaffordable luxury. And nowhere is the fruit of this perversion more sharply discernible than in the way in which, for instance, fundamental cosmological research is subordinated to supposedly more immediately pressing technological demands. Yet a wiser judgment would have recognized the extent to which growth in technical expertise may emerge as an unbudgetted spin-off of fundamental enquiry pursued for its own sake.

It was suggested above that a contemporary 'hermeneutic of danger' must be interrogative in style. But it must also be wide-ranging, aware that the perils which beset us include an obsessive preoccupation with supposed immediate advantage in a race that acknowledges the development of weapons systems and their cognates as morally sovereign, as supremely indicative of human achievement. To write in these terms is to run the risk of a charge of obsessive exaggeration. But there is a spiritual overspill between the pride we take in the supposed security conferred by advances in weaponry, to which no term can easily be set, and our frequent indifference to the claims upon us of the environment, even to the threat to the ozone layer. We turn our back too quickly on the question of the disciplines we should impose upon our adventurous interference, our wilful 'disturbance of the universe'.[9] In encouraging the re-birth of a mood of interrogation, in insisting that accelerating pursuit of uncritically accepted goals must be queried, our 'hermeneutic of danger' must always be disturbingly interrogative. The ridiculous charge that it is irresponsible to ask questions if one cannot foresee the answers must be dismissed, and likewise the suggestion that such a mood is akin to that of the man who would halt the world in its course because he wishes to get off, indulging a wild dream of protest. The illusion is rather that of those who construe the consequences of a vast number of human choices as if they belonged to the built-in fabric of the universe. And here the inevitably wide-ranging comments on contemporary cultural assumption join the questioning concerning the means of resistance to evil so continually raised in the pacifist tradition.

In conclusion it cannot be emphasized too often that the resource of the Christian churches resides less in the historically definable achievement of their structural embodiments than in the fidelity, often made possible by the Holy Spirit in spite of those same structures, to the mystery of Jesus of Nazareth. 'I have many things to say unto you; but you cannot bear them now.' '(The Spirit) will take of mine and show it unto you.'

2

A Theological View from the Non-nuclear World

SIMON MAIMELA

What does the debate about the problem of nuclear catastrophe which is of cosmic dimensions have to do with us who live in the non-nuclear world with our own unique problems to solve? For most people who live in the non-nuclear world, especially the third-world, the threat of nuclear holocaust is not uppermost in their minds. Rather the immediate threat is largely that of hunger, starvation, economic deprivation, lack of personal security due to the abuse of power under various authoritarian regimes. The temptation here is that people often think that the debate about nuclear holocaust has little to do with them. Against this tendency, it would be argued here that world security is indivisible. For there can be no security for the people living in the non-nuclear world unless there is security for everyone in the world. As a part of the human family that is trapped in a spiralling violence we – in the non-nuclear world – must become part of the solution of the problem of human violence of which nuclear arms is but an extreme form. Furthermore, as it should be clear from this and preceding chapters, global violence which threatens human security and our world consists of a set of interlocking processes and relationships such as unjust sociopolitical and economic systems, the tendency to provide for and defend sectional (parochial) interests at the expense of other people or nations, reliance on arms to defend the so-called national (read 'economic') interests without due regard for the security or economic interests of other nations, obsession with arms build-up which leads to regional and international insecurity – all of which are present in the non-nuclear world in one form or another. And there is no reason to believe that out of people's obsession with arms-guaranteed security the non-nuclear world will not develop nuclear weapons with which to threaten potential or imaginary enemies. Indeed, like a plague, the global violence and its concomitant threat to human survival signified by the nuclear weapons are likely to spread to every corner of the world, infecting both big and small nations with untold socio-economic repercussions – unless humanity resolves to confront and overcome it.

It must be stated at the outset that my interest in the debate about the nuclear catastrophe does not arise out of economic but out of the theological and ethical concerns. My reflections will therefore be of theological nature.

1 The illusion of arms guaranteed security

The problem of force and violence, in a world where war-making against seemingly countless numbers of one's 'enemies' and 'wrong-doers' seems inevitable, is as old as humanity itself. Indeed even Christians, the community called and committed by Christ, the Prince of Peace, to the vision of *'shalom'* and to the mission of peacemaking, have had to face the challenge of human violence as members of the human family in a world of sin. The so-called 'just war' theory was formulated in order to justify theologically their involvement, in potentially violent, war-making activities in the service of peace and justice when these values were threatened by aggression and injustice. In so doing, they yielded to the temptation of relativizing the demonic and destructive nature of war by suggesting that force and violence could be justified theologically because of the ends which war-making serves.[1]

The irony about human resort to one form of violence or another is that it is premised on the claim that its objective is to procure some good for some people. For instance, a resort to sociopolitical and economic repression might be said to bring security to the domi-nant groups, despite the fact that it often provokes outrage and counterviolence by the oppressed groups. Also, it is interesting to note that in the history of warfare the resort to armed conflict, violence, and killing that all war-making entails was premised on the human attempt to procure peace and security by destroying one's enemies. Accordingly, during the formation of modern national states, it became the fundamental task of every nation to use all the resources at its disposal to arm itself with a view to resorting to violence, if need be, to defend, protect and enhance its way of life or national interests.[2] As Goudzwaard[3] rightly points out, we have to do here with the emergence of an ideology of security guaran-teed by armaments, which leads to the manufacture, possession and use of more deadly weapons so as to create humanly manufac-tured peace. Obsessed with that ideology and trying to satisfy incentive to manufacture and use weapons which are judged by no other standard than by their maximum precision and destructive power, in order to protect their alleged national interests.

And the result of this human obsession with security has been a global militarization of unprecedented magnitude and scope as great and small states, the developed and underdeveloped countries engage in the global arms build-up presided over by the two super-powers, regardless of the threat that this poses to basic human rights and wellbeing. Indeed this global violence has become a social disease, a plague that has spread to every corner of the world, infecting both international and intranational political processes and structures during the 'postwar' period, leaving nations and groups more fearful, vulnerable and threatened than ever before. It seems to be impossible to assure one's national security without threatening the security of other nations, and by increasing their insecurity, more deadly arms are manufactured.[4] The futility of the ideology of guaranteed security and the impossibility of ensuring so-called national security without regard to the security of others is best exemplified by the two superpowers' irrational insistence on an ever-escalating build-up of more destructive weapons, in the hope that this will solve the problem of the arms race. However, no country today can provide absolute security because of the existence of atomic weapons which, to borrow Barnet's phrase, have burst the bonds of nationality.[5] All the arms build-up has managed to achieve is to make every human being more insecure, unsafe, and a victim of fear, the fear of a nuclear holocaust. In the meantime, while the nuclear missiles and warheads wait silently in their silos and submarines, whole nations, both in the Western and Eastern blocks, are held hostage through the so-called nuclear deterrent policies of the superpowers.

As Goudzwaard observes, this situation of total paralysis and fear because of the possibility of a nuclear holocaust is the price that humankind must pay for having created an idol, a golden calf, of arms-based security.[6] Whole nations have become victims of that idol worship, which not only thrives on terror and fear but also demands that people should sacrifice the financial resources of their country, the ecological wellbeing of their environment and their own personal freedom to that idol.

2   Implications of the nuclear holocaust for theology

The possibility that humankind could bring about its own total self-annihilation as well as the destruction of the world and most forms of life, brings humanity and human self-understanding up against their ultimate limit. It confronts humanity with an unprecedented situation, a situation which, as Thielicke and Kaufman rightly point out, raises theological and ethical questions for which there is no historical analogy.[7] These questions have to do with the meaning of human actions and of human life in the face of nuclear catastrophe, the responsibility that we humans must assume for our fellow creatures in view of our capability of destroying all of creation, and the possibility of changing our human ways of thinking and our collective behaviour. These and similar questions posed by our new religious situation demand theological answers if we are to cope effectively with the nuclear threat to our world and human survival.

Naturally, as Christians, we must turn to our primary sources, and to words spoken and written thousands of years ago, in order to draw inferences for our faith and life as we try to respond to the theological questions posed by our novel situation. However, it must be admitted that, even as we turn to the Bible for guidance, we will not find direct answers to the unprecedented problems we face because, as Lee points out:

> . . . the Bible knows nothing of nuclear weapons and nuclear warfare. War in biblical times was conducted with spears and swords, horses and chariots, battering rams and siege mounds. Only the most fanciful interpreter today would attempt to read into the apocalyptic imagery of the battle of Armageddon a portrayal or 'prediction' of nuclear war.[8]

Agreeing with Lee that we face a new religious situation without any historical analogy, a situation so novel that even the Bible knows nothing about it, Kaufman notes with sadness the insensitivity of some theologians to our new situation, who continue to theologize on the assumption that we have a given and existent deposit of values, norms or truths enshrined in some past revelation or religious tradition or book, rather than attempting to reinterpret Christian symbols in order to understand this new situation and to try to answer the questions it poses to us.[9] In a perceptive analysis of some of the theological positions which assume that truths or answers are already given in the Bible, and that the duty of theologians is simply to get hold of, transmit or apply those given truths and answers to particular human situations he points out that three serious theological errors are committed.[10]

First, theologians misuse biblical language about the so-called 'Holy War', which portrays God as taking part in battles on the side of God's people. Some Christians, even today, employ that concept as a justification for military preparedness, including the stockpiling of nuclear weapons. The assumption is that, in the struggle between Russia and America, it is their destiny to fight 'godless' communism. And because this is God's own battle they are fighting, they believe that they are justified in doing whatever is necessary to protect themselves, their national interests and 'Christian civilization' even if this might result in inflicting destruction on their enemies. In other words, the 'Holy War' concept is invoked to create the confidence that God is on their side and approves their resolve to destroy the so-called 'enemies' of God, however demonic their actions might be.

Secondly, theologians propound a theology based on the apocalyptic imagery of the battle of Armageddon, which strikes the imagination of some right-wing Christian groups in response to the nuclear holocaust that we face. Here God is portrayed as a Judge who is about to bring some catastrophic end to history by wiping out sinners and those evil powers that oppose divine purpose by means of a fiery holocaust.[11] As Jesus Christ, the messianic figure, came to overthrow all evil powers resisting the divine will and establish God's kingdom of peace and happiness in fulfilment of God's plan contemplated since the time of Noah, it is believed that God's faithful remnant would survive that catastrophic end of history and join the Saviour in his heavenly kingdom.[12] It is because the catastrophic end of history is understood as God's climactic end, one which believers look forward to with hope, that certain Christian groups urge Western nations to arm themselves in preparation for the coming nuclear Armageddon which, in their view, will be an expression of God's purpose.[13] Agreeing with Kaufman's observation, Simmons notes that some of these Christian groups actually wish for a nuclear holocaust so that Jesus will return.[14] This, as he rightly points out, is 'nothing but "Judas syndrome"', the belief that God's hand can be forced to bring destruction on the enemy and salvation to the righteous'.

Thirdly, some Christians invoke the doctrine of God's providential care for humanity and the world, arguing that God will not permit human beings utterly to destroy themselves and other forms of life or reduce the world to its original barren and dead condition. That is, it is believed that God, as Creator and Saviour, has so bound himself to humanity, to our world, and to human enterprises in the covenant mode in Jesus Christ, that he will do everything possible to ensure that any humanly initiated self-destruction and devastation of the world through a nuclear holocaust will never be allowed to take place. This is nothing but a theological affirmation of God's ultimate sovereignty over historical events, an affirmation that finds support in some biblical texts (cf Ps. 46.1–7; Rom. 8.28–39). There God is portrayed as the mighty fortress in whom the faithful can feel secure, one who is so faithful to those who trust in him that ultimately everything will work together for their good because nothing can separate them from God's love and salvation.[15]

Kaufman notes that while these theological positions might be biblical and able to provide some sort of comfort, courage, confidence and hope to believers in life's struggles against potential threats, they are misleading and dangerous if we invoke them in the face of the potential nuclear catastrophe that confronts us.[16] For, beside the fact that it is fallacious to claim that God is always on our side against our 'enemies', these religious affirmations fail to come to terms with an important and fundamental reality, namely, that nuclear catastrophe and its concomitant evils and destruction of all life on our planet will *not* be something that God brings about but will be solely a human act. A nuclear holocaust will never be part of God's grand plan to bring about the salvation of humanity, because it brings about the total annihilation of humanity, the irredeemable devastation of our world, and the end of all life. It is an event, therefore, which can never be conceived as having any positive meaning or redeeming value for us as human beings. Rather it has negative significance for us, namely, that we will be the ones responsible for bringing that ultimate and catastrophic evil on ourselves and our world.

Indeed, our situation is so novel and so unprecedented that we cannot adequately respond to it by merely repeating or invoking biblical, traditional beliefs about God's providential and yet catastrophic ending of history in order to realize some divine purpose. For while those beliefs might have been persuasive and truthful in the past, they have become problematical for us in our new religious situation because they are ignorant of the magnitude of technological power that gives human beings in our time the power utterly to exterminate themselves and reduce the world to nothingness. According to our religious tradition, it is God alone who has the power to bring history to its ultimate end. Though still valid, such an assertion cannot now be made without further qualification. Atomic weapons have turned things upside down, fulfilling that ancient human dream, one which for ages existed only in the imagination of the serpent, namely: human beings will one day become as gods (Gen. 3.22–23). It took the splitting of the atom for that dream to be realized, thus creating an historic divide between our religious forebears and ourselves. The world has never been the same since the detonation of the atomic bomb. For, as Fromm humorously points out, 'the serpent, who had said *eritis sicut dei* ('you shall be like gods') had been right'.[17]

Indeed, it is no exaggeration to say that technology and weapons of mass destruction have made the impossible possible: human beings, perhaps unwittingly, have been transformed into 'gods'. That is, humans are now endowed with the capacity to decide on the fundamental issues of life and death, of choosing between good and evil, to the point of destroying themselves and the entire creation. This is the reality of our new religious situation: the responsibility for the future of the world and of humankind now rests in human hands and no longer in God's hand alone.[18] This new religious situation is one which cannot adequately be grasped if theology continues to understand its function as merely the transmission of truths or answers deposited in the Bible, thereby calling for the blind adherence to and confidence in past formulations of truths or religious symbols. Put differently, we cannot uncritically take over traditional imagery that portrays God as the providential Lord of history and of nature, as the 'Alpha and Omega' who circumscribes everything else, as our merciful 'Father' in heaven, a King of Kings and therefore as a dominant male figure of great authority and power, as one who acts in particular ways to fix the lines along which the history of the world unfolds, and who is sufficiently powerful to ensure that cosmic and human history reach their predetermined goals.[19] For to accept such past formulations of truths uncritically is tantamount to ignoring the fact that those religious beliefs and imagery are themselves products of human creative imagination, constructed by men and women like ourselves, as they tried to find new ways of coping with new problems and crises in life. In other words, biblical symbols and images, portraying God as the omnipotent, divine King who guides history towards some purposeful end, have to be understood as the products of human imagination that go back to the early mythopoeic activity, in which a world picture was created depicting all of life as derived from and ordered by God, the divine Creator and King.[20] God was understood as an all-powerful being who is responsible for everything that happens in the world, making certain in divine providence that all things are ordered for the wellbeing and ultimate fulfilment of the faithful. The proper and only remaining thing for humans to do was to cultivate an attitude of obedience and subordination, of respect and devotion to that almightly divine figure.

However, like all other finite human products, this religious portrayal of God as a fatherly, loving and genial being who created the universe, and now rules it as a kingdom according to divine will, is totally inadequate in helping us to come to terms with the problems that confront us today – even though it might have provided security and confidence in the past. For it overlooks the fact that God is *not always* behind all that happens in the world. Rather it has become clear that, alongside God is the human being, who is endowed with enormous creative and destructive powers with the potential to destroy all life.[21] The production and possession of nuclear weapons is the clear demonstration of that power. Accordingly, the nuclear holocaust that confronts us today as a result of the transformation of human creatures into 'gods' requires that we come to terms with the novelty of our situation. It will be we humans, and not necessarily

God in divine providence, who will bring about our annihilation, and close world history – a possibility unforeseen by our religious forebears who bequeathed the Holy Scripture and its doctrines to us.[22]

3   The meaning of sin and salvation in the light of nuclear weaponry

In the light of the preceding discussion, it is clear that the newly acquired human ability to obliterate all of life through the use of nuclear weapons and technology demonstrates, religiously speaking, what is fundamentally problematic, wrong or sinful about human existence today. That is, sin and salvation have to be redefined in the light of the novelty of our religious situation about which the Bible knows nothing. In the past when God was conceived mythically as a quasi-political figure who works for divine purposes in history, what was problematic or sinful about human life was conceived in terms of loyalty or disloyalty, obedience or disobedience to the divine will (law), and in terms of fellowship with or alienation from the divine being, that is, innocence or guilt in the presence of God. Indeed, the fundamental question was: How do I find a merciful God who will rescue me from the sinful condition of disobedience and alienation, sin and guilt, divine wrath and eternal condemnation. Today, however, those are not our pressing questions – however important they might be in themselves. Rather our problems are: How can we control the enormous knowledge and power at our disposal, which have endowed humanity with the capacity utterly to destroy itself? How should we guide the technological power that steadily undermines the very conditions that make meaningful and fruitful human existence possible? What role must we humans, who have been transformed into 'gods' through technological revolution, assume in relation to the threat to our survival, to the survival of other living creatures, and to our world whose future rests in our hands as a result of technology and modern biological science?[23] How can we outgrow the tendency to work against 'God' (that is, those forces that make for life and our wellbeing) and overcome the evil we are doing by abusing our mother earth? Indeed, as Kaufman rightly points out, the greatest problem that we face today is: How do we bring about the re-ordering of human life and our social institutions so that we might be able to move away from the likelihood of utterly destroying ourselves either through nuclear catastrophe or the increasing impairment of our ecology?[24]

These and similar questions arise from our awareness that our thinking has been turned upside down by our possession of enormous destructive powers that have placed our fate on earth in our own hands. We must therefore take full responsibility for the possibility that it will be we humans who will bring history and our world to their catastrophic end. In other words, the ultimate violence embodied in the use of nuclear weapons and the fratricide that will ensue from that are human problems, humanly created evils, which should not be explained away as necessary or unavoidable sins or features of the human condition beyond human control. Rather, as human-made problems, and not inherent in human nature or something willed by God, they are evils which we must face as of our own making, evils for which we are responsible, unless we resolve to avert or overcome them.

When the ultimate violence and evil symbolized in the threat of nuclear holocaust are understood as fundamentally human-created problems or sins that confront us today, it becomes imperative that our conceptions of salvation from such sins should be reformulated. This holds true also for the medium or remedy necessary to overcome what we perceive to be today's problem areas or sins. In the past when sin was understood to be a condition of alienation from the divine King and Father, conceptions of salvation focussed on the view that Christ died for our sins in order to rescue humanity from the bondage in which humankind was trapped. That view of salvation rested on the belief that God intrudes into the historical process as, for instance, in the Exodus event, the return of exiles from Babylonian captivity, or in the Christ-event. In all of these events, it was left to God to take decisive steps to procure redemption for trapped humanity with or without their cooperation.[25] This view of salvation will not provide answers to the problems we face today, for it will tend to evade the problem that it is we humans, *not God*, who will bring disaster on earth by obliterating ourselves. We cannot leave everything in the hands of God as if it is enough merely to pray for our survival on earth rather than do something about the threat of a nuclear holocaust for which we are solely responsible. Indeed, to try to respond to the problems that confront us today by merely invoking conventional conceptions of salvation, will be tantamount to copping out, letting ourselves off the hook, and passing on our responsibility for our future on earth to God, hoping that God will do our work for us.[26]

Against the above possibility, we need to realize that, in so far as nuclear weapons have transformed us into 'gods', as it were, with the power to destroy human life on earth completely, it is our responsibility to work out ways and means which will procure salvation that is appropriate to contemporary problems. That is, rather than leave everything to God, we should take ourselves, as well as the enormous powers at our disposal seriously, by making ourselves accountable for the continuation of life on earth. We should engage ourselves in those activities which will help to overcome recurrent sinful conditions such as injustice and oppressions, insecurity and all forms of threats against our neighbours, fratricidal wars, disruptions and alienations, various exploitations and deprivations, the pollution of our mother earth and all activities which cause imbalances in the natural order – all of which will ultimately threaten the health and wellbeing of ourselves and of all other life in our world.[27] The upshot of what I am saying is this: in the light of the prospect of a nuclear holocaust, a human-created problem (sin), which threatens not only human life, but also the entire existence of the whole ecosystem, instead of fixing our gaze in the skies, we have to work for our salvation, for the blessing, the peace and the survival of the entire creation, as if we lived in 'a world from which the gods have fled'.[28] That is, we should resolve to find ways and means of ordering human life, including its customs, social practices, institutions and interpersonal relationships at local and international levels, fully aware that what we do or fail to do has significance of cosmic dimensions.

The preceding observations which emphasize the tremendous responsibility that human beings have in working for the survival of themselves and the entire creation whose fate is in their hands, flow directly from the biblical understanding that human beings have been elevated to the unique position of being bearers, makers and co-creators of history with God. That is, their role in relationship to the entire creation is that of trustees, stewards and divine representatives in the exercise of the power entrusted to them of caring lordship over God's creation (Gen. 1.28–30). As humanity must embody God's own way of relating to the entire creation, human actions must thus be both creative and redemptive. That is, men and women must engage themselves in activities that are life-giving, life-sustaining, life-affirming and therefore salvific *and not life-denying and destructive*.[29] Indeed, as they try to embody God's own dealing with creation, human beings are called upon to be champions and 'gods' that promote the wellbeing of their environment and the continuation of life on earth, fully aware that God's own being and destiny as well as honour with respect to creation is intimately bound up with human activities and the course of human history. That is, as Kaufman correctly points out, our actions as well as our fate on earth have become God's own fate.[30] What we do or fail to do as we act as God's representatives, could either spell disaster for all life and therefore spell disaster also for God, or could promote a further unfolding of creativity and thus help God to bring salvation to finite creatures. For in the final analysis, the journey to our survival on earth, to a future world without poverty and exploitation, without poisoning ourselves and causing the collapse of our ecosystem, a world freed from insecurity and the threat of a nuclear holocaust, will be brought about by human actions and hard labour as we confront the social evils of our contemporary world. God will not do our work for us without our co-operation and our getting our hands dirty.

4   Towards a theology of human responsibility

Admittedly, the remarks made in the preceding discussion which, by demonstrating the full implications of the human vocation of stewardship with respect to creation, indicating the enormous creative and redemptive responsibility conferred on humanity, will come through to some readers as overly optimistic, naive, and unrealistic. There seems to be a lack of awareness of the limits to human insight and human ability to redeem mankind from their sinful situation. For what is being suggested, marks a fundamental departure from the conventional theology which tends to put a heavy emphasis on human obedience to some divine will that we must submit to and yet cannot fulfil.

Accordingly, it becomes the function of theology to remind humanity of its fall, its weaknesses, its crippled powers to act creatively and redemptively in their humanness, to affirm that human beings are unable to choose life rather than death, to reprimand humans when they forget that they have no control over their destiny because the choice for the determination of humanity's future and of the world should be left in 'the hands of God'. In short, conventional theology aims no further than reminding humans that they cannot be trusted, because they are ill-equipped to care for themselves and their world.[31]

While this conventional theology sounds laudable and commands respect by trying to stress that God is everything while human beings and their achievements are nothing, I submit that this theology is not appropriate to the problems that nuclear technology poses to our survival, because it fails to come to terms with the enormous powers that have been thrust upon human beings over the years. Indeed, as Brueggemann rightly points out, this conventional theology, by belittling human effort and promoting despair, paralysis and a dim view of human activity, can only result in social indifference, defeatism, moral dullness and irresponsibility.[32] It encourages us to assume that our survival on earth and our future will come in some other way than by our willingness to commit our activities to those goals that make life possible and fulfilling.

Against this conventional theology and at the risk of being accused of heresy, we must rather call for a new theological approach appropriate to the problems and challenges that the enormous powers with which humanity is endowed pose for their own survival as well as for the future of their world. This calls for a theology of responsibility, one which acknowledges the powers that humanity has to destroy itself and which looks positively at those powers with a view to calling human beings to their senses by inculcating responsibility in their use of the powers entrusted to them as stewards for the entire creation. We need a theology of responsibility which acknowledges, on the one hand, the limitations of human knowledge and powers and, on the other, reminds us that within those limits God, who has endowed us with the ability to ensure the survival of creation, has pinned great hopes and expectations on us. And as trusted stewards, who must represent God in our dealing with creation, the fate of which is in our hands, we must act in ways that mirror that divine trust in us.[33] This theology of responsibility should teach us to believe in ourselves as special, endowed and enthroned creatures who must come to terms with the opportunities and responsibilities that come, along with our transformation into the glorious position of being little 'gods' (Ps. 8.1–10). It is a theology which calls human beings to take themselves seriously as those who can be responsible in their decisions and actions because they have real options and choices to make in the face of a nuclear catastrophe and other potential sociopolitical disasters that confront them. Therefore, they must never regard any of their decisions, choices and actions as trivial, because the future of the world and human survival is in human hands. For we live in a world whose future is not foreordained or mapped out by divine fate but is open to human intervention and is therefore alterable through human creative actions and decisions.

Furthermore, as Brueggemann points out, we need a theology which will remind us that Christ is not simply a Saviour from spiritual sins but is also a fulfilment of the summons made to Adam in Genesis to be a king of creation, a king with real powers of creativity.[34] Accordingly, in Christ in whose humanity we now share, theology ought to remind us that our nature, our sonship and daughtership to God, our distinct humanity, our dignity and nobility, lies in nothing other than the responsible and creative use of the powers entrusted to us, that is, in our ability to re-order and transform our social and natural environment for the sake of a healthy human community and the prevention of the destruction of our world. This theology of responsibility which is called for here, seems to be the only one appropriate for our time as we face the enormous powers that human beings now have to destroy God's creation entrusted to their care.

Put somewhat differently, what our world today needs is a theology that can inspire and move men and women to undergo a radical transformation (*metanoia*) so that they become agents in the transformation of their social, political and economic institutions, of their ways of thinking about global security and world-order, of their perceptions of their so-called enemies as well as national security; of their perception of their role in relation to creation and to God as well as to other processes that make human life possible and fulfilling. In short, in the threat of a nuclear holocaust we are faced with an essentially religious challenge, calling for fundamental changes in human collective behaviour, in our thinking and acting as well as in the transformation of the very structures of ourselves.[35] To be sure, the transformation which is called for here and which should be inculcated and nourished by a theology of responsibility is nothing short of the miraculous, because it involves a qualitative leap of the sort that our genetic forebears had to undergo when they moved from a watery environment to the land.[36] But it is a transformation which must come about by human creative, as well as redemptive acts because not only do human beings have the power to transcend tragedy but also because they are not fated to destroy themselves.[37] Indeed, it is the claim of the Christian faith that humanity and the world can be changed; they are renewable and transformable for the better (II Cor. 5.17–21; II Peter 3.13; Rev. 21.1–5). Therefore our world is not doomed to destruction. This faith is premised on the conviction that, in entrusting all of life and the world to the stewardship of men and women, God firmly trusts that humans can be responsible creatures who can live in the world without destroying or threatening to destroy one another.[38]

In conclusion, we must, with Barnet, emphasize that this future survival of humanity and of our world will be possible only when this present generation take their stewardship seriously by exercising responsibly the powers entrusted to them, through a resolute commitment to the 'salvation of the human family and our heritage, the earth'.[39] In doing this they will be working alongside, with and on behalf of God with a view to overcoming a human-created problem, that is, a race towards self-destruction through a nuclear holocaust for which they and they alone will be responsible. They can save themselves and God's creation, as sons and daughters of God on whom the entire creation has pinned its hope (Rom. 8.19–23).

3

Facing the Future: The Challenge to Secular and Theological Presuppositions

RICHARD BAUCKHAM

What if this present were the world's last night?
John Donne[1]

It is not yet the evening to end all days, every night still has a morning.
Ernst Bloch[2]

What is that lovely rainbow that abides
upon the dripping moments till it fades?
    God promised me, though I am old,
    if I will work this new-washed field
while my future vanishes past
something will come of it at last.
    This is the rainbow that abides
    on the dripping moments – till it fades.
        Paul Goodman, 'Noah's Song'[3]

If I knew the world would end tomorrow, I would plant a tree.
falsely attributed to Martin Luther[4]

In Albert Einstein's now familiar words, 'The power set free from the atom has changed everything except our ways of thought.'[5] The nuclear threat has by now provoked a great deal of political, strategic and also ethical rethinking, but its fundamental challenge to habitual ways of thinking about human destiny, about our place in history and our attitude to the future has barely begun to be faced. In this chapter I shall argue, first, that the nuclear threat is a radical challenge to some of the presuppositions of modern Western culture in its secularized form, and, secondly, that the resources of the Christian tradition can be retrieved as a more adequate source of hope, once the challenge to theological presuppositions is also appreciated and met.

I

The greatest challenge of nuclear weapons to all thinking about human life and destiny lies in the fact that they have created a radically new possibility in human history: the possibility that human beings themselves might put an end to human history. As Jonathan Schell put it, by inventing the capacity for self-extinction as a species, 'we have caused a basic change in the circumstances in which life was given us, which is to say that we have altered the human condition'.[6] According to Schell,

> The spectre of extinction hovers over our world and shapes our lives with its invisible but terrible pressure. It now accompanies us through life, from birth to death. Wherever we go, it goes too; in whatever we do, it is present . . . It is the truth about the way we now live.[7]

This takes for granted – what scientific discussion now strongly supports – that the use of nuclear weapons on a large scale could lead to the extinction of the human race, as well as to the destruction of many other forms of life on the planet. Of course, not any use of nuclear weapons would have this result, but it is within the capacity of the weapons now in existence. Nor should we envisage the nuclear holocaust in terms of that mythic image which Ira Chernus calls 'the big whoosh',[8] i.e. an image of instantaneous total annihilation. Chernus points out that probably many people have in their minds such a purely mythic image, such that (in the words of the song) 'we all go together when we go.'[9] The empirical reality of the nuclear holocaust would be quite otherwise, not a mercifully instantaneous big bang but a relentless process of annihilation. Many will survive the initial blasts but will die extended, painful deaths from burns, injuries and radiation sickness. In a devastated and radiation-contaminated environment survivors will be prey to innumerable threats to life. As the large-scale atmospheric effects of nuclear explosions take effect, the nuclear winter will engulf the world, including parts of the world not immediately affected by the explosions themselves, and will add the more ordinary effects of extreme cold and hunger to the mysterious deadliness of radiation. Finally, long-term effects on the environment, such as damage to the ozone layer, may well render the planet no longer habitable for human beings or most other forms of life. Thus the scientific probabilities are not for a mythical 'big whoosh', but hold out nonetheless a quite realistic prospect of human extinction. At any rate the *possibility* cannot be ruled out.[10]

As a possible threat to the continuance of the human species, the nuclear threat constitutes a unique kind of contradiction of human hope. It should not simply be put in the same category as other occurrences which in contemporary society threaten individuals with premature death (cancer, car and aeroplane crashes, and so on). In the face of death, individuals commonly find meaning in their lives on earth by reference to the corporate future of the family or society which will survive them. (This is true whether or not they also expect some form of individual life after death.) Hope for the future gives meaning to life by enabling it to be read as a *narrative* which continues, so that the fullness of meaning which has not yet been achieved may still be sought in the future. If an individual's narrative is broken off without achieved meaning, it may still have meaning in hope, because it flows into and can gain significance in the continuing story of the wider society. When the survivors of a tragedy feel the strong need to ensure that the dead should not have died in vain, they witness to this common sense that the continuing human story can give meaning to individual lives which have been cut short. But the unique force of the nuclear threat is that it threatens an end to the whole human future on earth. It therefore radically undermines the sense of meaning in life which is dependent on hope – the meaning, that is, of individual life in its interconnexion with the continuing life of the wider human society. Life as a narrative with indefinite space to develop collapses into the immediate present which could at any time be curtailed – not by a satisfying conclusion, but by a meaningless end.

The nuclear threat, in its cultural and religious significance, needs to be seen as one element, coincident with others, in the loss of hope in contemporary Western culture. It provides the most dramatic and final contradiction of hope. To some extent it should be possible to document the psychological effects of the nuclear threat, even though awareness of it is frequently repressed.[11] But for the full significance of the nuclear threat to be appreciated, it must be placed not only in the context of a general phenomenology of human hope, but more specifically against the backdrop of the significance of hope in post-Enlightenment western culture. In an important sense the nuclear threat shows how the western tradition of hope has come to undermine itself. (I use 'western' here, as in any but a narrowly political context one must, to include the Communist 'East' as well as the North Atlantic 'West': the nuclear threat itself illustrates how these two branches of modern western culture still grow from the same tree.)

For two centuries western culture has been strongly orientated towards the future, far more so than most human societies in the past. This peculiarly western sense of history as movement towards a new future was inherited from the Christian tradition, with its messianic-eschatological sense of history as unidirectional and moving in the providence of God towards a future fulfilment. In particular, western culture inherited from these theological roots a sense of the *transcendence* of the future: the future as no mere repetition of the past but as open to not yet realized possibilities of human fulfilment. This orientation to a future open to human hopes has in the last two centuries taken various forms, both evolutionary and revolutionary, which have in common the sense that much of the meaning of human life lies in hopeful striving towards a better life in the future.

In its Christian form, of course, the hope that history was leading towards a better future rested on a belief in the providential power and goodness of God: the role of human action in creating the future was subordinate at most. The secularization of the western sense of history through the Enlightenment eliminated a sovereign, transcendent God from the picture.[12] In place of the promise and providence of God as the ground for hope and the creative power of the future, the new philosophies of history substituted both human action and an immanent teleology within history. This combination is typical of nineteenth-century thought, is found both in the liberal idea of progress and in Marxism, and creates in both the characteristic tension between historical determinism – the future will result from an inevitable historical process inherent in the nature of things – and voluntarism – human decision and action create the future. The former, of course, was a secularized form of providence, and for all its difficulties, both in itself and in its relationship to human action, it played an immensely important part in the western sense of the future until recently. It meant that human hopes corresponded to the nature of things. Although the need for human action was stressed, confidence in the power of human action to create the future was underpinned by the sense of inevitable advance (whether progressive or dialectical).

Confidence in an inherent tendency of the historical process towards a future goal of greater human fulfilment survived long into the twentieth century, and to some extent can still be found, especially in Marxism. But it has suffered repeated blows – the First World War, Nazism, Fascism, Auschwitz, Stalinism – and has declined very considerably.[13] However, it is important to notice the initial effect of this decline. The western cultural drive towards a new future remained, but, deprived of an immanent teleology in the nature of things, required, even more intensively, belief in human power to control and create the future. The historical process has no humanly desirable direction of its own, with which we are or can be in harmony, but must be subjected to the human will to master and direct it to the achievement of humanly-defined goals of greater humanity. Here we notice the typical late-twentieth-century loss of any sense that the meaning of human life resides in the nature of things: meaning is humanly created and given to the historical process by the imposition of our purposes on it. Also it is at this point that humanity finally completely replaces God. By retaining a secularized sense of providence (immanent teleology) the nineteenth-century historicisms deified the historical process at least as much as humanity as such. It is with the loss of any sense of a direction inherent in the nature of things that everything now depends on human sovereignty over the process, and in place of the God who was once expected to establish his own kingdom in the future, humanity must now define and achieve our own utopia. (It is, incidentally, within this broader context that modern Christian theology now finds providence one of the most problematic of traditional doctrines.)

The loss of immanent teleology highlighted and intensified a feature present since the Enlightenment: that the modern western sense of history and the future is closely connected with the attempt to *subject* history to human control and to *master* the future. It is part and parcel of the culture of domination which stems from the Enlightenment. Modern humanity is 'Faustian man' bending the world to his will through power (and the sexist language is appropriate). But this has become more apparent in recent times for another reason too. Nineteenth-century hopes of progress had broad ethical and cultural goals of peace, brotherhood and freedom, which went hand-in-hand with the progress of science and technology. But disillusionment with these broader humanistic hopes has been more widespread than disillusionment with the purely materialistic progress achievable through technology. Technology, always important for both liberal progressivism and Marxism, now became the major focus of the will to control and create the future.

The development and deployment of nuclear weapons belongs within this context, but before considering them it will be useful to notice the extent to which technological optimism has now dissipated. This is the point at which the western tradition of hope finally undermines itself. Whereas scientific and technological advance had once seemed the hard evidence of progress and became the major means of mastering and directing the future, their ambiguity has become increasingly apparent. The same process which has relieved so much suffering has also made possible the sickening cruelties of twentieth-century wars and tyrannies. The ecological crisis has revealed how the same mastery over nature which has adapted nature to our benefit and seemed to free us, to some extent, from nature, at the same time threatens the natural conditions on which our survival depends. To many it seems that technological mastery has been flawed not only in its actual achievements but in its illusory aspiration to total control. As Christopher Lasch comments, 'The

development of modern technology . . . has improved human control over the physical environment only in a very superficial way, by
enabling scientists to make short-term modifications of nature, of
which the long-term effects are incalculable.'[14] The future, it seems,
reasserts its transcendence in retaining its unpredictability and
uncontrollability. Whether or not it is really open to human hopes,
it cannot be simply created by them.

In the nuclear threat the will to total control of the future through
technology both culminates and most dramatically reveals its own
impotence.[15] In the context of the messianic view of science as the
instrument by which humanity would master its own destiny the
development of atomic weapons was irresistible. In this context fear
of the incalculable destructive power of the weapons was bound to
weigh less than the impetus to grasp and wield the greatest physical
force in nature. Thus Robert Oppenheimer could justify the continuation of work on the atomic bomb in these terms: 'If you are a scientist
you believe that it is good . . . to turn over to mankind at large the
greatest possible power to control the world.'[16] Immediate American
comment on the awe-inspiring significance of the bombing of Hiroshima in 1945 turned to the image of Prometheus, who stole fire from
the gods: 'The atomic bomb can turn the world into a graveyard or a
garden, and the United States, the Prometheus who has dared the
heavens to invoke this power, has assumed first responsibility for
deciding which it shall be.'[17] In such comments it seems a virtually
divine omnipotence[18] that the new Prometheus has made his own.
The outcome of world history ('a graveyard or a garden') is now
wholly a human – that is, American – decision.

As a US senator put it in 1951, 'Mark me well: massive atomic
deterring power can win us years of grace, years in which to wrench
history from its present course and direct it toward the enshrinement
of human brotherhood.'[19] The ambition, it should be noted, is the
exact mirror-image of the Marxist aim with which it saw itself in
technological as well as political confrontation. But whether the
political end was as grandiose as this or the superficially more modest
desire to guarantee national security, the nuclear arms race of the
post-war period was propelled by the attempt to use supreme
technological power to attain and maintain mastery over the *political*
future. Nuclear weapons became the Faustian magic by which
politicians could transcend the intractable problems of human conflict. Ronald Aronson aptly calls them 'a technology of madness':

> A technology of madness is a technology formed to solve properly
> political problems, a technology the root of which is a break with
> the real nature of these problems and the determination to dissolve
> them in a scientific fantasy-universe.[20]

The fantasy lies in the illusion that the achievement of world-destructive power can give absolute security and total control, whereas in fact it has hung a sword of Damocles over the whole human race.

Omnipotence is an illusion, not because the power to make the world a graveyard is not there, but because it cannot be adequately controlled by those who have created and possess it. Not only might the technology itself deceive its human controllers, as in the outbreak of a so-called accidental nuclear war. Probably more importantly, the deliberate outbreak of nuclear war would be subject to all the unpredictable and irrational features of real human life. In a situation of international crisis, which could never be exactly foreseen, a very small number of political leaders would face the decision whether to use nuclear weapons, in a very short time, under extreme psychological pressure, their judgment swayed no doubt by quite accidental factors (such as their state of health) affecting their ability to think quickly and clearly. The collocation of circumstances which would lead to the use of nuclear weapons cannot be controlled.

One of the great dangers of the nuclear situation is in fact that the sense of technological mastery can lead to a neglect of the real limits of human control over the nuclear situation. The Cambridge seminar pointed out how dangerous this is in relation to American military strategists' plans for a limited nuclear war.[21] The strategists' belief that a limited nuclear war can be fought without escalating into the holocaust itself is based on the belief that war *plans* can be actually carried out. In the imaginary world of war games in which nuclear strategy is developed the strategists can control their weapons precisely as they wish. They assume that their will is supreme over the technology. But conventional strategic theory, based on the real world of real wars, always recognized that war plans are *not* usually carried out, because of the unpredictable elements in all real situations. In real nuclear war, the unpredictable could release the full potential of the technology without the generals' having intended it.

Thus the attempt to control human destiny with ultimate technological power rebounds on itself. Because those who wield this vast power cannot fully control their exercise of it, they have in fact created a situation in which accidental and unpredictable factors have correspondingly great significance. However much human control is extended and the elements of chance reduced, they can never become negligible, simply because so much is at stake. The irony of the nuclear situation is that our vast control over the forces of nature, which would have been unimaginable in the past, actually puts us *more* at the mercy of *un*controllable factors, including those which influence our own decisions, than the human race has ever been in the past.

But the use of the word 'our' in that sentence misleads – and reveals
one final respect in which the nuclear crisis throws the whole modern
attempt at total control of our historical destiny into doubt. Against
the claim that 'modern man' is the free creator of his own history,
Mircea Eliade observed:

> It is becoming more and more doubtful . . . if modern man can
> make history . . . For history either makes itself (as the result of
> seeds sown by acts that occurred in the past, several centuries or
> even several millennia ago . . .) or it tends to be made by an
> increasingly smaller number of men who not only prohibit the
> mass of their contemporaries from directly or indirectly intervening
> in the history they are making (or which the small group is making),
> but in addition have at their disposal means sufficient to force each
> individual to endure, for his own part, the consequences of this
> history, that is, to live immediately and continuously in dread of
> this history. Modern man's boasted freedom to make history is
> illusory for nearly the whole of the human race.[22]

Similarly, one of the burdens of Albert Camus' book *The Rebel* was
that the modern project to take control of history resulted in the
horrors of Nazism and Stalinism. At least it must be admitted that
the modern period has been characterized no less than previous
periods of history by political oppression, victimization through war
and other forms of suffering endured by the many because of the
policies of the few. Perhaps it may be suggested that since Eliade and
Camus wrote (in 1949 and 1951) greater democratization of the
process of history is apparent. But if the human future is threatened
by nuclear weapons, it is in the hands of the very few human beings
who can use them. The whole human future, including that of the
non-nuclear nations, is in the hands of the leaders of the nuclear
powers. Of course, in democracies the possession of nuclear weapons
could be subject to democratic veto, though in practice the development and deployment of nuclear weapons has been very little subject
to the democratic process. But, given the existence of nuclear arsenals,
their *use* is not only in fact not subject to democratic control: it is
inherently incapable of democratic control.[23] At the point where most
is at stake, in the crisis in which the weapons may be used, awesome
decisions must be made for which no democratic mandate can have
been given. Moreover, the majority of the victims of nuclear weapons
will not even have consented to their existence. Thus it now appears
even more true that 'Modern man's boasted freedom to make history
is illusory for nearly the whole of the human race' (Eliade).

The sense of helplessness and fatalism,[24] which is often said to be
a common attitude to the nuclear threat, is therefore understandable.
Opinion polls report that a considerable majority of people in Britain

and the United States expect a nuclear war in their lifetime, but do not think about it often.[25] The unthinkable is repressed, but the future is closed off nonetheless. Chernus speaks of 'the disconnected generation', concerned only with survival in its own lifetime, connections with past and future generations no longer felt. Fatalism is accompanied by an 'ethic of living for the moment' and 'a preoccupation with the ephemeral'.[26] Though cultural generalizations about the present can be made only with great caution, the collapse of the western tradition of hope coheres with Christopher Lasch's attempt to characterize contemporary western culture as one of 'survivalism'.[27] Technological optimism has dissipated and a kind of stagnation of society sets in. Although new technological possibilities abound, they seem no longer to produce hope for a different future: the vision of a new society created by the new technology, while nourished by a few, apparently inspires neither politicians nor people. Merely to prolong the present (or the past, as in 'economic recovery') seems the most that can be hoped for, despite the recent resurgence of national confidence in both Britain, where it is largely materialistic, and America, where a sense of national destiny struggles vigorously to survive.

The loss of the future is strikingly evoked in James Bertolino's poem, 'The American':

> He stands bent before negation,
> no way to straighten his bones, no hope
> of direction into death
> or life. He falls
>
> before negation, and before he knows
> anything he rises
> to stoop forward, to follow
> the long reaching of his shadow
>
> always before him. However he turns
> the dim light is behind.
> He kneels, begging to find a direction
> in dying, to leave his shadow
>
> for the light
> of burning. He lies
> before negation, he pleads
> for burning.[28]

The religious overtone – prostration before the annihilating future – should be noted.

The theological critique implicit in the preceding discussion must now become explicit. In reaching for deity – in the form of total control of their own destiny – human beings become subject to illusion. Technology is seen as a means of abolishing human limits. All the risks and struggles of life, the real unpredictability and uncontrollability of the future, are to be eliminated by the possession of superhuman power: technological impregnability. But this omnipotence is a dangerous illusion: human beings prove not only morally unfit to be their own gods, but actually, at the height of their powers, incapable of controlling the power by which they hope to determine their own destiny. In fact, so far from their achieving deity, absolute security through nuclear weapons becomes an idol[29] to which they are subject, helpless and resigned in the face of its threat to their future.[30]

The mistake lies in the aspiration to *total* control – absolute security – and the reliance on the sheer power of the bomb to this end. My point is not to deny the *real* power to shape the course of human history which human beings now have – or the responsibilities which go with this. But these responsibilities can be properly exercised only with a realistic awareness of human finitude. There is a restricted sense in which, in Bonhoeffer's phrase, we have 'come of age', but we have done so precisely as finite human creatures. As William Lynch points out in his study of human hope in relation to mental illness, omnipotence belongs to the illusory self-image of the small child, whereas maturity is growth into 'the finite but real self-image of the adult. . . . When we give up omnipotence we only give up fantasy'.[31] When technology becomes 'a technology of madness' (Aronson), it is comparable with the infantile dreams of omnipotence found in the mentally sick, who retreat into counterfeit hope because they cannot cope with reality.[32]

Accepting reality means living with 'the terror of history' (Eliade) and the real openness of the future: its unpredictable and uncontrollable character. With the loss of any, even a secularized, form of providence, twentieth-century humanity found it impossible to face the open future with *trust* and could continue to hope only by the attempt to create the future, which has destroyed hope. Renouncing the dream of omnipotence means acknowledging dependence, living in trust, openness to non-dominating relationships. These things are not weakness, servility or evasion of responsibility, but the conditions for the exercise of properly human autonomy and strength. Instead of aspiring to total control of the world, we need respect for the world as, in the last resort, a home we have not created and cannot replace but have been given. Instead of aspiring to total control of the future, we need to live in openness to the open possibilities of the future, *both* as a challenge to responsibility *and* as an invitation to trust – in others and in God. In this context technology can be rescued from the dream of omnipotence and restored to its place in a human dominion exercised within properly human limits. Instead of the vast risks which the aspiration to total control creates but cannot properly acknowledge, living in openness and trust means accepting the risks which are involved in all creaturely existence, but it also opens up possibilities for dealing with the real problems of human conflict in an appropriately human way.

Living hopefully before an uncontrollable future is not possible if meaning and purpose in human life are thought to be solely a human creation. The meaning and purpose we create must in some way respond to a meaning and purpose beyond ourselves, on which the future we cannot control depends. If the western tradition of hope has any future at all, it must recover its roots in the Christian doctrines of providence and eschatology. But this is not at all to say that we can uncritically revive these doctrines in their traditional form, for the modern world and the nuclear crisis constitute a challenge also to these traditional Christian responses to history and the future. In the next section we must consider this challenge, and ask whether the resources of the Christian tradition can be interpreted by the nuclear threat in such a way as to provide an adequate theological interpretation of and response to the nuclear threat.

II

In this section we shall consider two very different American theological responses to the nuclear threat.[34] In their different ways both bring to light the difficulties of interpreting the nuclear situation within the categories of the traditional Christian view of history (providence and eschatology). Criticism of them will lead to an attempt at a more satisfactory theological restatement.

In the nuclear nation in which Christian faith is most widely professed and most publicly prominent an extraordinarily widely accepted Christian theological response to the nuclear threat is so-called 'nuclear dispensationalism'.[35] It is arguably one of the most important factors[36] forming public attitudes to the nuclear issue in the United States and must therefore be taken seriously. As a school of interpretation of biblical prophecy, dispensational premillennialism originated with J. N. Darby in early nineteenth-century England, and partly through the influence of the *Scofield Reference Bible* (first edition 1909), had already made considerable headway in American evangelical Christianity long before the advent of nuclear weapons. Its relevant features are a pessimistic attitude to the course of history and an optimistic expectation of the escape of believers from history. A final crescendo of evil, under the Antichrist, will incur God's judgment in the period of seven years leading up to the parousia, which will inaugurate the millennium. But before[37] the 'tribulation' in which the rest of the world will be engulfed, Christian believers will be miraculously removed from the earth in the 'secret rapture', which could occur at any moment.

It is important to notice how this scheme has overtaken the older American postmillennial eschatology, which in the eighteenth and nineteenth centuries fostered the American sense of national destiny to bring about the kingdom of God on earth. In nineteenth-century liberal theology this older postmillennialism, with its optimism about the future of the historical process, merged imperceptibly into the liberal idea of progress.[38] Precisely this discredited it for conservative Christians, whereas the dispensational scheme cohered with a rejection of the 'social gospel' and a concentration on evangelism and personal salvation. Logically, it would seem to be the outlook of a Christianity disengaged from the public, political world. As far as the future of the public world is concerned it is fatalistic, leaving it to God's judgment, but it is far from fatalistic about the future of individuals, which, by means of evangelism, decision for Christ and the 'rapture', can be entirely disengaged from the future of society at large.

Thus the broadest effect of this theology is to express and strongly to reinforce the resignation which most people feel in the nuclear situation. Cautious as some dispensationalist leaders may be about identifying Armageddon with nuclear war,[39] the popularizers[40] and the people have no such hesitation. The plausibility of dispensationalist eschatology derives in large part from its coherence with the supposed inevitability of nuclear holocaust (as well as from the establishment and fortunes of the state of Israel, which also fulfil the dispensationalist expectation). Moreover, the scheme both rationalizes the sense of helplessness before the threat (God's righteous judgment on an evil world must be accepted) *and* provides something for individuals to do about the threat (one can save oneself from it by decision for Christ and save others from it by evangelism).

It is important to notice, because the point is often misunderstood, that dispensationalist eschatology *itself* has no political consequences except passive acceptance of the nuclear situation.[41] Of course, for most Americans who hold it, it is accompanied by – and certainly does nothing to detract from – more or less strong support for the government's nuclear policy for the usual reasons (defending American freedom against the communist enemy).[42] But the conjunction of dispensationalist eschatology and positive involvement in political policies relating to nuclear weapons is by no means entirely logical, as can be observed in the stance of the new Christian right and in the problem commentators have in assessing the significance of personal statements of dispensationalist belief by Ronald Reagan[43] and other prominent politicians. Fatalistic irresponsibility with regard to the public future is hard to translate into political acceptance of responsibility for the public future. The new political prominence of conservative Christianity is not only dangerous; it also embodies the ambivalence of American public attitudes to nuclear weapons, as the power which the American people wield in their own self-defence and as at the same time the power which is bound to destroy them before long.

The nuclear situation results not from faith in divine providence but from the aspiration to divine omnipotence. But nuclear dispensationalism, despite its faith in a divine purpose in history, offers no resistance to the nuclear situation. The more it moves from sectarian disengagement to political responsibility, the more it is guilty of complicity with the attitudes that have created the nuclear threat. Its doctrine of providence is at fault in two respects.[44] In its attitude to God's purpose for the world at large, it too closely resembles the unbelieving fatalism with which it so easily fuses. At the same time, it escapes fatalism in the sphere of the destiny of the individual only by means of an extreme disengagement of believers from the world. Both faults make it extraordinarily unfit to support and guide Christians who assume responsibility in the public sphere. Both faults might be corrected by subjecting its doctrine of providence to *christological* correction: any Christian assumption about divine purpose in history must relate to Jesus, who in Gethsemane rejected the option of 'secret rapture' and fulfilled his Father's purpose by suffering in loving solidarity with his Father's world.

If nuclear dispensationalism fits the nuclear threat all too well within a traditional theological scheme, Gordon Kaufman[45] sees it as a radically novel situation which demands radical deconstruction and reconstruction of Christian theological symbolism. Inspired by Jonathan Schell's *The Fate of the Earth* and persuaded by Schell of the epoch-making novelty of humanity's new-found power of self-extinction, Kaufman claims not only that this possibility was not foreseen in the Christian religious tradition, but also that it cannot be satisfactorily interpreted in terms of the tradition.

Of course, it is true that the tradition, in the form of apocalyptic eschatology, has long contemplated a cataclysmic end to human history, but Kaufman cannot, with the dispensationalists, assimilate the nuclear threat to this expectation, because the tradition expected an end of history brought about by God. The nuclear holocaust will be an end brought about by humanity – and this, Kaufman claims, makes all the difference:

In the religious eschatology of the West the end of history is pictured quite differently than we today must face it. For it is undergirded by faith in an active creator and governor of history, one who from the beginning was working out his purposes which were certain to be realised as history moved to its consummation. The end of history, therefore . . . was to be God's climactic act. A consummation of this sort was something that the faithful could live with – even look forward to with hope – for it would be the moment when God's final triumph over all evil powers was accomplished. In contrast, the end of history which we in the late twentieth century must contemplate . . . must be conceived primarily not as God's doing but as ours. Moreover, it is difficult to think of it as part of a grand plan bringing about the salvation of humanity: it is, rather the extinction . . . of human life on earth.[46]

This novel situation in which we have total responsibility for the holocaust means that we cannot appeal to divine sovereignty over history as a ground for hope. If we continued to believe in God's providential direction of the course of history, then we should have to think either (with the nuclear dispensationalists) that God intends and will bring about the nuclear holocaust, or that God will never allow it to happen. But both alternatives obscure the real novelty of the situation in which it is we human beings who are wholly responsible for nuclear annihilation, should it happen. In this situation any appeal to providence is an evasion of our own responsibility.[47] Therefore, the traditional image of God's providential care must be questioned. Kaufman in fact goes on to reject all personalistic images of God as King or Father, since they embody the idea of a divine loving purpose guiding history towards its goal, which is no longer tenable in view of the extent of contemporary humanity's power to determine the course of history. 'God' becomes a name for the processes of nature and history which have produced and continue to sustain humanity without the implication that these processes embody a divine purpose or imply a divine transcendence beyond them. The fate of humanity on earth will also be God's fate.[48]

This thesis has the merit of making us face squarely the problem which the possibility of human self-extinction raises for our understanding of God's relation to history. However, there are several serious weaknesses in the way Kaufman poses and resolves the problem. In the first place, the model of providence which he rejects is one in which God brings about and, in the most direct sense, wills everything that happens. He regards it as inevitable that this should produce the kind of fatalism which we have already criticized in nuclear dispensationalism. Whether this is in fact the case could certainly be questioned,[49] but even granting his point it is no ground for sweeping aside, without consideration, any possibility of a more acceptable doctrine of providence. That he moves immediately to the most extreme alternative – rejection of any form of providential purpose in history – is the more remarkable, since he acknowledges, in passing, that 'some [interpretations of the nuclear situation in terms of providence] can certainly provide powerful incentives to struggle against a nuclear disaster, as the widespread peace and disarmament work by religious groups shows.'[50] It becomes apparent that Kaufman's rejection of anything like traditional theism is not in fact *compelled* by the needs of the nuclear situation, but results from his seeing the nuclear situation within the context of his own theological development away from traditional theism.[51]

Secondly, so far from providing the alternative outlook which is needed in the nuclear situation, Kaufman actually capitulates to the fundamental attitude which has led to the nuclear crisis: the aspiration to human omnipotence. Although his clear intention of supporting the anti-nuclear movement puts him in a quite different category from the nuclear dispensationalists, he no more provides serious *theological* resistance to the nuclear threat than they do. He can offer the peace movement only the same presupposition as those who created the nuclear threat had: that our only hope lies in mastering the future.[52] In the first section of this chapter we have seen that what the nuclear situation demands is a quite different attitude to the future: a form of trust and hope which will enable us to exercise our real responsibilities without the dangerous illusion of omnipotence.

In fact, there are two important elements in Kaufman's own discussion which could have led in a different direction from the conclusion he reaches. In the first place, he does in fact recognize that human *finitude* emerges actually within and from our greatly enhanced power, as well as that the nuclear danger results from the temptation to neglect this finitude and attempt total control of the future.[53] But this observation does not contribute to his main conclusions, probably because he is so concerned not to detract in any way from the sense of human *responsibility* in the nuclear situation. What is needed here is a more careful distinction between the notions of human power, human control, and human responsibility. Human beings now have the power to end human history. They do not have complete control of this power, but this by no means diminishes their responsibility. If a nuclear holocaust happened, human beings could be held wholly responsible for it, since they have invented, manufactured and deployed nuclear weapons, trained other people to use them, and developed military plans for using them, all in sufficient knowledge of the consequences of using them. They have also deliberately created a situation in which they know that accidental use is possible. But, as we have seen in the first section of this paper, human beings are by no means in total control of the situation in which nuclear weapons may be used. Whether they are used, and therefore whether the human race survives, will partly depend on chance. It follows that a fully responsible attitude is possible only if the *limits* of human control are fully recognized. Emphasizing human finitude – in the proper way – does not detract from but promotes responsibility.

Secondly, Kaufman recognizes that much of what is significant in human history is not the direct result of deliberate intention and planning by human beings. For example,

> Though innumerable decisions and actions were certainly involved in the gradual evolution of modern democratic parliamentary institutions, no one simply thought out this mode of political organisation and then directly produced it.[54]

In other words, the consequences of human decisions and actions outrun human intentions and must be attributed to 'a hidden creativity at work in the historico-cultural process'.[55] Whether *purpose* can be attributed to this creativity (and therefore whether Kaufman is falling back on some kind of immanent teleology) is not quite clear. If not, he means no more than that chance determines much of the course of human history.

This point is more relevant to the nuclear situation than Kaufman realizes. We have already seen how the future use or non-use of nuclear weapons, assuming their continued deployment, depends on collocations of circumstances which cannot be planned. The same is true of a successful process of disarmament. Naturally, nuclear disarmament, by whatever route, could not come about without the responsible activity of large numbers of people, but it will also depend on a complex collocation of circumstances which no one can deliberately create. Human decision and action are essential but not sufficient for success. Moreover, the actual forms and structure of a nuclear-free world are not likely to be such as can be accurately predicted and planned in advance, important as planning may be to their emergence. The result will outrun human intentions.

Kaufman comments:

> Although we can and certainly should hope that the creativity working in history will bring forth possibilities we cannot now foresee or intend, a pathway through the innumerable potential disasters that lie before us, this is not something on which we may rely with easy confidence (in the manner suggested by the traditional image of a providential God). Rather our fate today is very much in our own hands, and we must take full responsibility for it.[56]

But this is to miss the real significance of the point which Kaufman himself has recognized. For successful avoidance of nuclear disaster, we not only can and should but *must* hope for more than we can ourselves ensure. Our fate is in our own hands in the sense that annihilation will not be avoided unless we act to avoid it, but it is not in our own hands in the sense that we can ensure the success of our attempts to avoid it. The future is partly in our hands, but partly in the hands of – either chance or some purpose beyond individual human intentions. This alternative is unavoidable. If providence is understood in this way, not as overriding or manipulating human decision and action, but as that creativity which constantly makes more of our decisions and actions than we can make of them ourselves, then trust in providence is the very opposite of fatalism.[57] To decide and to act responsibly without the illusion of human omnipotence we *must* either hope that sheer chance will happen to be in our interests or trust in a providential purpose that has our interests at heart. Clearly the latter alternative, so far from detracting from human responsibility, is more likely than the former to sustain and encourage human responsibility.

Kaufman rejects the personal images of traditional theism as appropriate symbols for the 'hidden creativity' he sees in history, because he associates these images of providential care with the notion of a divine sovereignty that contradicts human freedom and responsibility. In fact, what is wrong with that notion is not that it conceives God as a personal, loving agent but that God does not, according to it, treat *us* as persons. We are merely his puppets. But a divine loving purpose which sustains, elicits and requires our free action, allowing it its full finite competence, while at the same time including it in consequences which lie beyond our competence, is most appropriately understood in personal categories. Jesus' image of the divine parent is not, after all, obsolete in the nuclear age.

However, a further step is necessary for a doctrine of providence adequate to the nuclear situation. The greatest failing of the traditional doctrine of providence was in being insufficiently christological. A reconstruction of it for the nuclear age must submit it to the Christian criterion of God's love for the world: the life, death and resurrection of Jesus. This will relate in two important ways to the theological issues of the nuclear threat.[58]

In the first place, the real difficulty of the doctrine of providence in the modern period lies not in the extent of human power, but in the appalling effects of the human attempt to master history in modern times. It is the difficulty of continuing to speak of God's providential care in the face of Auschwitz and all the other horrors of twentieth-century history. The prospect of the nuclear holocaust is, from this point of view, the prospect of an, if possible, even greater obstacle to all theodicy. However much it might rightly be said that, if the holocaust occurs, human sin will have brought its consequences on itself, innocent suffering will also be vast.

The only possible response, problematic as it is, is to say that God's love for the world not only creates history but also suffers it. (Again, against Kaufman, this requires not a less but a more personal image of God's relation to history.) God's omnipotence is not to be conceived as that omnipotence of sheer coercive force for which humanity reaches in developing nuclear weapons. It is the powerful love which includes, on the cross, God's suffering solidarity with humanity in both the judgment they bring upon themselves and the meaningless agony they inflict on each other. Because the crucified Jesus was God's self-identification with all human victims he will, in Dale Aukerman's phrase, be 'the central Victim' of the nuclear holocaust, should it happen.[59] But precisely because of this divine solidarity with victims, we know that the nuclear holocaust cannot belong to his purpose. If it happens, he will suffer it and it will happen because he suffers it.

Secondly, however, does trust in God's providence mean confidence that the nuclear holocaust cannot happen? Since Auschwitz has happened, no one dare say that the nuclear holocaust cannot happen. But Christian eschatology which is founded on the cross and resurrection of Jesus – God's identification with humanity in the depths of our suffering, failure and judgment and God's new creation of humanity out of the worst that can come to us – offers hope in two senses. It offers, in the first place, ultimate hope – that, should evil do its worst, it will not finally defeat God's purpose of establishing his kingdom. This requires a really transcendent God who, though he suffers the holocaust, will not, like Kaufman's God, perish with us in it, but, beyond the possibilities of our history, will raise our world and us into his glory in the new heaven and the new earth. In a sense, such radical hope deprives the nuclear threat of its *ultimate* seriousness (as belief in God must deprive evil of its ultimate seriousness), but not of its real seriousness nor of our motivation to avert it. God's purpose is not the holocaust but his kingdom which, even should the holocaust happen, he will establish *in spite* of it.[60]

The assurance of ultimate meaning which radical hope in the God of resurrection gives is a sustaining context for 'hoping against hope' in our efforts to avert the holocaust. A truly human future of peace, justice, friendliness and freedom cannot be achieved by the attempt to master history and control the future. The illusion of human omnipotence only frustrates these aims. Rather these are qualities of God's kingdom, which lie beyond the limits of our unaided competence, but can be received in trust and promoted in hope. Of our actions in faith and hope, the Spirit, who is God's providential love mediating the future of the resurrection into our present, can make more than we can make of them ourselves.

4

The Use of the Bible in the Nuclear Debate

JOHN-RICHES

The last few years have seen a number of weighty and considered church contributions to the nuclear debate. None of them, in my view, has drawn great support or insight from the Bible, though some acknowledgment of its relevance to the debate is generally made. Has the Bible nothing very much to contribute? Or is its effective neglect more the result of confusion about how it is to be read and its insights properly applied?

Let me start by considering one of the major church reports in this field, the Church of England General Synod's report, *The Church and the Bomb*.[1] The remit given to the Working Party which produced the report was a broad one. It encompassed both questions of Christian discipleship and advice on how Christians should best participate in public debate on the issue. In the end, it might seem, it was the latter which captured the attention of the working party. Its recommendations are concerned principally with matters of public policy, though there is a section on the churches' involvement in the peace process. This interpretation of its remit is not unimportant as it means that the report is addressing itself both in its recommendations and in its reasoning to those who have influence on decision making in matters of military policy and who cannot be assumed to hold Christian convictions.

This may well account for the structure of the report. Its opening four chapters address themselves to questions of technological and historical fact: the nature of nuclear weapons and their effects, the development of strategies for their deployment and the changing political context in which such strategies have emerged. It is then that its major assessment of the value of such policies is offered on the basis of a reading of the 'just war' tradition and conclusions drawn 'regarding the legitimacy of nuclear weapons, nuclear deterrence and nuclear war'. In so doing the report consciously appeals to what it refers to as 'the common ethical tradition, in part expressed in international law'.[2] Only then does it go on to discuss the 'principal theological themes which have shaped our approach'.

It has to be said that this chapter,[3] in marked contrast to the rest of the report, betrays a lack of cohesion. There are six sections, whose interrelation is not altogether clear: 'Ethics and the Gospel', 'Technological Progress and the Will of God', 'Peace, Love and Justice in the Christian Tradition', 'Principalities and Powers', 'Pacifism' and 'The Role of the Church'. The justification of the approach taken in the rest of the report is offered in different ways. Its appeal to the common ethical tradition and to a careful scrutiny of the facts is linked with the use of the Wisdom tradition, not only in the Old Testament, but also in the New by Jesus. The exact point made is worth noting. The Wisdom tradition, it is said, had two characteristic features: 'observation of the facts of nature and human life, and the quest for patterns in events . . . Wisdom, in the sense of understanding and respecting the given order of creation, and of living in harmony with it, is goodness'. Such wisdom was not always easy to find and therefore 'humanity needed a share in the mind of God, an endowment of his Spirit and Wisdom, a revealed knowledge of his laws'. But important though this was to Judaism it 'never superseded the keen eyed study of both humanity and the world order, and it is this which has given Jewish religion and morality its vitality and sympathetic quality to this day'. (Is this intended to imply that where Judaism deals with specific matters of Torah it is neither vital nor sympathetic?) Similarly we are reminded that Jesus in the Gospels owed a great deal to the Wisdom tradition.[4]

The conclusions drawn from this are, first and foremost, that a proper study of the world is part of the Christian vocation and will give us an insight into the nature and will of God. Christians are not, that is to say, committed to an authoritarian view of ethics but must give themselves more thoroughly to the study of the 'facts of the situations in which moral dilemmas occur'. This is clearly reassuring to the writers of the report because it allows them to participate on equal terms in a general moral debate. What is less clear is the role of that specific revelation of God's will which even the Wisdom tradition recognized was necessary, particularly in matters of deep complexity. This problem is not directly addressed, though we are told that 'except in the most general sense there are no timeless moral conclusions of Christian ethics in regard to nuclear weapons'.[5]

Now the fact of the matter is that the report has up to this point presented a very compelling argument based on the 'just war' tradition, in which, after careful consideration of the nature of nuclear weapons and the strategies which presently govern their deployment, it concludes that in the light of the 'just war' theory both their use and their threatened use is unjustifiable. To have introduced further theological considerations into the debate at this point might well have been to darken counsel. But, as we have seen, appeal to the Wisdom tradition in the Bible also involves an appeal to the legal tradition, to the knowledge of God's will revealed in Torah. By the same token it is hard to appeal to Jesus' use of proverbial sayings and parables without closer consideration of his teaching and preaching of the kingdom and of related apocalyptic material in the gospels. There is thus a strong sense in which the report's argument demands more sustained treatment of these matters; while prudence would dictate less. What the report in effect does is to neutralize Jesus' teaching.

In the first place the report effectively dismisses the relevance of Jesus' ethical teaching to this present world: in his ethical teaching he was looking away from the present world to the kingdom which was to come.[6] Thus his followers subsequently had to find answers to questions about their relation to the state which Jesus had turned aside. That is to say, the report regards his teaching about the kingdom as being concerned with a future world and therefore not strictly applicable to this. In their belief that this world would pass away Jesus and the earliest Christians were mistaken[7] and so the early church had to find its own ways of dealing with day to day problems. This implies that Jesus' ethical teaching is of no immediate relevance to our present concerns.

Nevertheless at two points the report does consider Jesus' teaching on specific topics: the relation of love and justice (referring to Matt. 20.1ff.)[8], and the question of love of enemies and non-retaliation (Matt. 5.38–48).[9] However, the direct bearing of Jesus' teaching on present decisions is left less than clear.

Jesus, we are told,[10] confronted and challenged contemporary notions of justice. He went beyond an understanding of justice simply as fairness: in the parable of the Labourers in the Vineyard (Matt. 20) the 'landowner chose to reward the labourers according to who they were, rather than according to what each had done'. In this Jesus points to the love which should lie behind justice, motivating and indeed criticizing (the report says; 'purifying'[11]) it. And this, rather surprisingly it might seem, is why Jesus concerned himself with love rather than justice as such. To get more specific teaching about the actual exercise of justice we should rather go back to the eighth-century prophets.

The discussion of Jesus' teaching on love of enemies and non-retaliation is subsumed in a general discussion of pacifism. Jesus, it is agreed, taught his followers to love their enemies and to return good for evil. Moreover in the Matthaean Sermon on the Mount love of enemies is linked with non-retaliation. It is on such teaching that pacifists of principle draw in their 'radical dissatisfaction with the world as it is . . . insist[ing] that nothing less than a renunciation of all use of coercive force will ever be able to bring about peace'.[12] Pacifists of this kind believe that 'the laws of the Kingdom, such as those of the Sermon on the Mount are literally binding in the present age, without exception or qualification. They reject the idea that God has made special provision for governing a fallen world between the Fall and the coming of the Kingdom'[13] (the report here makes reference to the Lutheran doctrine of the two kingdoms). From its own favouring of a more selective form of pacificism it is clear enough, though the case is not extensively argued, that the authors in the main took the view that Jesus' teaching could not be seen as 'literally binding in the present age'.[14] To do so, it is implied, would be to ally oneself to that radical dissatisfaction with the world as it is which would effectively cut one off from significant political interaction with those who presently have to take decisions about the development and deployment of nuclear weapons.

But what is being said here precisely about the teaching of Jesus? On the one hand it is suggested that his ethics were not intended to be/cannot be applied in the conditions of this age: they are more concerned with the kingdom which he expected to come with power. On the other hand it is said that his expectations of the coming of the kingdom were mistaken and that the church therefore had to set about making its own ethical rules as best it could. Put like that one might be forgiven for wondering whether the authors of the report have not cut away most of the ground on which they might reasonably be thought to have to stand as Christians. Of course it is not put like that and my construction of their rather disjointed remarks may therefore not represent the views of any member of the committee. Nevertheless it does raise questions, not exactly new ones, about the relation of Jesus' ethics to his preaching of the kingdom. (1) Are his ethical injunctions and reflections to be understood to apply to a future age which he expected to dawn imminently, or are they to apply to the lives of his followers in the present evil age? (2) In what sense, if at all, does the disappointment of Jesus' hopes in an imminent coming of the kingdom invalidate his ethical teaching? More generally there are I think questions to be raised about the whole framework within which the report interprets Jesus' teaching which is in no little way responsible for this strikingly negative interpretation of Jesus' teaching.

Let me turn first to the more general question of the interpretative framework. Christian interpretations of biblical texts are, in very broad terms, offered within a narrative framework which provides an account of universal history embracing creation, fall, the covenant with Israel, the incarnation and redemption in Christ, the church, judgment and the world to come. Within such a framework Jesus' teaching is seen as the authoritative revelation of God's will and purposes for his people – relating, that is, to their present duties and their future hopes. The report clearly reflects such a view when it speaks of Jesus' teaching as 'authoritarian', less so when it attempts to relate Jesus' teaching about the kingdom to the world to come, though even here it still works within the traditional framework.

There are, however, difficulties with such a framework when it comes to seeking guidance from the Bible in relation to pressing matters of state, such as military armaments and defence. In the first place, there have been in the course of history many views of what the church's relation to the state should be. At times the church has aspired to some form of theocracy; at others it has been happier to accept some kind of role division, such as is implied in Lutheran forms of the doctrine of the two kingdoms.[15] In the former case, the laws of the church were seen as binding on all aspects of life. In the latter case, theologians have tended to distinguish between 'natural' ethical teaching which was normative in affairs of state and the specific teaching of the church derived from the Bible which was binding on individual Christians, rather than on society at large. The report seems largely to opt for this second view and therefore to deny or play down the direct relevance of Jesus' teaching to affairs of state and international relations.

But secondly, there have been since the eighteenth century a series of sustained attacks on the biblical narrative which have shaken Christian confidence in it in a more fundamental sense.[16] Above all, the attack was directed against the notion that the Bible contained a divine and therefore infallible revelation – on the grounds both of the contradictions and errors to be found in the Bible (the report speaks of Jesus' mistaken beliefs) and on the grounds that such a revelation is heteronomous, that it requires men's and women's obedience without question and so undermines their moral integrity and autonomy. (This too is echoed in the report where it speaks of Christians not being committed to an authoritarian view of ethics.) Lessing in particular attacked the notion of such an authoritative revelation of divine truth. True human dignity lies not in the imagined possession of some truth; but in the continual striving for the truth, even though in the process one may always err.[17]

Such an attack on the authoritative character of Christian theology and ethics can, however, lead in different directions. On the one hand it may lead to a rear-guard action, as theologians attempt to retreat to some suitable high-ground from which to defend an albeit reduced doctrine of the Bible's authority. Christ may have been mistaken in some respects; much of what he taught may have been drawn from the common stock of human wisdom; but at least in certain key areas, concerning eternal salvation, he spoke with divine authority. Here the Lutheran doctrine of the two kingdoms may prove a valuable ally. On the other hand, it may lead bolder spirits, of whom Lessing was probably one, to see the teaching of the Bible as itself also part of that common search, not beyond criticism or error, but containing nonetheless important insights which should be drawn on in the general search for truth. This is not an option which many church theologians have felt able to take;[18] but it holds out greater prospects of being able to allow Jesus' voice – and indeed other Christian voices – to be heard within contemporary ethical debate. Nor, importantly, does such a view of Jesus' teaching require those who hold it to take any particular stance in regard to the question of naturalism and supernaturalism. To see Jesus' teaching as part of the human quest for truth and meaning does not mean that such a quest is or is not conducted under the guiding providence of God. Maybe that in such providential guiding God's hand is perfectly hidden; but maybe, too, to those who hear and seek to work out such teaching in the lives of their communities it does indeed become a 'light to their feet'.

It should be fairly clear that the report on the whole remains within the traditional framework of biblical understanding and it is this, coupled with its espousal of the doctrine of the two kingdoms, which, I would suggest, leads it to discount the relevance of much of Jesus' teaching to present matters of concern. At this point we may return to the questions raised above about the relevance of Jesus' teaching to this world and about the way in which his mistakenness about the coming of the kingdom affects our view of the validity of his ethical teaching.

I would agree with the report that Jesus' belief in the imminent coming of the kingdom was mistaken. But how are we to evaluate such mistakenness?

Let us first be as clear as possible about the nature of the mistake. Jesus believed that within his listeners' life-time God's rule would be established fully (Mark 9.1). In his exorcisms and healings he saw evidence of the binding of Satan and the overcoming of his power. At the least, we should suppose, this must have meant that opposition to God's will would cease, as would suffering, disease and sorrow. Manifestly that did not and has not occurred.

A number of questions arise: Was Jesus mistaken about every aspect of his belief in the coming of the kingdom – or only about its timing? Even if he was completely mistaken about the coming of the kingdom of God, does this invalidate all his other beliefs about the nature of God and his will? And, what significance should we attach, even to such mistaken beliefs about the future?

First, we know tantalizingly little about Jesus' precise notion of the kingdom of God come with power. His choice of Twelve seems to indicate his belief in a restoration of the kingdom to Israel, albeit in a rather different form, now ruled over by Galilean fishermen and artisans. Similarly, his action in the Temple, though deeply obscure, suggests some hope for radical change in the life of the nation, rather than simply an end to this life and the beginning of a totally new world. Thus his vision seems closer to the visions of Isaiah 40 and 60 of the restoration of national glory and independence, than to the visions of Mark 13 and Matthew 24–25 of a total transformation of the world. If this is the kind of belief that Jesus entertained – some radical renewal of Israel, [19] in which his chosen Twelve would play a role – then it is fair to say that it was in major respects mistaken: the Twelve did not sit on twelve thrones; there was no restoration of sovereignty to Israel, and there was no immediate end to suffering and disease.

If then Jesus was – literally – mistaken about the imminent coming of the kingdom, was he mistaken about everything else? Of course if one were to regard Jesus' teaching as true if and only if he was an infallible divine revealer, then one serious mistake would be sufficient to discredit him. If on the other hand, one sees Jesus as a major figure in the common search for truth and meaning then one will expect and be able to countenance a measure of error. The question then is: to what extent are those beliefs of Jesus which can be shown to be false to be numbered among the truth conditions of his other beliefs? Or do his other beliefs stand on their own?

First, it is I think misleading to see Jesus' beliefs about the future as the central or pivotal points of his teaching. If Mark 13.32 is original to him, then he there expressly disclaimed knowledge of the timing of the events of the end.

Further, his general style of teaching distinguishes him from other apocalyptic seers who received visions of the coming end of the ages. Indeed, as the report points out, he makes considerable use of Wisdom motifs based on observation of the world (cf. Matt. 5.38ff. with Sir. 4.10). While the use of such motifs is not unknown in the apocalyptic tradition (e.g. I Enoch 2–5) where it may serve to expound the nature of God's actions which have been revealed to the seer, in Jesus' teaching it serves to *ground* the injunctions which he gives to his hearers. In this sense Jesus' teaching is argumentative, addressed to all those who will hear; not, as for example in Qumran, an esoteric teaching addressed to the initiates.

The point is important: it suggests that Jesus' teaching should be carefully distinguished from that of apocalyptic visionaries. It also suggests, by contrast with what is said in the report, that in combining Wisdom argumentation with strong eschatological beliefs Jesus is

not simply concerned with 'understanding the given order of creation' but with renewing things in the light of God's underlying will.
And it is this vision of God's will which drives Jesus. His beliefs about
the future are – secondary – expressions of his desire to see God's
will realized.

Finally, a broader observation may serve to suggest that Jesus'
teaching is by no means centred on or logically dependent on his
beliefs about the future. The fact is simply that a great deal of what
is preserved of his teaching is concerned with practical matters
relating to the conduct of affairs in this world, not with details about
the future. On all these counts, it is unlikely that the truth of his
beliefs about such matters was conditional upon the truth of his
beliefs about the future coming of the kingdom.

Thus there is a strong *prima facie* case for not disregarding all Jesus'
teaching, simply because he was wrong about the future. At the same
time we also need to ask, as the report does not, what significance
we may attach to Jesus' beliefs about the future, *even though they were
mistaken*.

It is clear that expectations of some sudden and dramatic end to
the present age were common among Jews (and others) in the first
century. Such beliefs were mythological in the sense that they
involved the intervention of divine powers in the affairs of this world.
They were of course falsified by history. But that does not mean that,
because their sense was in fact false, they did not therefore have an
important function, or indeed functions, in the societies in which
they were advocated. Belief in some coming major societal crisis,
brought about by God himself, freed people from the control of their
traditional beliefs and enabled them to contemplate and adumbrate
changes to come as also willed by God. Thus, interestingly, while
those who held such beliefs were deeply critical of the present order
in which they lived, they were in no sense otherworldy in their
attitudes. On the contrary they eagerly looked forward to the renewal
or restoration of this world.

Thus such mythological beliefs may quite properly be said to
represent a belief that important changes were underway and the
role of the prophet was often to begin to spell out what those changes
would be. In this respect Jesus' teaching offers a remarkable range of
ethical and theological perceptions which will indeed form the basis
of the new age which is inaugurated by his disciples. Not that such
perceptions come to us as fully worked out programmes of legislation.
Rather, such figures, as Victor Turner has argued, are the 'unacknow-
ledged legislators' of humanity.[20] It is for their followers to attempt
to embody their teaching in social and constitutional form.[21] Jesus'
achievement is to have quickened and inspired the common search

in a way that has continued to engage people in a struggle for justice and peace.

This may be the point at which to address the difficult question of the use of such apocalyptic ideas in contemporary debate. It is, it seems to me, one thing to say that they had an important function in advancing contemporary aspirations and making people more receptive to innovatory ideas; quite another to move from that to employing them in contemporary debate. And the variety of uses to which they are put should serve to make us cautious.

On the one hand, there are those who argue that Christians should not accept the existence of large stocks of nuclear weapons as if they were simply a fact of life. They should rather respond positively to the gospel's call to establish a new order of things, for the gospel is not solely a call to personal renewal or transformation but a call to bring about a new social order.[22] Here, as occurs also within Liberation theology when arguing for the need for radical transformation of the world economic order, the apocalyptic tradition is being used to reaffirm that transformation of the existing social world is a central Christian concern.

This is certainly a faithful reflection of Jesus' prophetic role in pointing his people towards new worlds, even if the process of appropriation is not always clearly expressed or indeed understood. A caution, however, should be entered. While it is right to appeal to the apocalyptic tradition to justify the concern with radical social change it would not equally be justified to identify with the kingdom itself *any* particular state of affairs which might be brought about. There is a possible danger here that liberation theologians might identify particular revolutions with the ultimate realization of God's will, rather than seeing the kingdom as a reality that always has to be worked for. Similarly, it would clearly be a mistake to suppose that any kind of arms agreement on nuclear weapons, even if it involved the agreement on all sides to renounce all nuclear weapons, would represent a final solution to the problem. That of course does not mean that it is not something devoutly to be striven for! Rather, the apocalyptic tradition should serve to remind us of two things: of the need to be constantly on guard against those forces in society which tend to corrupt; as well as of the need to be constantly searching for more and more effective ways of instantiating those fundamental insights into the nature of God's will which lie at the heart of Jesus' ethical teaching. The 'kingdom' is not something that we shall ever see fully realized; it does stand over against all human efforts to realize justice and peace in the world as both a critique and a spur to action.

Other uses of the language of apocalyptic have tended to concentrate more on its ability to characterize the sinfulness and corruption of the present world and thus to help people loosen their commitment to existing forms of political order. Thus Daniel Berrigan[23] has drawn powerfully on the image of the beast to characterize political regimes which threaten mass destruction. This is an aspect of apocalyptic which has also fascinated writers, artists and film makers, (Büchner, Golding, Schiele, Bergmann, Fellini). The reason for this fascination lies, I suspect, in the inadequacy of our commonly accepted ethical language to express the depths of depravity to which people individually and corporately may fall.

The power of such rhetoric is undeniable; as are its dangers. In the first place the rhetoric is as easily used by those with great moral insight as by those with little or none. Alongside Berrigan stands Reagan whose talk of the 'evil empire' was all too effective in communicating a sense of outrage and rejection. And in both cases the use of such biblical language invests the utterances with a measure of theological authority. Secondly, it is again too easy to move from use of such language as rhetoric to a literal belief in the demonic nature of those so characterized.

Where of course apocalyptic darkens counsel beyond any redemption[24] is where it is taken as giving a set of predictions about what is – shortly – to come. Current belief in Armageddon and the Rapture among some groups in the United States and in the UK gives a vivid example of the dangers of such uncritical use of Revelation. The error of such an approach is clear enough. If apocalyptic texts of, for example, the synoptic gospels are to be interpreted literally then they clearly predicted the end of the world within the life-time of Jesus' followers and have therefore long since been shown to be false. No attempt to reschedule or to reapply them should blind us to this obvious point. The question is not how to demonstrate their falsehood but how to counter such erroneous understandings.

But even those who reject literalist uses of apocalyptic language in favour of its rhetorical use need to be critical of the ethical content of some forms of apocalyptic tradition. There can be no disputing the fact that the apocalyptic literature of the intertestamental period was full of visions of the violent destruction of the seer's enemies. Doubtless for those suffering from various forms of oppression this had its own consolation. But it does mean that there is a sharp ethical dissonance between Jesus' teaching of love of enemies and sentiments to be found in books which draw heavily on the tradition, such as Jude and Revelation.

An example here is provided by Andrew Chester who seeks to play down the predictive aspects of apocalyptic by emphasizing its visionary nature and its concern with a particular historical situation.[25] But in attempting to rescue the book of Revelation Chester is too quick to point up the applicability of some of its themes to our present situation. Here I have particular objection to the claim that the two witnesses in Rev. 11 'denote ideal witnesses, and . . . represent the true prophetic role exercised within the community'.[26] What does this mean, said without further explanation, of figures of whom we read: 'And if any one would harm them, fire pours from their mouth and consumes their foes; if any one would harm them, thus he is doomed to be killed' (Rev. 11.5)? Taking that seriously in the present nuclear debate might have more serious and detrimental consequences than the belief in Armageddon.

Thus my own view is that we should not try to salvage the apocalyptic element in the New Testament in any but the most rigorously critical way. And that means, on the one hand, being quite clear about the falsehood of apocalyptic predictions, and on the other, recognizing the danger, to which apocalyptic literature was prone, of drawing on a rich vein of tradition which rejoiced in the destruction and torment of one's enemies. It would be better, as *The Church and the Bomb* writers clearly felt, to distance oneself from the tradition altogether, than to run the risk of using it uncritically. But it would be better still to be able to draw on its power to alert us to the gross immorality of much present political policy and to spur people to work for the realization in society of those values which are centrally advocated in the New Testament.

Perhaps one final observation on apocalyptic may be in place. One of the most intriguing aspects of apocalyptic literature is indeed, as Chris Rowland has argued perhaps too forcefully,[27] its visionary nature. These visions draw strongly on dualist language and imagery, though such dualism is ultimately contained within a burning vision of God's sovereignty and power. The evil in the world, that is to say, is seen as starkly contrasted with God's will and nature – but also as ultimately subject to him. One of the issues to which those who acknowledge such theological views have to turn is the manner in which the sheer destructiveness of nuclear weapons and the actual use of them against fellow humans may affect our understanding of creation. Can we any longer see a world which contains within it such awe-inspiring destructive forces as good, as the creation of the ultimately good God? Or does the blame for Hiroshima and Nagasaki lie not with God but with those who unleashed such forces, truly reflecting the very power of God, *for such ends*?

A most illuminating treatment of these issues is to be found in Chaim Potok's *The Book of Lights*.[28] Potok draws on the resources of the Zohar to make us ponder the awesome destructiveness of the physical world of God's creation, and the sense in which men and women are involved in the continuing work of God's creation. And thus he raises the question how we are to undo the damage which has been inflicted on human history and consciousness by the guilt of Hiroshima and Nagasaki. Again this is a profound question about the kind of world we are to build. Is it a world in which we accept without repentance the horrors inflicted on innocent people? Or can a new world be built only when the stain of that crime is expunged?

The argument thus far has been as follows: Jesus was mistaken in his belief in the imminent radical restoration of Israel. He was however 'correct' in so far as he looked forward to radical cultural shifts in the Jewish tradition. While he was mistaken about the coming of the kingdom, even such beliefs expressed a deep awareness of the corruption of the present and the need for change. Nor does the mistakenness of such beliefs mean that he was mistaken about everything else. The main weight of his teaching, indeed, seems to have lain elsewhere. In his ethical teaching he points to a new understanding of human relations rooted in a vision of the mercifulness of God, who sends his rain upon the just and the unjust. In all this we may see him, not so much according to the traditional picture as the infallible revealer of divine truths but as one of the great searchers for truth in human history. In such a quest men and women may never penetrate to the ultimate truth which is beyond all error. That, as Lessing suggested, is for God alone. In so far as they are human they are limited by the particular beliefs of their own age and culture. But they may nevertheless in their searching see and learn things about God, the world and humanity which remain as signposts for future generations.

The question which then arises is this: if Jesus' teaching is to be seen as one of the major contributions to the human quest, under God, for truth and meaning: how far was it related to and can it be presently related to the conditions of this world? How far, as the report puts it, is it 'literally binding in the present age'?

Much here depends on how closely the various aspects of Jesus' teaching were linked. Did Jesus' ethical teaching relate exclusively to the kingdom come with power? This seems highly unlikely. The commands to love one's enemies and to turn the other cheek suggest a context more to be expected in the period which will usher in the kingdom than in the period of its realization. Similarly one may assume that in the kingdom all will be properly cared for and that there will be no need for almsgiving or for concern about where one's next meal is coming from. Injunctions about such matters, which occupy most of the Sermon on the Mount, are for the period of 'seeking the kingdom' (Matt. 6.33). There will indeed have been a correspondence between the actions and attitudes which were enjoined for the period before the coming of the kingdom with power, and those appropriate thereafter, but the immediate relevance is for the present.

But, in what sense was Jesus' ethic realistic, appropriate to the social, political and economic conditions of his age? Here some consideration of the immediate circumstances in which Jesus enjoined Jews to love their enemies is necessary. The Jews had long been living with powerful neighbours who had occupied and ruled their country for considerable periods. At the time of Jesus all Palestine was moving towards direct Roman rule which would be followed by two disastrous Jewish revolts. Many of Jesus' contemporaries would have cherished stories of the victorious Maccabaean revolt and wished to redeem the defeats of the followers of Judas the Galilean at the beginning of the century. Others responded to encroaching Roman rule and influence by putting up the barriers, reinforcing Jewish separation from Graeco-Roman culture and redoubling their efforts to maintain their own cultural rules and values. ˙

Thus in Jesus' day many will have been scandalized by Jesus' call to 'love your enemies', not so much because of the cost that such an invitation implied – where risks were concerned there were clear parallels in the Zealots' call to discipleship[29] – as because of the manner in which Jesus suggested that people should respond to the threat of Roman domination. To urge people to adopt open and friendly attitudes to those who sought to dominate them, who were perceived as threatening their own values, and who would not scruple to use all necessary coercive force against those who opposed them, would have appeared to many either as an act of betrayal or of folly.[30]

Why then did Jesus advocate such a policy and how did it relate to his belief in the coming kingdom? Jesus' own justification for the command to love one's enemies was given in the form of a wisdom saying: 'so that you may be sons of your Father who is in heaven; for he makes his sun to rise on the evil and the good, and sends rain on the just and on the unjust,' (Matt. 5.45). It is because such behaviour is in fundamental accord with the will of the creator as that can be inferred from the course of natural events. This is the way that men and women should behave because it corresponds to the way things – really – are.

But of course that was certainly not the way they may have appeared to be to many of Jesus' contemporaries, or indeed to Jesus himself. His observation of the world must have told him all too readily that such openhanded behaviour might well be taken advantage of and he clearly longed for a world where this would no longer be the case, where God's will would indeed be done. Thus in his preaching of the kingdom he announced the coming of a new age where the divine will – as he perceived it – would be realized. And much of his teaching in parables was an attempt to spell out what such a world would be like, on what notions of God's justice, mercy and love it would be founded.

In that sense it is right to say, as the report does, that the notions of justice which are explored, for example, in the parable of the Labourers in the Vineyard are concerned with virtues which, for Jesus, will be fully realized only in the age to come; not right, even in Jesus' own terms, to suggest that he was only interested in the future manifestation of such virtues. He called people to follow him in such a path even in the present age, knowing that the conflict between this age's values and the values of the kingdom would bring suffering, but believing that such a path would lead to the new age. Jesus is a liminal figure in his society: a prophet who stands at the margins, dreaming of new worlds to come, giving voice to the values of such a new age in metaphor and ethical injunction. But even so, his commands bear a direct relation to the present behaviour of his disciples: this is how they are to act now. They are themselves part of the reality of that new age which is already dawning.

Jesus' command to love one's enemies represents, I believe, a significant development of Israel's traditions. It is certainly not without precedence in laws which prescribed the just and open-handed treatment of strangers within the Jewish community; but as a command to love those outside the community, or those with evil intent towards it, it is novel. It is also intensely difficult to apply to human and social situations. How can you go on forgiving someone who misuses your forgiveness to disrupt and destroy the life of the community? It is not, as I was suggesting above, so much its huge cost as the apparent conflict of such a policy with other goals: the maintenance of one's community itself, that makes it seem impossible. In what sense can communities dispense with the use of coercive force?

Put like that, it is hard not to side with those who argue that it is an unworldly ethic, not – literally – applicable to his own or indeed to ours. At best it may be thought to act as a spur to greater moral effort, while for the majority 'God has made special provision for governing the world between the Fall and the coming of the Kingdom'.[31] But to take such a view is to blunt the force of Jesus' command and to invite us to seek guidance elsewhere.

It may be that the account we have been offering of Jesus' prophetic role can help resolve this dilemma. On such a view Jesus is neither to be seen as a legislator, laying down a detailed code of laws for the new society which he expected; nor is he to be seen as solely describing the conditions which will obtain in the 'spiritual kingdom' whenever it may come. He is a prophet proclaiming the fundamental principles which will have to be given detailed instantiation in the new age which his followers are called to 'seek'. It is, in other words, an invitation to seek forms of society, national and international, based on moral authority rather than on the readiness to use coercive force. That search is still ours and can only be pursued by detailed efforts to bring legislation more into accord with his vision. This does not mean that the need for the use of force will vanish overnight. What it means is that we should be working for a society where its use is the exception, rather than the norm.

It is of course clear from Jesus' own history that the cost of such policies is high. Jesus' own longing for a new world where the forces of evil would be finally overcome is itself testimony to his desire to see the end of those forces which opposed him. And yet he did, as far as we can know, remain true to his own precepts. He did not 'revile again'. And in this he won a strange victory: not the victory of the imposition of his will on his oppressors – quite the contrary, he was delivered up into the hands of wicked men. But his victory lay elsewhere: in the triumph of his spirit over temptation, in the living out of his vision of God's will to the end (John 13.1). It was in that finishing of his work that his glorifying of the Father lay, that he gave form to, embodied the divine purpose. To speak thus is of course to abandon the language of humanist social history for the profound meditations of the Fourth Gospel. But such a move is a necessary step in understanding the kind of commitment and understanding which underlies the way of the cross. It is a way which can only be embarked on by those who are fired with a vision of God's ultimate love for all men and women (John 3.16) – and who are prepared to allow that vision to take root in their lives (15.5). It is this vision of the holy, living God which empowers and sustains Jesus and his followers and which gives them the strength to stand firm.

And yet it is of course one thing for an individual to commit herself to ways which can lead to martyrdom: how can such an example inform the policies of groups and nations? It is clear that, from the start, even within the community of Jesus' immediate followers, attempts at embodying Jesus' precepts in social form encountered great difficulty. The tension between the vision of an all-forgiving God and the need for community discipline is vividly expressed in Peter's question: Lord how often shall my brother sin against me and I forgive him?[32] And there is in the Matthaean resolution of that question an element of accommodation: the one who cannot learn forgiveness when he himself has been forgiven so much is himself cast out. And there is a sense in which the history of the church, and even more so of Christian societies and states has been a history of such accommodation. But that is not to suggest that all such attempts at realizing Jesus' precepts in social form are simply betrayals of the original ideals. Some may indeed so far abandon the original ideal that little recognizable is left. In others a creative tension may be achieved which gives birth to policies and forms of life which do indeed reflect something of the original. In one sense it is clear that there is a great gap between Jesus' command not to resist evil and the notion of a just war. In another the development of such a theory represents a substantial achievement in tempering aggression and limiting the damage and destruction which men inflict on their enemies. Such attempts at the social embodiment of Christian precepts are marked then by a realism which takes seriously both the realities of human aggression and depravity *and* the sense in which, as creatures of God, men and women have it in themselves to rise above such powers.

And because such Christian realism takes seriously the *prevailing* realities, even such relative successes are in need of constant revision. The conditions, economic, political and military which produced the just war theory are not ours. It may be that once there was indeed a sense in which the use of limited and carefully directed force could be seen as the least damaging and costly way of resolving serious situations of conflict between the great powers. This century has already shown how in a world grown so small any conflict, however limited, can easily spread to engulf all. But now not only have advances in communication and the consequent enlargement of political spheres of influence made the localization of conflict increasingly difficult; the advent of thermo-nuclear war has made the costs of any globalization of conflict impossibly high.

In such a situation the just war theory still fulfils an important function. It demonstrates, as the report clearly shows, the unacceptability of any nuclear war and of any policy based on the willingness to employ nuclear weapons at any stage. What in a sense it does not do is to point the way forward to a new moral base on which international affairs may be conducted in present conditions: though even here we may learn from it. We may appeal to it, justly enough, as part of our common ethical inheritance, born out of the creative encounters of Christian precept and historical realities. But we need again to engage creatively with our own situation. How can the centuries of Christian experience of attempting to forgive the unforgivable, of encountering fear, aggression and destructiveness with love, courage and patience, inform present negotiations and armaments policies? Where is the place for the creative act of renunciation? Where the place for prudence and calculation? Answers to such questions may indeed be worked out in fear and trembling and a wider framework achieved perhaps only after a protracted period of debate. But there is at least a strong case for saying that in our present situation where the use on a super power level of counterforce carries with it such possibilities of global (and therefore also self-) destruction, considerations not only of the limitation of force, but of its voluntary renunciation must be given full weight.

In any such attempt we shall be wise to bear in mind the great variety of Christian attempts to live out and embody Christ's precepts. Whatever the failings of Christian history, and they are many, we must not overlook those who have striven to give political and communal form to such insights. Whether at the level of the family, the small community or indeed of the state there are important lessons to be learned perhaps not least from those who have been considered radical and been largely marginalized by the main stream of Christianity, among whom, importantly, are the pacifists. Now is not the time to abandon such attempts to live out Jesus' radical insights, just at the point where they are of particular and pressing relevance, as indeed the report acknowledges at one point.[33]

The reference is to a speech of Dr Runcie in which he suggested that if peace is to be achieved we need to learn to see things through Russian eyes and to avoid the rhetoric which suggests to us that threatening their mass extinction is in some way part of the 'normal' world. Such an affront to existing and accepted attitudes and beliefs is precisely what is required if we are to break free of the cold war which locks us into two conflicting worlds. But how specifically can appeal to the command to love one's enemies help us to move forward in the present situation?

In the first place I think it is important that we should have this ethical goal very clearly in view in any practical discussions of these issues. What I have been criticizing in this chapter is the tendency to dismiss such ethical goals from 'realistic' discussions of technical issues of thermo-nuclear warfare in the interests of remaining within a shared field of common ethical insights. I have argued both that Jesus' call to love one's enemies has in fact played an important role in forming our common ethical traditions and that it should continue to act as a spur to ethical reflection, precisely because of the changing nature of our world.

Secondly, I think that we need to challenge arguments which suggest that love of enemies is either impossible or unrealistic. Even in Jesus' day, as stories in Josephus make clear,[34] non-violent resistance was not by any means ineffective. Today this may be all the more true. For if in past ages it was possible to resolve international rivalries and conflicts by military engagement, by the use of coercive force, it is now in the last resort no longer so possible. What may have looked impossible, because detrimental to national security and survival, is now perhaps the only chance left for survival. That should challenge us both to look to our traditions, in so far as they have sought to find ways of instantiating that command of Jesus, and to seek boldly and creatively new ways of following it in the present situation of nuclear confrontation.

Thirdly, the importance of such goals lies in their ability to widen and criticize the goals which we might otherwise set ourselves. Nuclear arms limitation talks are, no doubt at all, important. But the continued threat of the use of such weapons, even after the success of such talks, makes it only too clear that we need to remove not only the means of inflicting such appalling destruction, but also any reason for so doing. We need, that is, to seek all possible ways of making peace between East and West, both within and outwith the context of official diplomatic relations. Here the past record and experience of the Christian churches may have much that is valuable to contribute, both by way of warning and of encouragement.

Such suggestions remain of course at the level of considerable generality but are not, I hope, without a certain cutting edge.

How negotiations are to be conducted; how crises and emergencies are to be managed; what risks we can afford to take; what ways may be found of overcoming the 'natural' aggression of nation states and discovering new forms of international co-operation: all these questions require detailed expertise and discussion. But in each case we cannot afford to rest until we have answers which allow us to create structures of trust in our national and international life.

5

Nationalism and Internationalism: A Theological Critique

KEITH CLEMENTS

'We are coming to a time when national sovereignty is no longer a helpful ingredient in the management of world affairs.'[1] This recent comment by an Anglican bishop typifies much of the concern which prompts the task assigned to this chapter: to enquire what theological resources there are for relativizing the interests of state or nation, in view of the tendency for thinking about nuclear weapons to elevate the concept of national security to that of an absolute value. In fact criticism of the assumed status of 'the sovereign nation-state' has been typical of peace-movements since the turn of the century. Nuclear weaponry, however, appears to mark the ultimate apotheosis of nationalism, signifying as it does a willingness not only to raise the stakes of conflict to mutually genocidal proportions, but to inflict upon the rest of humankind and planetary life, not parties to the particular conflict, the threat of extinction.

1 The nation above all else?

Loyalty to the sovereign nation-state as an absolute or supreme value has not, of course, had to wait for the advent of nuclear weaponry. In his *Mein Kampf* Adolf Hitler laid it down as a basic item in the National Socialist creed that: 'Whoever is prepared to make the national cause his own to such an extent that he knows no higher ideal than the welfare of his nation; whoever has understood our great national anthem, 'Deutschland über Alles', to mean that nothing in this wide world surpasses in his eyes this Germany, people and land – that man is a [National] Socialist.'[2] But neither has it had to await the arrival of Nazism or other forms of fascism. It is instructive, if disconcerting, to place alongside Hitler's phraseology the more

familiar poetry of Cecil Spring-Rice, which to many British people is
still the most eloquent expression of national loyalty:

> I vow to thee, my country – all earthly things above –
> Entire and whole and perfect, the service of my love.
> The love that asks no question: the love that stands the test,
> That lays upon the altar the dearest and the best:
> The love that never falters, the love that pays the price,
> The love that makes undaunted the final sacrifice.

Taking these statements in themselves, it is hard to be certain of
any fundamental difference in basic sentiment. Hitler ('nothing
in this wide world surpasses . . . this Germany') and Spring-Rice
('. . . my country, all earthly things above') alike regard nationality
as an unquestionable, absolute claim upon loyalty and conscience,
repellent though it may seem to place a poem found in many English
hymn-books in the same camp as, say, the *Horst Wessel Lied*. The
sentiments of the respective authors, it will be argued, cannot be
separated from their practice. Hitler was a brutal dictator, Spring-
Rice a gentle, indeed gentlemanly, English diplomat. That, however,
simply recasts the criticism: for all their differences, does not any
statement of human loyalty, however seemingly grotesque or
refined, which assumes the nation as an absolute ideal, sanction
violence as an inherent feature of human existence with ultimately
genocidal consequences? The case of Hitler and Nazism might be
extreme, but is it not the extremity of a road on which we are all
travelling if we take national tribalism for granted? What is to
distinguish the evil of the holocaust being prepared for in our missile
silos from the holocaust actually perpetrated at Auschwitz?

It is not hard to see that nuclear weaponry, the ultimate in armed
force, is bound up with the absolutization of nationality (or what the
country, or 'the free world' – for of course we are also dealing with
transnational empires and alliances – 'stands for'). It both feeds, and
is fed by, the demand for national security as an unquestionable
value, and all the attendant symbolism and emotions of 'patriotism'.
Reinhold Niebuhr's comment, made over fifty years ago, has therefore acquired a new level of confirmation in the nuclear age:

> the modern nation is the human group of strongest social cohesion,
> of most undisputed social authority and of most clearly defined
> membership. The church may have challenged its pre-eminence
> in the Middle Ages, and the economic class may compete with it
> for the loyalty of man in our own day; yet it remains, as it has been
> since the seventeenth century, the most absolute of all human
> associations.[3]

In face of this description, the prescription of the ultimate Christian commitment can be baldly stated: the kingdom of *God*, which, precisely because it is the kingdom of *God*, is universal by nature and transcending all particular loyalties. It does not merely exist alongside these 'lesser' loyalties but engages with them in judgment and grace, and thus forbids their absolutization or idolization. As Wolfhart Pannenberg states, 'A world in which national interests dominate diplomacy and politics is one which has no room for the Christian expectation of a kingdom of God which will be a system of justice and peace for the whole human race'.[4]

However, even if it is agreed that the ultimate necessity of war is 'a logical conclusion as long as one sees the world as made up of rival nation-states',[5] this is only to make the merest beginning of an engagement with the issue of the absolutization of nationhood. The 'sovereign nation-state', as was stated earlier, has long been a familiar target of anti-war argument, but such arguments are notoriously short on prescriptions for alternative structures for international life – or at least those which can conceivably be implemented. At the risk of being accused of accepting too readily 'the world as it is' this chapter will argue that Christian theology does indeed offer insights and axioms which can counter the absolutization of nationhood, but only if first it recognizes that the 'sovereign nation-state' does exist, and that no amount of wishing it away, however passionately and eloquently expressed, will make it cease to exist. We should rather examine more carefully just what constitutes national existence in the modern world and how – on the assumption that it cannot be conjured out of existence overnight – it might be subjected to a new evaluation so as to be brought within the purposes of justice and peace instead of oppression and violence. Elsewhere, using the thought of Dietrich Bonhoeffer as a foil, I have explored at greater length what 'love of country' could mean today not as a contradiction of, but as an aspect of, one's commitment to a world of justice and peace and in opposition to nationalistic idolatry.[6]

A convenient way of beginning the analysis is to examine the term 'sovereign nation-state' itself. That we require three words to describe an apparently obvious fact of contemporary life, should be enough to warn us against any simplistic notions of what we are dealing with. In fact, the more the concept of nationhood is examined, the more one is inclined to despair of reaching any satisfactory definition of what it means to be, or to belong to, a nation in the modern world.[7] The term we are dealing with, however, is the *nation-state* and we should therefore first attend to 'the state'.

2   The state

By state is understood here 'the organized political community with government recognized by the people, commonwealth, nation'.

Now the term 'nation-state' itself indicates that we are dealing with an ambiguous or at any rate a complex phenomenon. In the modern world 'nation' and 'state' can rarely in actuality be separated, but must be distinguished. A nation requires some sort of legislative, judicial and administrative structure to function on the contemporary scene. Equally, a state without a society to govern would be an absurd abstraction (even 'governments in exile' lay claim to more than paper constitutions). But our wish, sometimes only partly articulated, to distinguish 'nation' and 'state' while hyphenating them, witnesses to a recognition that they cannot simply be identified or wholly subsumed one in the other. We cannot therefore abstract consideration of the 'state' from the 'nation'. Neither state nor nation comprehends the totality of what it is to be human, nor should the state be considered the supreme sphere of national existence.

3   Nation

'Nation' denotes that complex of objective and subjective features whereby people identify themselves as 'a people', and it cannot by any means be entirely comprehended within the 'state'. It typically includes attachment to and occupation of a specific geographical territory, a common language (or possibly more than one), the subtle fabric of 'culture' inherited from the past and enriching the present, and the barely definable but vital collective memories and shared historical experience out of which the national story or 'myth' is composed and by which, at profound and barely conscious levels, the national identity is shaped. It is, in short, communal rather than organizational existence. It is a concrete form of human social life, and simply to dismiss its significance in face of the need to affirm a 'global human solidarity' is to ignore how human history and human society operate. Any who would dismiss regard for it out of hand as 'chauvinism' should ponder how many of the aspects of their lives which they value highly, or simply take for granted, would even be possible but for the operation of the institutions and services which arise and are sustained within the context of a particular national tradition and culture: not least in academic life.

We shall examine certain theological evaluations of 'national existence' later. For the moment, it suffices to emphasize again that national life cannot simply be equated with membership of the state. For one thing, a state may include more than one nationality within it, as seen for instance in the United Kingdom (though the English are largely unaware of this fact). For another, loyalty to the state on the one hand, and 'patriotism' conceived as loyalty to one's 'people' on the other, can at times be in conflict. In nineteenth-century German history, for instance, the uneasy tension between the autocratic Prussian state, and the pan-German nationalist movement, would offer a constructive case-study which has been obscured by the later fateful course of German history whereby state absolutism and populist extremism have been fused in a single image of 'nationalism'. However, a further factor must be noted. Not only is the nation distinguishable from the state, but in modern times the nation as a 'people' has often undergone an absolutization of its own, distinct from that of the state. A widespread tendency of national sentiment has been to conceive of the nation as a kind of 'person': and all this, while there has been developing in western thought the deeply rooted tendency to emphasize the unique individuality of each 'person' who has a right to his or her particular 'fulfilment'. The modern nation has therefore received powerful ideological backing from those philosophies (such as romanticism) and religious trends (such as pietism) which see each person or specific group as possessing a unique individuality, an inner 'soul' struggling to find its unique expression or salvation. It is but a short step from the rights of the unique individual in society, to the rights of the unique nation in the world. So we find Friedrich Schleiermacher, pioneer of modern Protestant theology, hailing the eve of Prussia's liberation from Napoleonic dominion in 1813:

> God has imparted to each its own nature . . . In rising up to cast this [domination] utterly off and to keep it away from us for the future, we become once more a kingdom that trusts in the Lord; for in him is that nation trusting which means *to defend at any price the distinctive aims and spirit which God has implanted in it, and is thus fighting for God's work*; and only as we succeed in this can we become as a tree planted by the waters, that fears not when heat cometh, and brings forth its own fruit without ceasing.[8]

We shall deal presently with some of the later fruits of this theology of nationality. It has kinsfolk in all attempts to invest the nation with some unique, quasi-mystical character requiring 'purification' or at least preserving 'at any price'. In still more extrovert and confident form, it manifests itself in a messianic consciousness as a 'chosen people' called to fulfil a divine (or perhaps secular revolutionary) role in the world at large, as in some self-perceptions in the United States today, possibly also in the Soviet Union, and certainly in the high days of the British Empire. Thereby the state is supplied with a most potent pretext for justifying its own power and means of 'security' at any price. In promoting the overriding aim of 'national security' as *itself* the chief moral consideration, by nuclear arms and by other typically modern means, the state will not in fact overtly appeal to its own unchallengable claim, as a *state*, to conscience and allegiance, nor to *its* insatiable drive to ensure *its* own survival. Rather, it will claim to be acting in the interests of 'the nation' and its ideals, and, in the case of idealistic, messianic nationalism, in the interests of humanity at large. It will be prepared, moreover, should it feel the need to arise, so to influence and maybe to direct the organs of education and the media as to ensure that its own image of what the nation 'stands for' is projected upon society. Theology therefore will have to engage with both the related but distinct facets of 'state' and 'nation', each with its own forms of self-promotion to 'all earthly things above'.

4   Sovereign

'Sovereignty' has become something of a hate-word among peace-campaigners and internationalists, conveying as it does the image of nations being laws unto themselves within their own domain, and acting purely out of self-interest, as power and opportunity allow, on the wider world scene. Nothing is more provocative of conflict, apparently, than the felt violation of a nation's 'sovereignty'. It seems logical, therefore, that 'sovereignty' should be rendered obsolete for the sake of a safer and more sane world order in which 'international law' or even 'world government' becomes the order of the day. Unfortunately, the word carries a spectrum of meanings in inter-national political parlance and debate. Loosely, and especially by its critics, it is taken to mean the right of a nation or state to act in whatever it imagines to be its best interests, regardless of the consequences for other parties. On this view it is yet another symptom of the elevation of nationhood to a unique and unquestionable value, disregarding any sense of accountability to the wider human community.

However, it is possible to agree (as I do) with a rejection of that form of national egoism, and at the same time to identify a perfectly legitimate and indeed vital notion of 'sovereignty'. This has nothing to do with the 'power' or 'freedom of action' which a nation may wield in the outside world, but everything to do with what actually constitutes the nation as such. To quote Alan James in his recent study *Sovereign Statehood*,[9] the sovereignty of a nation-state, which qualifies it for participation (regardless of its 'power') in international life is its *constitutional independence*: 'the distinguishing characteristic of a sovereign state is that it possesses a set of legal arrangements relating to fundamental matters – its constitution – which exists in its own right.'[10] Or, as another theorist puts it, 'To say that a state is sovereign means that it decides for itself how it will cope with its internal and external problems.'[11] Far from being inimical to the notion of international law, it is the presupposition of such law, which can only take effect as it is recognized by nation-states – and such recognition implies their sovereignty. This bedrock understanding of sovereignty can be seen as analogous, at a more intimate level, with the presuppositions required about the status, dignity and moral autonomy of the individual person. This need have nothing to do with 'individualism' or 'egoism', but is simply the recognition that only real persons can form genuinely *interpersonal* relationships, and can do so only by commitments entered into with a real measure of freedom respected by others. On the level of world order, to ignore this has profoundly undemocratic, indeed oppressive or even tyrannical implications. Far from inducing an ethical tone into international affairs, therefore, unqualified condemnations of national 'sovereignty' and glib talk about 'world government' can be recipes for catastrophically amoral views of national and international behaviour.

Any relevant theological critique of nationhood must therefore engage at these three related but distinct levels: the state, the nation, and sovereignty. It is of course possible to suggest that conflict is endemic in these very concepts themselves, and that these entities cannot be reformed or controlled, only abolished, in the interests of peace. What follows in this chapter assumes that theology is to provide a framework of understanding which accepts the need for the state as a means of ordering a world of justice and peace, which recognizes the place of nationhood as a valid structure of human social existence, and which recognizes that such communities of human existence as do exist, should be responsible for their own life. What is required is a theological perspective which prevents these features from becoming so exalted as to become demonic instruments of destructive power. The Christian theological resources which can give nationality its due, yet keep it in its proper place, are located not in any esoteric feature of the tradition or of contemporary thought, but in the central items of belief in the kingdom of the triune God.

Implicit throughout this relativization of nationhood within the divine ordering, is a recognition that in the biblical record 'nationality' (assuming in any case that one is not using the word anachronistically) plays a not insignificant but ultimately incidental role in the drama which moves through creation and fall to the final consummation of God's purpose in a new heaven and a new earth. One can hardly endorse the comment of a British politician who recently claimed that 'The idea of "the nation", indeed, has the most far-reaching biblical endorsement'.[12] In the biblical story, 'nations' or 'peoples' do not appear till well after the 'fall' (or the judgment at Babel). Israel occupies the centre of the stage in the Old Testament, not on account of any supposed 'national genius' of her own, or anything else distinctive about her, but simply because of the sovereign and gracious calling of God to be his servant people. Nor does Israel exist for herself alone, but to be the light that will lighten all peoples, for all are within the care of the one God. And when St Paul speaks of God 'fixing the bounds of the peoples' (Acts 17.26) he does so only in the context of asserting the fundamental *unity* – 'of one blood' – of all humankind. In Christ, the New Testament proclaims, the kingdom of God has been inaugurated, in him one new humanity is being created instead of the old enmity (Eph. 2.14–16), and at Pentecost the confusion of Babel tongues begins to be reversed. At the end, the kingdom of this world becomes the kingdom of our God and of his Christ. The nations walk by the light of the new Jerusalem and offer up to it their glory and honour (Rev. 21.24–26). In biblical perspective, then, national existence is neither an original nor a final state of humanity. It is provisional. As such it is recognized but also transcended in the kingdom of God. There is a proper glory and honour of the nations, but these are to be submitted to the one God, in whom alone sovereignty ultimately resides, who alone reigns for ever.

The main theological resource with which Christian theology is equipped to attack the false elevation of 'national security' to absolute status, is the concept of the kingdom of God as the power of transcendence. It is not simply that this kingdom is 'other than' the kingdoms of this world. It is the kingdom which calls and enables people to live in the way of transcendence, that is, to be open to what, or who, is other than themselves. It is opposed to ways of wholly immanent living, that is, ways which seek to embrace the whole of truth and reality within self-contained finite entities. It can be expounded in terms of the three main credal items.

(a) God the Father Almighty, Maker of heaven and earth: the critical significance of transcendence

Nationality, we have seen, is a historical fact and a means whereby human society and culture are sustained. We have seen, too, how the absolutist claims of the state have fed themselves on an exalted view of 'nationhood' as something as sacrosanct as the unique individuality of a person, and thus with a 'right' to exist, to survive at all costs, and to 'fulfil' its special destiny. In turn the state bolsters its claims to absolute authority by claiming that it is itself the guarantor and protector of the nation's character, cultural heritage and moral aspirations (generally summed up as 'our freedoms') and hence the means whereby the nation's future is assured. Theologically, whether or not (as has often happened) these claims are expressed in religious terminology, they represent an attempt to find within the structures of this world a source of power and security which belongs to God alone. If not actually confusing the creature with the Creator in idolatrous fashion, they at least attempt to find direct access to salvation through a finite, natural or man-made structure.

A prime case-study of where theology not only failed to resist, but actually encouraged, the absolutism of nationhood and national loyalty is provided by the nationalist Protestant theology in the days just before Hitler's advent to power and in the early days of the Third Reich.[13] Many Protestants were wholly behind the new nationalism and justified it with a chauvinistically-oriented use of the concept *orders of creation*, that is, the doctrine that certain structures of human life are not just biological or historical phenomena, but are deliberately ordained of God as essential and immutable conditions of human life without which humankind cannot fulfil its divine calling. Christian doctrine has indeed traditionally understood certain human features to be specially indicative of the 'image of God'. But the nationalist theologians made a much freer and arbitrary use of 'orders of creation', and above all claimed that *the* supreme order of creation is the people, race or nation to which one belongs and owes loyalty. Thus, for example, the credal confession of God the Creator now means belief that God has created me with my particular nationality and its special characteristics, and has bound me to submit myself to the forces working out the destiny of my nation, and to cooperate with its spirit. Indeed in the flowering of a nation we see what creation really is, and so as part of their reverence to the Creator Christians must play their part in affirming the distinctive nature of their nation as God's creation, which means safeguarding its racial purity and preserving it from 'alien' elements. The so-called Faith Movement of German Christians made the racial implications of this the main plank in their attempts to gain control of, and to nazify, the Protestant Church.

Such theology claimed to be able to discern the will and purpose of the Creator by an observation of 'creation' as it now is. What *is*, the nationalists had argued, evidently *must* be and is therefore ordained of God. To such as Karl Barth and Dietrich Bonhoeffer this was to commit the cardinal error of ignoring that what *is* exists as part of a fallen, sinful world, and that only in Jesus Christ, the Word of God, can the will and purpose of the Creator, and hence the true shape of human existence, be truly discerned. For Bonhoeffer, however, who at that time was deeply involved with the ecumenical peace movement, this did not mean any other-worldly escape from or abstract dismissal of these concrete structures of human existence. It meant a different theological evaluation of them. Instead of 'orders of creation', Bonhoeffer proposed instead the concept of *orders of preservation*. He reported on his own address to a church gathering on this theme:

> The difference was that in the light of the concept of orders of creation, certain ordinances and features of the world were regarded as valuable, original, 'very good' in themselves, whereas the concept of orders of preservation meant that each feature was only a feature preserved by God in grace and anger, in view of the revelation in Christ. Any order under the preservation of God should be carried out by Christ and only preserved for his sake.[14]

Nationality, on this view, can be gratefully accepted as a sustaining, enriching form of community which fosters values and forms a kind of matrix for the reception of the gospel, but is never allowed to become an end in itself, or an absolute good in itself. '*Any order* – however ancient and sacred it may be – *can be dissolved*, and must be dissolved when it closes up in itself, grows rigid and no longer permits the proclamation of revelation.'[15] Later, in his *Ethics*, Bonhoeffer would speak of such structures as part of the 'penultimate' matters which necessarily precede the 'ultimate' word of the gospel. (He would also speak of the 'mandates' of church, marriage, labour and *government* – the last-named being distinguished quite sharply by him from that of state.) There is certainly room with this theological approach for the 'natural' gratitude for, identification with and enjoyment of, the distinctive culture and life of a people which constitute the core of a genuine 'patriotism'.

Paradoxically, this way of gratefully living and loving the national distinctiveness is *prevented* by undue elevation or idealization of the nation. The absolutization of nationality in practice prevents any real, spontaneous 'loving' of people, culture and heritage because every energy is progressively sucked into the 'defence' of the realm, every imaginable threat to 'national security' is in turn discovered and frantically countered, every possible rival has to be outmanoeuvred, to the exclusion of all other considerations. One of the casualties of the armaments spiral therefore is in fact 'love of country', however much the 'defence of our way of life' may be invoked as its justification. In a parallel context, in South Africa more than one commentator has remarked on the relative poverty of modern Afrikaner culture, and ascribed it to the fact that every energy has been invested in the promotion and maintenance of *apartheid* with the result that little has been left over for *being* Afrikaner, and for drawing the creative possibilities out of that heritage. Put another way, to make an absolute ideal of the nation, is to disregard history, as may be seen from the tendentiously mythicizing accounts of the nation's past which so often accompany it. In fact it fears history, attempting to foreclose change, development and the future by presuming to uphold fixedly the 'order of creation' rather than accepting and participating in the dynamism and openness of providence.

(b) The person and work of Christ: Life from the Other, Life with the Other

The Christian gospel announces that our salvation has been won 'for us' in the incarnation, cross and resurrection of Jesus Christ. It is good news, the news of superabundant life. But the news comes with a cutting edge of offence, the obverse of the grace expressed by the 'for us'. It is not of our own devising, making or possession, it breaks in from outside us and from beyond us. It causes the greatest offence to the 'natural man' to whom nothing is more dear than the illusion that his existence can be completely self-enclosed and self-sufficient. The absolutization of the nation-state represents one of .the natural man's most sophisticated forms of this illusion of 'aseity'. As stated earlier, this absolutization has both produced and been concretized by the nature of nuclear weaponry (the 'independent deterrent'). A nuclear nationalism both feeds and requires a massive effort at national self-justification. It demands that the unequivocal rightness of the nation's cause be asserted and, concomitant with this, the inherently evil threat posed by the enemy.

Nuclear weaponry is thus associated with the most extreme efforts at national self-justification, to the point of a pyschopathological attempt at projecting all that is evil on to the 'other'. Whereas, in theory at least, in former ages war was seen as some kind of appeal to divine arbitration in which certain rules had to be obeyed and in which victory would be accorded by destiny, the nuclear nation has effectively already arbitrated in its own favour. Hence, such as Karl Barth refer to the sheer 'godlessness' of reliance upon nuclear weaponry.[16] A national self-idealization thus takes place, in face of which any critical stance is seen as 'betrayal'. The last thing that can be admitted is any suggestion of guilt.

The Christian gospel with its note of 'for us' instead of 'of us', claims that it is impossible and futile to attempt to legitimate one's existence in this way. The cross of the incarnate Son of God exposes the sinfulness endemic in all human endeavours, including the political and even (or especially) the religious endeavours, and enacts God's forgiving grace to all. Communities, in the ways appropriate to them, no less than individuals, are therefore invited to let go of the futile efforts at aseity, that self-existence which is God's alone. And even God's 'aseity', even if it is described as 'existence out of himself' is not 'existence by himself', but an existence with others as expressed in the traditional doctrines of the Holy Trinity and the incarnation.

Communities no less than individuals can enter into the liberating and humanizing – if sometimes painful – encounters with others, and with themselves as seen by others. That means a relativization of perspective, the de-throning of the unchallenged rights of the view from one particular corner of the world, the recognition that 'the world' requires to be seen from Red Square as well as Parliament Square.

It is from this angle that a more penetrating critique of the notion of 'sovereignty' can be made, than the unqualified condemnation which, as we saw earlier, is unable to recognize the proper sovereignty which *must* exist if there is to be some kind of moral order among nations or peoples or states or communities of whatever kind which actually exist in this world. That proper sovereignty, we saw, is a matter of the constitutional independence of the government of the country. Nation-states have it simply by virtue of their being nation-states, recognized as such within the international community. But sovereignty conceived as the free exercise of power in the wider world is, in practice, a wish rather than a fact for most nations, even the most powerful (witness the significance of Nicaragua and Afghanistan in relation to the United States and the Soviet Union, respectively). The point is that the absolutization of 'sovereignty' as a value, conceived of as the free exercise of power and dominion over others, or irrespective of the claim of others, and thereby the realization of total security, is at most a *dream* of nation-states – but a very powerful dream none the less. The significance of nuclear weaponry is that it vitalizes this dream considerably without in fact being able to guarantee its realization. It confers the ability to annihilate utterly, but only at the risk of being annihilated in turn.

Behind this dream of sovereignty lies, at root, the urge to be alone, without threat, rivals or indeed others of any kind. That is, after all, the ultimate security for the natural man. The theological insight calling to be heard here is not new. Fifteen centuries ago, Augustine – the nowadays much-maligned Augustine who has allegedly bequeathed so much pessimism and distrust of the world to the Christian west – perceived this attitude to have lain at the root of Rome's eventual inability to maintain its empire. The utter defeat and destruction of Carthage as a means to 'security' through unopposed sovereignty, argued Augustine, deprived Rome of 'both a convenient tutor and a necessary terror' and it was from that point on that Rome's internal moral and social dissolution began. 'This desire of sovereignty is a deadly corrosive to human spirits.'[17] Note again – the *desire* of sovereignty, not the fact of it. This particular absolutization, taking the form of a projection of the nation-state into a world of fantasy, is analogous to the individual who wishes to escape from the actual world where existence is continually confronted by the otherness of other people, to a realm where there are no claims, no responsibilities, no threats (real or imagined) from others. The desire for 'sovereignty' as an absolute ideal is thus highly ambiguous. Clothed as lust for power and dominion, it is in fact at root fearful and weak, for it is the desire to be by oneself as the only assured means of security. The Christian understanding of salvation, however, offers no hope for the self-enclosed existence whether of the individual or the group. Nation-states have all the sovereignty they need – for conformation to what is ultimately sovereign, that which is just and makes for peace. 'There is no way to peace along the way of safety. For peace must be dared. It is the great venture. It can never be safe. Peace is the opposite of security . . . To look for guarantees is to want to protect oneself. Peace means to give oneself altogether to the law of God, wanting no security, but in faith and obedience laying the destiny of the nations in the hand of Almighty God, not trying to direct it for selfish purposes.'[18]

(c) God the Holy Spirit: the new community of the Body of Christ

We have talked much about the need to relativize the claim of national loyalty, in face of the ultimacy of the kingdom of God. Such relativization, however, can only be effective if there is some equally concrete embodiment of this 'higher loyalty'. Christians claim to belong to the universal church of Christ, the *una sancta*. That being so, the implications of membership of the universal church for attitudes to national identity and citizenship of a particular state need to be explored. The very existence of the transnational community of the Christian church, potentially at least, should place a question-mark against any absolutist claims of the nation-state. That being said, historical legacies are still powerful. The mighty edifice of the Christianized Holy Roman Empire has arisen and crumbled. For a thousand years Christendom provided the west with an identity in which Christian allegiance and worldly citizenship were fused. Then came the fragmentation of the sixteenth and seventeenth centuries, with the rise of the nation-states and frequently the national churches as well – not to mention the churches and movements which rejected any state patronage or coercion of religion as incompatible with the entirely spiritual nature of belief.

The relation between religion and national identity in the west is highly complex and far from uniform, but on the whole it can be said that Christianity has more often served to support and at times to consolidate national causes (especially in wartime), than to assert an inclusive Christian identity transcending national frontiers. So powerful has been the sway of the nation-state that probably most members of the churches will identify themselves, within the global perspective, as citizens of their particular country who are Christians, rather than as primarily members of the Body of Christ in the *oikumene*, the whole inhabited earth, who happen to live in the United

Kingdom, or wherever. That weapons of mass-destruction are means of rending the one holy church as yet counts for little. The truly confessional note in Christian identity – that to be Christian is to belong primarily and exclusively to the one Christ who has given himself to all – has still to be heard. It is exceedingly doubtful whether any effective deflation of the absolutizing tendencies of the nation-state will be made from the Christian quarter, however eloquent its theological critique may be, unless and until this truly ecumenical consciousness grows and finds concrete expression in the life of the churches, and still less will there be any hope of confronting the crusading self-righteousness of messianic nationalism unless the churches are able to witness to their own role in the universal *missio Dei*.

This ecumenical consciousness will not, however, constitute a kind of pan-Christian nationalism over against the divided, sinful and unredeemed world. In his novel, *The Heart of the Matter*, Graham Greene describes how during the Second World War an English colonial police officer in an African port discovers a Portuguese sea-captain attempting to smuggle a letter to his daughter in Germany. The distraught man finds with some relief that the Englishman is, like himself, a Roman Catholic. 'For the first time he began to plead. He was like a man who meets a fellow countryman in a strange continent.' What is thereby being described, however, is allegiance to a certain religious culture held in common across national boundaries, inducing a certain fellow-feeling which can be exploited for personal ends. And as such it is not to be despised. But it is hardly the full reach of what is meant by *koinonia*, membership of the body of Christ and participation in the Spirit, which is a sign of the unity intended by God for the whole human community and the cosmos. That participation, for the present, is never joy unmitigated by pain.

If I may be personal, I have vivid recollections, on a visit to the Soviet Union a year ago, of the warmth and sincerity of welcome from fellow-Baptists there, summed up by the wordless greeting in smile and gesture of an old lady after I had preached through an interpreter at a village just outside Moscow. One felt that membership of the body of Christ was indeed a miracle transcending language, geography, and national and ideological divides. The problems came with fellow-believers who *could* speak English, for in conversation one quickly found oneself, if not speaking *for* western defence policies, then at least in trying to present a rationale for them in the face of sheer disbelief that anyone could remotely consider the Soviet Union a threat to world peace. Ecumenism does not mean the suspension of such differences stemming from our national and ideological conditioning, but a willingness to remain together at a profound level of trust and respect as Christians in order that the differences may eventually be overcome through being understood, not evaded.

Therefore the ecumenical qualification of national loyalty and identity most truly occurs not when one seeks to drop one's national identity and opt for some simplistic 'Christian alternative', but when one exposes the perspectives of one's particular national and cultural situation to the critique of the kingdom of God – which in practice involves exposure to how the world and the kingdom are seen on the other side of the ideological and political divides of the world. Kark Barth's call, made in his famous correspondence with Joseph Hromadka of Czechoslovakia twenty-five years ago, still remains challenging: 'I wonder if anyone (in western or eastern fashion) really interprets the historical situation in such a way that *in* that same situation . . . there can be spoken and heard the Christian *witness* to the kingdom which, deriving from neither the western nor the eastern world, seeks to be heard and spoken in both.'[19]

6

Confrontation and Peace in the Nuclear Age: An Analysis

GEOFFREY PRICE

I

The questions which I attempt to address in this chapter are all interrelated:

To what extent are the terms of the long-standing debate about war within Christianity any longer capable of comprehending and moderating the form and scale of potential world conflict?

Can the ethical and theological issues raised by nuclear weapons be fully understood if the threat and use of such weapons are considered in isolation from the conditions of war as we have known it in this century?

Why does the conduct of war now tend to blur the distinction between civilian and combatant, and thus become 'total'?

What are the philosophical and religious origins of the political movements in the last two centuries which have tended to precipitate and sustain total war?

Where now can we find the foundations of peace? Is it achieved solely through political action? Is peace simply the absence of overt hostility between rival nation-states? Or is the pattern of peace to be found rather in that sphere where we live not through the impersonal relations of power, but in relationships: the sphere of the family? Is the coming of peace among mankind most truly envisaged as a union of families under their creator?

First let us review the ways in which debate about war has been conducted within the differing strands of Christianity. Three main positions can be discerned. Borrowing the terminology of A. D. Nock,[1] we may say that a 'conversionist' account of faith underlies the view that the early church was united in its opposition to war, and that the practice of subsequent generations represents a failure to live by the ideals of its founder. On this view, the church represented a 'counter-kingdom', bound by ties of love unknown to Roman civil society; having rejected their 'old life', its members would sooner endure martyrdom, than break the injunctions of Jesus against killing. As Helgeland[2] has shown in a recent review, writers from this school differ on the degree to which this original purity of commitment was universal. Bainton,[3] while sharing the pacifist views that underlay the account written by Cadoux[4] in the aftermath of the First World War, was forced by the evidence to modify his claim that the early church was consistent and united in its opposition to war, and posited different levels of commitment among early Christians.

By contrast, however, the willingness of Catholic and state-church Protestant historians to recognize and accept early Christian involvement in the Roman armies,[5] stems from a quite different historical experience. Their traditions have witnessed differing degrees of compact between the church and civil society. Their conceptions of faith have placed a much greater emphasis than the 'conversionist', upon the guidance and transformation of the conditions of human life and community in the present. To a first approximation, the term 'adaptive' might be used to describe the outlook of these traditions; towards the evidence of early Christian involvement in war, they both tend to be more tolerant.

However, within this 'adaptive' stance, there are marked divergences of experience and outlook. When a civil society engages in outright conflict with its neighbours to the point of imperial conquest, it will often seek to strengthen its internal unity by invoking the symbols of its predominant religion to justify its actions and to denigrate its enemies. When, in addition, the attempted conquest crosses marked cultural and religious boundaries, it is particularly likely that the issue will be presented as a battle between strongly opposed forces of good and evil. The historical examples are well known: the aggressive missionary expansion of Charlemagne against the Saxons; the conflict between Christian and Islamic cultures in the Crusades; and the conflict between nascent nation-states, divided by adherence to now-divergent doctrinal systems within Christianity, that led to the wars of religion of the sixteenth and seventeenth centuries. Under these circumstances, 'adaptive' forms of Christianity require strongly polarized forms of theological reasoning to justify the actions enjoined by the civil community. Contrasting sharply with the pacifist position, these outlooks represent 'adaptive' Christianity in aggressive mode, which we may more simply term 'conflictual'.

At other periods in the history of 'adaptive' Christianity, attempts have been made to regulate and moderate war. From the eleventh century, the reformatory monastic movements in the West urged restraint from war, and the developing legal system of feudal society set severe constraints upon the size and duration of standing armies. With the subjugation of Saxons and Celts largely completed, Europe became sufficiently unified in culture and religion for wars to arise only in the course of settling limited diplomatic and dynastic disputes. In restating and refining the earlier teaching of Augustine that the proper civil authorities might be justified in waging limited wars to rectify injuries and incursions suffered at the hands of their neighbours, Aquinas[6] gave classic expression to the third main approach to the problem of war, which we may term 'regulatory'. His argument is rooted in 'adaptive' Christianity; the juridical terms in which it is formulated, assume widespread agreement between civil and ecclesiastical authorities, resting on a shared moral and religious outlook. However, in contrast to the conflictual approach, Aquinas' argument is addressed to the situation then developing within Europe, where the prospect of overwhelming superiority by one kingdom had receded, rather than to that which prevailed on her borders. His legal formulation of conditions to regulate just war was not addressed to the issue of the Crusades.

II

Debate between these three Christian positions on war – pacifist, regulatory and conflictual – has been greatly intensified since the use of atomic weapons against Japan in 1945. For those who hold the pacifist position, the problem has increased in magnitude but not in kind. There are many who, holding that position, have not withdrawn from public affairs, but have been spurred to efforts of the highest ethical value in the attempt to moderate international conflicts. Moreover, the radical pacifism of the nuclear protest movements has served an important role in moderating political opinion in the two post-war periods when the deployment of atomic weapons seemed most threatening. Nevertheless, it is not clear how the task of moderating the sources of war in the modern world, can be resolved through the pacifist outlook. As in *The Brothers Karamazov*,[7] the problem of human aggression remains, despite the other worldly idealism of Father Zossima, so our century has witnessed the outbreak of wars of bitter national and racial competition at least as severe as those of the sixteenth and seventeenth centuries, despite the influence of the radical Christianity of the pacifist position.

Because it recognizes the persistent problem of human aggression, the 'regulatory' approach to war has attracted much attention in theological debate. In this volume, Ronald Preston applies this approach in its classical form to the nuclear weapons problem, by defending the need for structures of restraint to secure society against endemic conflicts of power and interest. He admits the possibility of using so-called 'battlefield' fission weapons, after due assessment of the risk of escalation, but he denies the legitimacy of ever using megaton fusion weapons, on the grounds that they are inherently indiscriminate and disproportionate.

The formal terms of the just-war approach are also invoked by Hugh Beach in this volume, but here the argument is applied to considering whether there might be circumstances in which the use of indiscriminate megaton weapons against enemy cities would be justified as a last resort. This use of the argument is set in the context of a strongly confrontational view of international relations; the 'Russian empire' is described as 'alien, feared and hated'. Hence, although the form of the just war analysis is used, the underlying assumptions are characteristic of the conflictual, rather than the regulatory, approach to war within Christian reflection. The territory occupied by NATO countries is assumed to constitute the modern equivalent of 'holy land', to be defended from the influence of enemy beliefs, even if the cost is the death of tens of millions of the opposing population.

The fact that the formal structure of the just war approach can be invoked in these two divergent ways, highlights the issues which this chapter seeks to address. In its classical form, the regulatory approach of the just war tradition is only enforceable if there is an underlying moral and religious consensus among combatants. In our own day, can we still argue as if the regulatory approach would be observed, restraining the use of indiscriminate weapons?

On that issue, the historical precedents are sadly negative. The form which war has taken in the last two centuries has increasingly been of the type first seen in the aftermath of the French Revolution, when the raising of large conscript armies caused great extensions in the power of government over daily civilian existence. After 1815, calm returned for a period. The rule of Metternich in Europe allowed a degree of moderation in international conduct to be re-established, and professional, long-service armies tended to reappear. Nevertheless, the small nation of Prussia, seeking to recover from her defeat at Jena, developed the idea of universal military training in peacetime. In the campaigns waged by Prussia against Austria and France in 1866 and 1870, as well as in the

American Civil War, there occurred a fresh outbreak of the revolu-
tionary-Napoleonic pattern of conflict between mass armies fuelled
by fierce popular passion. After 1870, other European nations hast-
ened to establish their own standing armies.[8] As a result, when
conflict broke out in 1914, the field armies that confronted each
other numbered over two million. The need to supply those armies
with vast quantities of food, armaments and medical services meant
that civilian populations were closely involved in the cycle of war
from the outset.

Under these circumstances, the moral consensus between combatants upon which the regulatory approach of the just war tradition depends, was very easily undermined. Albert Marrin's study
of the changes in both public and ecclesiastical attitudes in the
months after the declaration of war in 1914, shows how, very
quickly, principles of restraint in combat were abandoned. Justifications were found[9] for the severing of food supplies to the enemy
population by the naval blockade of Germany, for the use of chlor-
ine gas in trench warfare, and for bombing raids in deliberate
reprisal for attacks on civilian targets. Moreover, there is evidence
both in Albert Marrin's study[10] and that of Alan Wilkinson[11] that
while the true costs of war were concealed, political leaders encouraged the belief that the German opposition was wholly evil, and
bent on enslaving the world. As well as many examples of political
language of this kind, there is evidence that clerical descriptions of
the situation in the language of the 'holy war' were by no means
infrequent. So, under the conditions of war, the tradition we have
called 'conflictual' superseded the careful moral evaluation called
for by the 'regulatory' approach. The symbolism of Christian sacrifice was invoked to nerve men for the front, and the language of
opposing political absolutes was used to reassure the consciences of
those who remained. Opposition to this language from the pacifist
position was weak, unorganized and late in developing. We know
also from such detailed descriptions as those of Robert Graves[12]
and David Jones,[13] what it was to endure the conditions of trench
warfare amid high explosives and gas – conditions which for many
of those who survived made a mockery of the Christian language
of noble sacrifice.

When war erupted again in Europe in 1939, the public mood in
England was greatly sobered.[14] Nevertheless, ideas of total war
involving both combatant and non-combatant had taken strong
root in military circles in the intervening generation. The Royal Air
Force in Britain had designed aeroplanes for systematic air-bombing campaigns, exemplifying a commitment to war conceived as a
total attack on the population of the enemy. Tony Carty has shown
through a detailed account of official papers how, irrespective of

military necessity, the British cabinet persisted throughout the 1939–1945 war with a policy of indiscriminate air attacks, killing 300,000 people and injuring 780,000.[15] He shows how the same premises underlay the United States' policy of air attacks on Japan; in the Tokyo fire raids of 8–10 March 1945 alone, one million were rendered homeless, 83,973 were killed and 40,918 wounded.

The decision to use atomic weapons against Japan in August 1945 was, as Carty[16] rightly argues, simply an extension of the prevailing policy of seeking to crush the will to resist of an entire nation without distinction. President Truman later described this action as if it had been employed as a last resort to shorten conflict against a ruthless aggressor who had pursued total war. But in truth, the United States possessed the atomic weapon precisely because of its own prior acceptance of the principle of the unrestrained development of armoury, representing the utterly changed climate in which war had come to be conducted since 1870 and 1914. In 1939, the economist Alexander Sachs at first had difficulty in gaining the attention of President Roosevelt to the letter he carried from Einstein and Szilard on the military potential of uranium fission. Eventually he succeeded, by recalling Lord Acton's judgment that England had only been saved from defeat by Napoleon, through the shortsightedness of Napoleon in refusing the offer of Robert Fulton to build him a steamship fleet. The point intended, that Roosevelt was foolish to reject the possibility of pursuing war by means unimaginable before, was taken.[17] Thus the principle of unrestricted warfare was implicit from the very beginning of the project to investigate the feasibility of atomic weapons.

Given this background, how can it be maintained that decisions affecting nuclear weapons are likely to be contained within the framework of proportionality and restraint required by the regulatory, just war tradition within Christianity? The weapons themselves would never have been developed and used, nor would the high-explosive air-bombing campaigns that preceded them have ever been conducted, if the premises of that tradition had been influential. Carty[18] quite rightly says that

> The foundations for total war waged with nuclear weapons, bringing with it the complete physical destruction of one's enemy, were firmly laid in 1945, for the US, and very shortly afterwards for the other nuclear powers. In fact they amount to nothing more or less than a continuation of strategies used during the last war, resting on identical political presuppositions, the ideology of total war. The doctrines associated with nuclear deterrence come later and have not modified the essential strategic assumptions nor

what the armed forces are actually organized to do. Questions of the credibility of the deterrence, the morality of a conditional threat to carry out an act in itself admitted to be immoral, and even the issue of unilateral nuclear disarmament come along when there is already a commitment to a type of war in which the absolute destruction of one's opponent is regarded as the orthodox and normal form of conduct.

Theologians and moral philosophers may refuse to recognize the changed situation, but in practice the existence and deployment of nuclear weapons is only an extension of the outlook that has become dominant in warfare over the last two centuries: the outlook that assumes war to be a conflict of wills involving the whole population, to be pursued by strategies of total, indiscriminate destruction. The only language within Christian theology with which such strategies can be 'justified', is the conflictual language of holy war pursued to the death.

Yet how can that language be employed, except in despairing disregard for everything in the created order, and for the untold millions of people who would die in such a conflict? Is the Western ideal of freedom not brought into a disrepute as great as that suffered by Christianity through the Crusades, if we contemplate the deliberate destruction of multitudes of defenceless persons, in order to defend that ideal?

III

I have argued that the form of war that has come to predominate in the last two centuries is such as to undermine any realistic application of the regulatory, just war tradition within Christianity. It is apparent, moreover, that justifications for future instances of such conflict, now involving nuclear weapons, can all too readily be developed within the conflictual, holy war approach that Christianity has invoked at earlier periods of acute conflict of belief. In this *impasse*, how may we proceed in the search for the sources of peace? In what follows, I offer a possible explanation of how the predominant modern form of war has arisen; the issues which this enquiry raises may serve to widen discussion.

In 1939, Denis de Rougemont[19] put forward the thesis that the passionate intensity with which war had come to be practised, represented the modern counterpart of the form of love first practised in the courtly circles whose ideals were symbolized in the Tristan legend. Figured in that legend, he argued, was a form of love which was not a love of the other's concrete reality as neighbour. The union that it longed for was not concerned for the needs of the other; rather, it sought, through love, to be united with the ideal realm of the spirit. Because it longed above all for this passionate fusion, this love would court suffering and risk death if need be, rather than renounce its goal.

As an interpretation of the mediaeval courtly love tradition, de Rougemont's work has remained controversial, and it now seems probable that his historical reconstruction was too greatly influenced by his knowledge of the form taken by romantic love in the last two centuries.[20] However, his thesis concerning modern war opens up a valuable line of enquiry. De Rougemont concluded that the force of modern revolutionary war arose because in modern times whole populations had acted out the forces of rebellion and negation that had previously been concealed within the formalities imposed on war by the chivalric codes derived from the courtly love tradition. With the murder of the king of France in 1789, he wrote,[21]

> – a deed which in a primitive society would have had a sacred and ritualistic significance – the violence that had long been pinned down by the classical formality of warfare, became once again something horrifying and alluring.

Writing a generation later, Albert Camus arrived at a similar diagnosis of contemporary political movements quite independently, through his study of *The Rebel.*[22]

> Seventeen eighty-nine is the starting point of modern times, because the men of that period wished, among other things, to overthrow the principle of divine right and to introduce to the historical scene the forces of negation and rebellion which had become the essence of intellectual discussion in the previous centuries. Thus they added to the concept of traditional tyrannicide, that of calculated deicide.

I submit that these diagnoses need to be taken seriously, in any argument about how international relations may move beyond the present stage of instability towards total war. They imply that the reasons why the modern nation may engage in revolutionary war at almost any cost, do not simply represent the failing influence of what we have called the 'adaptive' forms of Christianity. Rather, they imply that the political development of modern nations has been increasingly influenced by a current of romantic rebellion which is both ecstatic and world-defying, setting the pursuit of its ideals above immediate circumstances and limits.

To whom is the force of such national passion addressed, we may ask? De Rougemont[23] maintained that

> Nationalistic ardour . . . is a self-elevation, a narcissistic love on the part of the collective self. No doubt its relation with others is seldom averred to be love, nearly always hate is what first appears, and what is proclaimed. But hate of the other is always present in the transports of passionate love.

Should its aims be thwarted, a people moved by this form of love will meet death gladly, rather than surrender the fulfilment of their desire to achieve the beckoning glory of abstract political ideals.

Now, transposed into philosophical terms, this form of argument is influential in the currents of thought that underpin nineteenth-century nationalism.[24] Romantic idealism asserted the priority of a transcendent spiritual realm as the true home of humanity. In the hero – whether artist, statesman or politician – it found the perfection of humanity. Imagining history as a public stage, it saw the hero acting upon that stage as in a universal realm, in which alone the truly significant acts are played out. Only this, the realm of ideals, offers the promise of liberation and glory. Only by acting in this sphere is humanity truly free: only here can its leaders gain the applause which is everlasting. 'The world's history is the world's judgment', declared Schiller in his inaugural lecture of 1789.

In the philosophy of the idealist, history is above all the history of states. Consequently, the imagination of the nation's youth must be directed to the goals that lie ahead. Germany was strongly influenced by the ways in which this spirit had moulded life in revolutionary France.[25] So Fichte[26] urged the nascent nation to build itself up through an educational programme designed to evoke the strength of character needed to reaffirm the ideals of the people. Were those ideals mere fictions, or did they indeed reach to the heart of reality? Hegel[27] affirmed that nothing was more real.

> On the stage on which we are observing it – Universal History – Spirit displays itself in its most concrete reality . . . The truly good – the universal divine reason – is not a mere abstraction, but a vital principle, capable of realizing itself.

In this way, the passion to realize the transcendent world within the earthly that pervades the legends of courtly love, is transposed by the philosophy of idealism onto the achievements of the State. So, Hegel[28] maintained,

> The State is the spirit that dwells in the world and realizes itself

through *consciousness*; . . . It is the course of God through the world that constitutes the State.

Now the commandment that is central to both Judaism and Christianity is a twofold command to love God and to love the neighbour whom we find in the particular, concrete circumstances of our life. By contrast, the creed of political idealism holds that human responsibility is fulfilled by attuning each life to the universal course of an abstract idea. Correspondingly, each human life is considered as the material in which the essence of history is to be worked out; each person's citizenship is fulfilled in response to the call of duty proclaimed by the state.

Yet success in achieving this realm of ideals through art, philosophy and music can only be for a few. Nevertheless, the creed of political idealism could readily be democratized. For unlimited numbers of men could be called to abandon the sphere of home where they live with their immediate neighbours, to act as universal citizens by enlisting in the service of the state. In that way, they too might participate in the creative life; they too could fight for high ideals. What higher aim was there, they would begin to think, than the freedom of their nation upon the world stage? How else might they become free, but through their own action?

The popular implications of idealism are thus a militarism which feeds upon and systematizes the philosophical disjunction of reality into private and political spheres. The symbols of monarchy, presidency or party leadership, the colours and ceremonies of the flag, and the rhythms of the national anthem, are used in the training of soldiers to unquestioning obedience to military command. The division between ideal and material, universal and particular, is constantly represented and reinforced, until loyalty to the universal purpose is complete.

To what forms of war does such a popular idealism lead? At first, those who take their own creative action – expressed in symbols of nationhood – as the centre of meaning, may believe that they are only seeking to assert their own identity in the face of history. They soon find, however, that their project only makes sense in opposition to the existing scheme of things. They rebel: and their rebellion is as that of young men who turn against the way of their fathers: it leads on to a revolution which seeks their father's death. On this issue, Camus made a diagnosis which goes beyond the earlier argument of de Rougemont. In the limit, Camus maintained, those who take this revolutionary path will be led to seek the death of God. Choosing to seek acclaim in the realm of time, they will exclude themselves from trust and faith, in order to live solely by their own strength. But what will they find confronting them, beyond the death of God? All that will remain to them is 'mankind' – an abstract, anonymous mankind whose history they must now understand and shape. Their plans for domination must become prodigious: and with them, the prospect of greater and greater wars. So, Camus continues,[29]

> The society born of 1789 wanted to fight for Europe. The society born of the 1917 revolution is fighting for universal dominion.

In this way, believing that they exist by their creative powers, the young rebel-soldiers of modern idealism are always fighting for existence: in order to be, they must act. They act as upon a stage, seeking to impress an imaginary audience whose applause or disapproval is the 'verdict of history'. But if history is indeed the repository of all meaning, then the demands which can be made upon them for action are potentially unlimited.

In formulating this argument, Camus[30] noted how, after the first collapse of Germany in 1918, just such unlimited demands began to take hold, through the influence of Hitler's style of leadership.

> Action alone kept him alive. For him to exist was to act. That is why he and his regime could not dispense with enemies . . . Perpetual strife demanded perpetual stimulants.

But, Camus sensed, it was in the writings up to 1935 of Hitler's critic and eventual opponent Ernst Jünger, that the real logic of such dynamism was formulated, in plans for a technological world empire. Under the statutes of this new authoritarian regime, the worker would be subject to 'total mobilization', acting within a hierarchy of labour dedicated to production, transport and management. Camus considered[31] that if such a rule should be achieved, it would constitute ' . . . simultaneously the factory and the barracks of the world, where Hegel's soldier worker reigns as a slave.'

How does the technology of war appear, in the imagination thus dedicated to political domination? Jünger[32] described the modern battleship as

> . . . the embodiment of an icy will, all coal and steel, explosives and electricity, manned by specialized positions from admiral to boiler heater, the image of the latest precision mechanics, served by workers and directors, functional in the highest degree . . .

The development of aviation was more than a triumph of science:[33] it was 'the living expression of a powerful life force', signifying 'far more than the merely technical. Its soaring flights stake out the districts of a cultic world', and in this way would be an integral part of the fulfilment of Germany's national destiny.

At this point, the creed of political idealism overlaps with the pursuit of unrestrained technical efficiency in the conduct of war. In Germany, it was but a short step from the figures of limitless efficiency and national pride that Jünger's writings extolled, to the development of technical triumphs like the V2 rocket. In the same way in Britain and America, the battle of opposing national wills was taken as providing overriding justification, in the sequence of decisions that led to the building, testing and use of atomic weapons. In each case, it was taken for granted that nations must rely on the building of ever-larger instruments of total war, in order to maintain their supremacy upon the 'stage' of history.

Today, despite conditions of formal peace, the structures of loyalty that Jünger knew to be necessary for worker-soldiers in a unified technological state, are enjoined on the members of societies which are formally democratic. The state, taking for granted the idealist's disjunction of reality into the political-historical and the mundane, enjoins its citizens to believe in the technical necessity of nuclear deterrence, in order that their way of life may continue. Thus in Britain, the annual *Statement on the Defence Estimates* has repeatedly presented the argument that our political security depends upon foreseeing every possible threat from an expansionist, powerful and hostile Soviet Union, and blocking it with risks of retaliation that are sufficient to deter it from taking chances. By acceding to this counterbalance, the British people were told[34] in 1981,

> It is entirely possible, if we plan wisely, to go on enjoying peace and freedom – that is, to avoid the bogus choice of 'Red or dead'.

In 1987, the same case was made that the West should not lower its guard, in an essay[35] on the Soviet Union entitled '70 Years On: A Country or a Cause?'.

These arguments presuppose that our freedom is achieved solely through the might of our collective representation in the State, and that peace is constituted merely by the absence of active hostilities. They address us as citizen-soldiers, assuming us to be willing to arm ourselves with the instruments of total war in order to counter the revolutionary ambitions of our opponents. They take the international situation to be dominated by ideological competition; consequently, they presume, we will employ means that court our collective death, rather than give up our attachment to the world-transcending sphere of political values, in which it is supposed that our meaning is anchored.

IV

The central problem posed to theological reflection by the development and deployment of nuclear weapons is then, I submit, an
extension of the problem posed by the development of political
idealism in the last two centuries. Through the all-embracing
ambitions of the modern nation-state, the competition of war has
intensified into a conflictual pattern comparable to that seen in
earlier centuries, in the Crusades and in the wars of religion of the
sixteenth and seventeenth centuries.

How then, amid these developments, are we to find the foundations of peace? The task is daunting. The modern creed of political idealism asserts that our highest fulfilment as human beings
lies in our creative activity, practised at their highest level through
the realms of national politics. The universalizing technological
empire, whether in its western capitalist or its eastern planned-
socialist form, assumes that its citizens have goals which are no
wider than its own.

Against the grain of these beliefs, I suggest that some radical
questions need to be asked,[36] if theological and ethical reflection
are to begin to master the problems posed by threats of nuclear
warfare.

Is reality indeed pervaded by a polarity between the ideal and
the mundane, in the way that both modern revolutionary politics,
and some forms of Christian spirituality, tend to assume? Or is
the world one and indivisible, because it has been created and
pronounced very good?

Do human persons find significance by reaching out towards
a transcendent world of values through their own creative and
imaginative ability? Are they beings who if necessary must court
death rather than abandon their affirmations and their search? Or
does each person have meaning and dignity from the beginning
as the evident creation of God?

Is the world a neutral arena, a mere 'theatre of war', whose
incidental destruction is insignificant in relation to the acts of conflict through which human beings seek to establish themselves and
their nations in the immortal realm of history? Or is the world a
creation which has been given into the hands of men and women,
to be cared for and continually returned in thanks and worship to
their creator?

Is God merely the verifier of the political ideals that human
creativity conceives and pursues? Or is God truth, justice and
mercy itself, beyond any ideals which we may imagine? Is any act

of abstract heroism in loyalty to the nation, greater than the deeds of love with which we are commanded to care for the needs of our neighbour?

Is it true that human persons are free only in so far as they are creative? If so, can we infer that each of us is a potential worker-soldier, whose purpose is fulfilled in service to the goals of the state? Or is our freedom rooted in our membership of a family which is prior to, and independent of, the state – a family whose coherence is assured by God, who is ever capable of drawing it out of slavery to political ideals?

Do the symbols and ideals of political language represent the sum of our collective existence? Or are the living human persons who make up that collectivity, the only true reality within it?

How, the reader may ask, will our answers to these questions affect the problems posed by the invention of nuclear weapons? It is certainly possible for us to continue to live as if the fragmented world of political idealism was the only reality. We do so when we measure those we meet simply in terms of their political power and loyalties, or when we see them only as clad in the uniform of friend or foe. We do so whenever we act as if the organization of everyday life for the needs of political and economic survival constitutes the paramount and final measure of value. We do so whenever we respond to each situation merely in terms of the implications of those we meet for our needs as members of our own class, party or nation, rather than in terms of others as our neighbours.

Accordingly, we are all capable of arguing that it is for the good of the whole that our enemies should die. We all know what it is to elevate conflict to the level of regrettable but tragic necessity. We are all capable of suppressing our reaction to our neighbour as a human being, in order to thrust him aside as we pursue our calling in history. So we are all vulnerable to the voices that seek to persuade us that there are situations in which the protection of our political ideals will leave us no alternative, but to employ such force against our opponents as will destroy the innocent and leave the created earth scarred and barren.

Is it not time, then, if we are to face the issues that have now been focussed through the invention of nuclear weapons, for us to remember that political idealism does not have the last word in representing the world we live in? We know that our hearts are capable of pursuing political ideals with the single-minded devotion of the ascetic revolutionary rebel: but we know also that our hearts can hear the voice of God. For we can hear the voice of conscience that protests when we neglect our neighbour through our fragmented view of life. We can find happiness in trusting God who lives beyond the changes of history. So, given our appalling capacity for pursuing war with destructive passion, is it not time for us to find that the absolutes of political existence which drive us to conflict, are not absolutes at all, compared to the Creator whose love undergirds us all?

7

Styles of Documentary Engagement

ANTHONY DYSON

Nothing, it seems, can staunch the flow of church reports and pronouncements, of one kind and another, on one subject or another. Especially in the last decade or two, on a number of major issues such as economics, racism, inner cities, development, sexuality and the family – and of course war and peace – denominational and ecumenical bodies have become increasingly active, often with great skill and sophistication, in engaging with their own constituencies, with secular decision-makers and, to a lesser extent, with the general public. The motives for such engagement may vary. There may be the intention prophetically to point to a present, or coming, social evil and to stir consciences about it. There may be the intention on the part of church leaders to update and modify Christian social teaching, taking account of new knowledge and experience. Or, conversely, there may be the intention to remind the faithful of, and to call for renewed obedience to, a belief or practice which is held to be of unchanging value in a rapidly changing world. There may be the intention to react to a trend, an event, a piece of legislation, which apparently runs counter to Christian values. There may be the intention in certain cases to act as a straightforward pressure-group alongside other secular pressure-groups. Some critics have discerned more sinister intentions.[1] Granted the far-reaching effects of secular-ization which has greatly diminished the prestige, influence and power of the churches, setting them on the margin, are these many reports and pronouncements subtle ways by which some measure of the older *ex cathedra* control of the people typical of a 'Christendom' polity may be restored?[2]

How do the denominational and ecumenical bodies appeal to their various audiences? They surely have every right to address their own members, even if only a very small percentage of those members take any notice. We shall see that most styles of documentary engagement are directed at the highly literate. What assumptions does this make about the standing of, and contributions from the thought and experience of, those who ignore, and are ignored by, these sophisticated documents? Added problems arise when the documents set out to address secular experts, leaders, and members of the general public who may not share the Christian beliefs which presumably inform the documents. If in fact these documents actually appeal to the authority of the Bible, Christian tradition and religious experience, how are they to communicate to a public which simply does not understand these matters? When the churches try to overcome the problem by couching their reports in the language of reason and common experience, have they thereby evacuated what they want to say of its Christian content? Further, in many cases there is no agreement within the church bodies about what they want to say. Underlying that disagreement may be wide and apparently unbridgeable differences of biblical and theological interpretation, as well as notable differences of cultural outlook. Is the report or pronouncement going to strive for consensus? Is it to give equal space to every point of view? Is it to recommend or require, by synodical fiat or magisterial imprimatur, only one point of view? In all these processes, what is to be made of the relationship of Christian judgments to so-called secular experts who are rarely agreed among themselves and who are of course guided to no small extent by their own value-assumptions?

These are just a few of the considerations which can be introduced in a general way on the subject of 'styles of documentary engagement' by the churches in the socio-political realm. Nuclear disarmament and other nuclear matters are no exception to this general picture. Reports and pronouncements in the nuclear field, often the result of extremely complex and highly polemical bureaucratic processes, have been one of the principal means by which factual, ethical and religious perspectives have been communicated to different constituencies. The denominations and ecumenical bodies together can point to a large body of material of this kind. These documents serve as important sources for understanding how the churches as institutions try to involve themselves, and form their own mind as well as the minds of others, in these quite momentous issues of life and death.

But in this chapter I want to explore in some detail the hypothesis that the 'message' of the document may depend as much or more upon the *form* and *style of engagement* of the document and upon the *form* of the procedures which antedated, attended and followed its production than upon the overt subject-matter of the text. It would be, therefore, incorrect to treat these differences in style and form as marginal. In one sense they are only bearers of the explicit content;

in other ways they dictate and decide the content which is perceived, the outreach and outcome of the document, in a striking way. The style and form of engagement can point us to issues which lie below the surface of Christian involvement in the nuclear disarmament debate and which in fact deserve close attention if that debate is to be rescued from the risk of a certain myopia and superficiality. In this chapter I shall analyse and comment on *four* documents which illustrate different forms and styles of engagement with their audiences. They are just some of the many documents which might have been chosen for this purpose; they are not necessarily the 'best'. The subject-matter is too bulky to permit point-by-point comparison and contrast. So a limited number of themes are selected for discussion.

The four documents are as follows: *Before It's Too Late: The Challenge of Nuclear Disarmament* (hereafter cited as *BITL*), edited by Paul Abrecht and Ninan Koshy, which is the record, published in 1983, of the Public Hearing on Nuclear Weapons and Disarmament organized by the World Council of Churches, which took place in Amsterdam in November 1981;[3] the Pastoral Letter of the United States National Conference of Catholic Bishops, *The Challenge of Peace: God's Promise and our Response* (hereafter cited as *TCOP*) Washington DC, USCC, 1983;[4] *The Church and the Bomb: Nuclear Weapons and Christian Conscience* (hereafter cited as *TCATB*), Hodder and Stoughton, London, 1982, being the report of a working-party set up by the Board for Social Responsibility of the General Synod of the Church of England;[5] and the Report of the Consultation on *Violence, Non-Violence and the Struggle for Social Justice* (hereafter cited as *VANV*), convened by the Church and Society department of the World Council of Churches, and held in Cardiff in September 1972.[6]

Before It's Too Late had its origins in the request by the Central Committee of the World Council to two of its Sub-units to arrange 'an international Public Hearing on the current threat to world peace with special focus on the increased danger of nuclear war, where authoritative witnesses can be cross-examined in an effort to assess the present situation'.[7] The Central Committee approved the proposals of the planners of the Hearing as to theme and date. More than five hundred prospectuses to explain the projected Hearing were sent to six categories of person, namely to church leaders, theologians, representatives of governmental and non-governmental organizations, members of peace-movements, and experts in nuclear development, strategy and disarmament. Thereafter, the planners examined the replies to the prospectus, agreed on the subject-areas, proposed a panel of eighteen persons selected according to geographical and denominational interests, and began to select witnesses. In the event, some forty witnesses testified to the Hearing which was under the moderatorship of the then Bishop of Durham, Dr John Habgood.

The principal parts of *BITL* are the Report of the Hearing (31 pages), the three opening statements (19 pages), the forty edited testimonies, with questions and answers (332 pages), and the account of the subsequent Central Committee's action on the Report (2 pages). The edited statements by the witnesses, based on earlier submitted papers, oral presentations, and questions and answers, form the heart of the record. They are presented in seven chapters: Theological and Ethical Concerns in Relation to Nuclear Weapons; Driving Forces in the Development and Introduction of new Nuclear Weapons Systems; the Strategy of Limited Nuclear War and the new Debate about Deterrence; Views of the Third World Countries on Disarmament and Proliferation; Negotiations for Arms Control; Approaches to Disarmament – Multilateral and Unilateral; and the Witness of Public Interest Groups (mainly from the peace movements).

One of the notable strengths of *BITL* resides in the attempt to give the Hearing an international character. In particular, the Hearing Group was not dominated by any one cultural or national perspective; the members came from UK, USSR, Sweden, Japan, USA, India, Zambia, GDR, Canada, France, Lebanon, Indonesia, West Germany, Fiji and Hungary. There were four women in the Hearing Group. The speakers and witnesses were mainly drawn from Euramerica; only three were women. The international element in the Hearing made possible expression and argument that crossed East and West, Northern and Southern hemispheres.

Though the nature of the contribution made by witnesses can be pre-planned by *who* is selected, nonetheless the format of a public hearing makes for a breadth and an interaction of testimony. However, the testimony is not swallowed up as in the appendices of a working-party report; the testimony is the main subject-matter of the record. It seems that, at the time, some senior World Council officials were disappointed by the failure to achieve radical consensus. Certainly the mode of operation meant that the pluralism could not be denied or concealed, unwittingly or wilfully.

From another standpoint the above-mentioned international character of *BITL* can be construed as a weakness. This relates also to the consultative character of the World Council of Churches. As a document coming from an international body, *BITL* was not likely to receive a public welcome on any scale or of any intensity in any one country. The Central Committee did the only positive thing which it was empowered to do with the record of the Hearing, namely to receive it, and to commend it 'to the member churches and affiliated councils and to all concerned people'.[8] The World Council had little control or influence on the afterlife of the Hearing. In any case, which wider public might it have been expected to address? Much of it is demanding reading; some of it is very technical. But a good deal is accessible to the concerned reader. The record cannot, and ought not to be seen as an harmoniously balanced whole which makes for smooth reading. It was, and is, essentially the product of what the witnesses wanted to say and of what the Panel elicited from them. Its passion, which comes through at many points, arises from a conviction that it was part of an 'opportune moment'; for 'decisions are being taken which will have immense impact on the prospects for world peace and security'.[9] Equally, the churches cannot accept being 'passive witnesses to the steady deterioration of the prospects for world peace'.[10] Perhaps the Report of the Hearing could with profit have appeared on its own. It makes a very direct appeal to the churches, based on the general burden of the Hearing: '[for] the political and social impact of these developments requires the churches to rethink, not only their theological and ethical approaches, but also their commitment to appropriate and effective strategies in response to them'.[11] This twofold appeal reflects the structure of the document. The theological issues in chapter two and the questions about the churches in chapter eight have to speak both to and from the detailed nuclear conditions in chapters three to seven. This combination of *attitudes* and *strategies* will be discussed later in this chapter. By this structuring, the witness of the historic peace churches and of the contemporary popular peace-movements is deliberately brought into a key theological relationship with the technical and ethical sections of the document. A similar movement will be apparent in *TCOP* and *VANV*.

At first sight, *BITL*'s style of engagement is very open and democratic. A hearing is, in one sense, anti-elitist. This contrasts sharply with the secretive character of much secular and ecclesiastical politics. In a hearing, the panel is not in a conventional power-relationship with the witnesses. This more or less non-hierarchical form begins to raise interesting questions about where a Christian moral magisterium really lies, upon whom it depends and how it operates. A hearing is a type of dispersed authority. Connected with this, if a mature Christian judgment has to appeal to, among other sources, up-to-date knowledge, *BITL* is apparently a fine example of the attentive and sustained listening that is involved in collecting and sifting that knowledge. But maybe all is not as healthy and straightforward as it seems.

One of the key problems focussed by *BITL*'s style of engagement concerns the witness of experts. The decision to hold a hearing does not of itself guarantee the wider ability, reliability and disinterestedness of witnesses. *Public Policy and the Expert: Ethical Problems of the Witness*, by Daniel D. McCracken and others, discusses some of the major themes involved here, in particular 'how the expert witness should attempt to relate his technical expertise to the broader social context, and how decision-makers should attempt to evaluate testimony from this standpoint'.[12] 'It is still sometimes said that the experts should stick to the facts and leave the value-judgments to the decision-maker. But this amounts to carving the universe of discourse into watertight compartments, rigidly separated from each other'.[13] In the same volume Perkiss draws attention to other aspects of the expert as witness, especially the relation between the expert's *interests* and the democratic process. He points to the danger 'not so much that any group of experts will come to dominate decision-making and elbow democratic leadership aside, but that the increased reliance on expert opinions and supposedly scientific data to bolster one's position will so diffuse and undermine the decision-making process itself that the basically important decisions will be made by default'.[14] Perkiss asserts the importance of a 'working adversary system' in these respects.

In the case of *BITL*, as in any comparable case, we are also thrown back upon the basic consideration as to who are chosen as witnesses, and as to the criteria on which this choice is made. The Report does not vouchsafe this information. It may be right to argue against Perkiss and others that in a *Christian* context a deal of trust and goodwill must be presupposed, and that there are limits to be placed upon the adversarial mode. But the style of Christian self-involvement which the model of a hearing implies also requires a readiness to exist amid constantly competing interests in a realistic and truth-seeking way.

The Central Committee's subsequent action on the Hearing seeks to grasp two controverted issues. On nuclear weapons it says: 'we believe that the time has come when the churches must unequivocally declare that the production and deployment as well as the use of nuclear weapons are a crime against humanity and that such activities must be condemned on ethical and theological grounds.' On disarmament, staying within the pluralism of the Hearing, the Central Committee affirms: 'all means leading to disarmament, both nuclear and conventional, should be welcomed as complementary and mutually reinforcing – multilateral conferences leading to effective decisions, bilateral negotiations pursued with daring and determination and unilateral initiatives leading to the relaxation of tensions and building of mutual confidence among nations and peoples.'[15] Again, attitudes and strategies are held together.

The American Bishops' *The Challenge of Peace* is deeply indebted to the Second Vatican Council's *Constitution on the Church in the Modern World*, both in method and attitude. It believes that because Vatican II took its first and primary cue from the 'signs of the times', so the

US bishops, faced by new 'signs of the times', are licensed to go beyond Vatican II. Certainly, from the late 1960s many American bishops had become increasingly active and outspoken on nuclear issues – not least after Reagan's election. A notable landmark in this respect was the Bishops' 1976 statement *To Live in Christ Jesus*. This spoke out strongly against the use of nuclear weapons and against the use of deterrence arguments to justify threats to bomb civilian populations. It should be noted that the US bishops saw themselves as charged with a special moral responsibility, in view of the United States' role as one of the two major nuclear powers.

TCOP had its immediate origins in certain initiatives in 1980 asking that the National Council of Catholic Bishops should undertake the composition of a statement on the ethics of war and peace, and should consider means for the better dissemination of this aspect of Catholic teaching. A committee (four bishops with Archbishop Bernardin – known for his skills as a consensus chairperson) was appointed. The principal staff included Fr Bryan Hehir, upon whom the Bishops were to 'rely heavily'[16] for the direction of their deliberations, and Dr Bruce Russett of Yale, editor of the *Journal of Conflict Resolution*, who was external consultant and drafter. Evidence was heard from thirty-six formal witnesses and three drafts of *TCOP* were produced. A meeting with some West European bishops and curial officials (including Cardinal Ratzinger) materially shaped the form of the final version.

The Vatican meeting raised two kinds of critical questions, one relating to the moral and ecclesial authority and stands taken in the text, and one on matters of theological and ethical substance. It is probably correct to say that in Ratzinger's mind both kinds of question had a common foundation. Is or is not the church to keep its teaching within the boundaries defined by the historic norms of Roman Catholic moral theology about peace and war (summarized on p.102 below), or can, for example, new biblical study or a new experience and re-evaluation of the pacifist/non-violent traditions lead to those earlier boundaries being redefined? The questions about ecclesial authority in relation to the prerogatives of a national bishops' conference are of course also questions about the relation of such a body to the papal magisterium. But another important question, which will occur again in even sharper form in *TCATB*, concerns the theological and ethical propriety of moving from general principles to the application of those principles in practical options. Ratzinger's questions here[17] seem to imply that a certain dilution or contamination of the faith is risked when this occurs. Be this as it may, the American bishops agreed to take account of these criticisms in the third and final draft. The two hundred and forty-seven bishops, after two and a half years' work and hundreds of amendments, voted in favour (238 for and 9 against) of the final text in May 1983.

The document of about 30,000 words is divided into a Summary (6 pages), an Introduction (2 pages), four main Chapters (78 pages) and a Conclusion (3 pages). Chapter one deals with 'Peace in the Modern World: Religious Perspectives and Principles', which includes the chief biblical content. Chapter two discusses 'War and Peace in the Modern World: Problems and Principles'. Chapter three addresses 'The Promotion of Peace: Proposals and Policies'. Chapter four turns to much broader themes concerned with 'The Pastoral Challenge and Response'.

TCOP has many unsatisfactory features, but these should not distract attention from its strengths. Chief among the latter is the much-noted openness of the *process*. 'That process was almost as important, for both bishops and laity, as the document produced. The process was open, something unusual in the production of church documents. It involved experts of every possible kind . . . and, above all, those who both agreed and disagreed with the general direction that the document traversed.'[18] The bishops, as authors of *TCOP*, certainly saw themselves in a traditional teaching role but, at one and the same time, showed themselves to be of a teachable spirit. Over an extended period of time, in the process of absorbing responses and redrafting, the bishops exposed themselves to all kinds of criticism from all sorts of quarters. This is reflected in the tone of modesty which the document communicates. It is, for all its wordiness, a tentative first word.

The question of *authority*, as we have seen, hangs over the document. On one reading, *TCOP* bases itself on traditional Catholic norms of moral theology – the presumption against war and for the peaceful settlement of disputes, the right and duty of self-defence against unjust aggression, the moral unjustifiability of offensive war, the moral wrongness of intentional killing of innocent civilians and non-combatants, and the restriction to the limits of proportionality in defensive response to unjust attack. The difficulty is of course whether and in what way these norms, evolved out of a history of localized, conventional warfare, can apply to the nuclear situation. If these norms have to be accepted at the outset as the authorized *a priori* principles from which moral attitudes to nuclear war must be deduced, and all other considerations are regarded as no more than opinions, then the possibility of breaking new moral ground is restricted from the outset. At one level, *TCOP* loyally follows this path, especially in the final draft; but it also wishes to try to give substance to other sources of authority. Schneiders correctly observes that the Bible is not brought into the central structure of the bishop's argument.[19] Yet the type of authority which the Bible possesses begins to be understood. '[The] scriptures do not provide us with detailed answers to the specifics of the questions which we face today. . . . The sacred texts do, however, provide us with urgent direction when we look at today's concrete realities.'[20] One of the effects of the Vatican's early 1983 intervention in the formation of *TCOP* was to require the authors to distinguish much more carefully the levels of authority in different statements. But the formal Catholic authority of *TCOP* remains unclear. Even if the early 1983 meeting's criticisms of the second draft were accepted, the bishops still affirmed their right and duty to make moral judgments about concrete policies 'as moral teachers'.[21] These judgments 'while not binding in conscience, are to be given serious attention and consideration by Catholics as they determine whether their moral judgments are consistent with the Gospel'.[22]

To whom is *TCOP* addressed? The body of the text gives different answers to this question. Sometimes it seems as if American Catholics are the addressees. At other times, experts, leaders and the whole nation are included. *TCOP* should 'speak both to Catholics in a specific way and to the wider political community regarding public policy'. Neither audience and neither mode of address can be neglected.[23] In one sense, compared for example with *BITL*, the Pastoral Letter had a ready-made audience of those who had actively followed its process of formation over thirty months; the publicity had been of epic proportions. So for the Catholic audience there are biblical, theological, and pastoral passages using concepts and images of the Christian community. But the document also took the view that it had to *mediate* the church's evangelical beliefs and principles to the wider political community through the natural-law ethic of the just war. 'The natural-law ethic is designed to provide a mediating instrument which allows an ethic rooted in a faith perspective to be explained and expressed in a way which others could grasp and support.'[24] This raises an at once intellectual, linguistic and theological problem. In practice the natural-law ethic, codified in the tradition, has represented *the* Catholic mediating conceptuality. But that conceptuality has already widely broken down as a *lingua franca* in the intellectual community/ies. Furthermore, is not the manner of presentation of *TCOP* carrying the clear if patronizing signal that the secular American reader, in some residual way, shares the faith-assumptions of the document? Is the reader, in Rahner's terms, here treated as an 'anonymous Christian'? The problems of mediation stated thus are, of course, not unique to American Catholic Bishops and their Letter; they relate to all public initiatives in Christian social ethics.

At a practical level, one of the weaknesses of *TCOP* derives from one of its major strengths. The collaborative and revising mode of formation has resulted in a document which is too long, often confused, and which bears the visible scars of its many redrafts. And, even if 'the bishops went through a (democratic consultative) process unprecedented in the history of the American Catholic Church' there are still important questions to be asked about whether the use of a bishops' conference for this purpose reflects the correct relationship between laity and clergy in today's church. It also effectively reduces the initiating and decision-making role of women to a minimum.

TCOP's content has chiefly attracted attention to two counts. On the *use* of nuclear weapons, it strongly rejects first use and expresses extreme scepticism that any use can be kept limited. But a less obvious feature which is probably as important lies with the relationship of the document to pacifism, non-violence and the peace-movements. The 1937 Oxford Ecumenical Conference had stated three attitudes to war in Christian tradition, namely (virtually) unconditional obedience to the state, just war theory, and pacifism of various kinds.[26] These three positions, as enunciated by Oxford, had been repeated in subsequent ecumenical statements on war and peace, but their relationship to each other had not been explored – if they were conceived of as related at all. In both *BITL* (as noted above) and *TCOP*, the pacifist position and the peace-movements to some extent 'come in from the cold', in the process opening up for the just war tradition rich veins of spirituality and personal witness. As Hollenbach pithily observes: 'the link which binds the two perspectives together and prevents them from being simply contradictory is the presumption they share against the use of force'.[27]

As I shall discuss in my later remarks on the feminist critiques of the war-culture, it can be argued that, through abuse, the just war theory has lost most, if not all, of its moral energy. The first draft of *TCOP* seemed to regard 'just war' and 'pacifism' as something like two equal traditions in church history, in some sense complementary the one to the other. The document may well have overstated its case here, but in any case, a lot of material along these lines was dropped in deference to the strictures of the Vatican meeting. Some have suggested that this upgrading of the pacifist outlooks in the document betrays an acceptance of an 'emotionalist' element into the debate about peace and war. This is probably a misinterpretation of *TCOP*'s intentions. I judge that the document is attempting to affirm, again and again, that alongside of, and interwoven with, the chiefly cerebral and external character of just war *theory* there is a Christian practice of peace-making in which the content of Christian faith in the death and resurrection of Christ is actualized. It is not therefore a question of cool reason versus emotional rhetoric, but rather a matter of the way in which the practice of Christians is nurtured, radicalized and rendered actively responsible in everyday life. This has to be understood as a theological objection to a view of peace and war which renders ordinary people passive and helpless victims whose faith cannot, in the nature of things, be effectively operationalized. Seen in this context, the apparently abstruse objection of the Vatican meeting to the draft's treatment of eschatology becomes a matter of central importance. For if one lives in a world viewed eschatologically, then the action of God radically to change human history through radical human action becomes conceivable. By contrast Dougherty, for example, in practice emasculates pacifism by treating it as acceptable as a pious interior witness and as unacceptable when it takes political form.[28] Further comment will be made about this feature in my discussion of the Cardiff consultation.

The method which produced *The Church and the Bomb*[29] seems far removed from the open, public, collaborative processes of, in their admittedly different ways, *BITL* and *TCOP*. By comparison *TCATB* seems altogether a more muted exercise. It employed the traditional working-party method, was small in membership (an episcopal chairperson, with five other members and a Secretary), yet attracted a degree of publicity similar to that achieved by the American Pastoral Letter. In 1979 the General Synod of the Church of England had requested its Board for Social Responsibility to explore further aspects of the nuclear debate in 'the theological debate relating to discipleship in this field'.[30] This debate should moreover be undertaken 'in the light of the witness and insights of the whole ecumenical movement'.[31] This ecumenical dimension was personalized in the membership of the working party: the Anglican chairperson/bishop who was a systematic theologian, an Anglican philosopher of religion and ethicist, a noted Quaker expert on nuclear questions, an Anglican priest well-versed in international affairs, who was a pacifist and a member of the Society of Friends, a trained philosopher specializing in war studies, and a distinguished Roman Catholic moral theologian. The setting-up of this working party illustrates in a organizational way the question posed above as to the weight to be given to the several sources of Christian authority and as to the relationships between them.

TCATB arose out of the work of a previous working party which published a report in 1979 under the title *Christians in a Violent World: Defence and Disarmament: An Analysis of Current Issues, with some Recommendations*.[32] This is in many respects an unsatisfactory document, disjointed, sometimes incoherent, with a theological content strangely remote from considerations of defence and diplomacy. It appears to be the voices of the 'professional military men' on the working-party which are predominant. This raises again the question of the role of experts in relation to wider theological and social horizons. This seems to some extent to explain the nature of *TCATB*'s terms of reference which invite the formulation of *critical* analyses. Thus the first two terms of reference: (1) 'to study the implications for Christian discipleship of the acceptance by the major military powers of a role for thermonuclear weapons in their strategy'; and (2) 'to consider the bearing of this on the adequacy of past Christian teaching and ethical analysis regarding the conduct of war'.[33]

TCATB is effectively divided into two parts. The first (125 pages) presents in six chapters the processes and consequences of nuclear fission and fusion, the then current nuclear weapons strategies, the liabilities and risks involved in reliance on the nuclear deterrent, key political developments since 1945 and the importance of the perceptions which each of the power blocs have of each other, a detailed analysis of just-war thinking, and the principal theological themes which shaped the working-party's approach to nuclear weapons. The second part (38 pages) consists of an analysis of the principal policy options available (chapter seven), and conclusions and recommendations (chapter eight).

Chapters one to six offer what amounts to a highly skilful 'teach-in', summarizing and explaining various aspects of essential background knowledge. This immediately makes *TCATB* the most sophisticated and useful for educational purposes of the four documents under discussion in this essay. This feature is intrinsic to the document's urbane and self-controlled style of engagement with its audience. Much of the pessimism and optimism which surrounds the subject of nuclear weapons may be prejudiced or misinformed or misplaced; cool-headed, accurate description and comprehensible explanation is a Christian duty, and so a theological and ethical desideratum. This holds particularly true of the discussion in chapter four of the mutual perceptions of the world power blocs. 'Both sides feel it necessary to assume the worst of the other and to build policy on worst case scenarios.'[34] (*TCOP* had also emphasized the need for a demystification of the supposed attitudes of the Warsaw Pact countries in the eyes of the United States (paras 245–258) and was sharply criticized by some for so doing.) But 'to believe we are condemned in the future only to what has been the past of US-Soviet relations is to underestimate both our human potential for creative diplomacy and God's action in our midst which can open the way to changes we could barely imagine'.[35] This potential is now partially realized in the INF Treaty of May 1988 and the subsequent USSR commitment to unilateral cuts in its conventional forces in Eastern Europe.

The most controversial aspect of *TCATB* was its proposal of a policy for Britain that it should surrender by stages its own nuclear capability, locating this unilateral action in a wider hope about the progress of disarmament at large. It is not within the scope of this chapter to discuss that proposed policy from strategic and other standpoints, but to comment on the issue of adopting a detailed policy recommendation as a Christian form of engagement in the nuclear debate in the churches and in the wider society. Before thus commenting, two preparatory observations are in order. First, *TCATB*'s qualified unilateralist proposal was not arbitrary; it was based upon the perceived convergence of several kinds of consideration – ethical, philosophical, theological, strategic, diplomatic, etc.[36] Second, the authors clearly did not believe that renunciation was the only imaginable alternative. It was commended by them for study and consideration, after great wrestlings and even changes of mind, on the basis of how it conscientiously seemed to them at the time.

It is incorrect to suggest, as some have done, that the Report considers only one alternative. Other options, namely negotiation from strength, 'balanced force reduction and multilateral disarmament with unilateral stages, are analysed in chapter seven. Or should the working-party have been expected to set out the pros and cons of each policy option without expressing any preferences of its own? But this would have been to deny the purpose of the working party and its carefully chosen membership – namely to frame and communicate reasoned judgments. A stronger objection to presenting policy options is to be found among those thinkers who commend the formulation and use of so-called middle axioms. The bare bones of the argument is that the churches should seek to arrive at intermediate moral objectives which, on the one hand, are certainly less general than the most general ethical norms but which, on the other hand, are certainly less specific than detailed policy options which may have to change from place to place and from time to time, and which in any case are the work of the relevant experts. The objection, then, would be that *TCATB* has acted *ultra vires* in presenting a policy option at all, let alone spelling it out in some detail. This is not the place to rehearse the arguments for and against middle axioms.[37] It is a notion which has certain uses in finding consensus positions in, say, ecumenical debate, where to be more specific about policy objectives would be divisive. Employed as a method of Christian socio-ethical reflection, however, it runs into serious difficulties as it seeks to unite one 'essence of Christianity' with the changing views of experts. Certainly, a problem for *TCATB* was that, in showing a preference for, and detailing, one policy option, some people might reject the entire report out of hand either because it (improperly) did not confine itself to general norms or because these people did not approve of the policy option presented. It is clear that potential readers may have been put off *TCATB* as soon as they were aware from the media of the character of the recommendations and so may have missed a sight of the other jewels in the crown of the report.

But the style of engagement of documents like *TCATB* which

express a preference for a certain policy option can justify itself at a much deeper level of theological seriousness. One of the forceful objections registered by the contemporary theologies of liberation against the traditional Christian arguments about peace and war concerns their generality and abstractness. This generality and abstractness in turn reflects a dualistic attitude to reality which in fact implies that the action of God cannot really enter the realm of human ahistoricity in all its finitude and contingency. In the last hundred years it is notable how many Christian thinkers have employed an a historical Idealist philosophy as a framework for conceptualizing the relationship (or lack of relationship!) between God and the world. The transcendent dwells in a supernatural realm and cannot be really instated within concrete worldly historicity. The only way in which the transcendent can therefore express itself in human life is at the level of interior faith or inward subjectivity. In theological and ethical circles this dualism links up with the influential 'two kingdoms' doctrine where the Christian does not act *qua* Christian in the public realm. The liberation theologians would therefore take extreme exception to the kind of outlook noted by Preston in an essay on 'Middle Axioms in Christian Social Ethics' which runs: 'the Christian way of life is so far-reaching that it transcends any particular embodiment either in personal life or social structures'.[38] The liberationist would argue that if the Christian way of life cannot be concretely embodied in personal life and social structure with a very high degree of specificity, then it lays itself open to the Enlightenment/Marxist/Nietzschean charge that Christianity distracts attention from, and weakens commitment to, the characteristically human responsibilities in this world. To say this is not to make the rather silly statement that no theological or socio-political discussion is valid or useful if it does not *always* include detailing of policy options. As Deem has said; 'the claim that knowledge and explanation of an existing situation is of no importance unless accompanied by policy suggestions is equivalent to arguing that only a limited number of people are capable of deriving ideas from information about a particular state of affairs'.[39] What the liberationists *are* insisting on is that there is something deeply problematic and sinister about the view that theological assertions must of their nature hover above, and never really enter into, the untidy and ambiguous realm of human historicity.

TCATB, like *TCOP*, clearly seeks to avoid this whole body of accusations. It appears to want to say that the grace and presence of God is immanent to the processes of human *action* in history. There is therefore a profound sense in which we can be said to have taken *full* responsibility for a course of action not only in giving an intellectual and emotional assent to it, but when we have also been prepared to commit ourselves to the activity and consequences involved in that course of action. *TCATB* is eager, it seems, to suggest that the Christian ethical reflection about war and peace has to be concretized and operationalized if it is to be faithful to the contours of the *historical* destiny of Jesus the Christ. So the last two sentences of the first part of *TCATB* affirm: 'What is required is something more specific, something which takes all the relevant information into account, which dares to make technical judgments and *shuns the immunity afforded by more general statements*. This can be achieved only when Christians relate the Church's general teaching on war and peace to the circumstances of the present and have *the faith to come to specific conclusions*, however provisional and even imperfect they may seem to be.'[40]

My choice of a fourth document upon which to comment may seem somewhat unusual; it seems something of a wild card in the pack of four. I have selected it because it explicitly opens up for attention a feature of recent church pronouncements on war, violence and peace – and specifically nuclear matters – which has become increasingly prominent in the last two decades or so. This concerns issues of individual and group peacemaking and peacekeeping, the varieties of pacifism and non-violence, the spirituality of disarmament and the justification of personal involvement in violence in situations of embedded oppression, and so on. This was ventured upon in chapter eight of *BITL* and in section four of *TCOP* (though in a rather muddled way). It is more submerged in *TCATB*, perhaps connected with the report's rather severe intellectual manner and rational tone.

It was in response to the troubled beginnings of the Programme to Combat Racism and also to the memory of Martin Luther King following the 1968 Uppsala Assembly of the World Council of Churches, that the Central Committee moved to set up a programme dealing with the ethics and strategies of violence and non-violence. The Cardiff Consultation on *Violence, Non-Violence and the Struggle for Social Justice* came half-way through the programme.

The participants, 'academics (theologians, peace researchers, political scientists), church leaders and activists were present – sometimes in the same person!'. Outside Euramerica these participants came from Chile, Uruguay, Zaire, Dahomey, Lebanon, Philippines, Tanzania, Japan, Czechoslovakia, India, Brazil, New Zealand, South Africa and the USSR. Out of forty-three participants, eight were women.

The report of this consultation did not appear in book-form and was circulated on a limited basis. It consists of thirty-three mimeographed pages. It is dated 20 November 1972, under three months from the time of the consultation. It is a raw document; 'what follows should be read therefore not as a finely honed record of consensus, but as a listing of issues and a gathering of ideas, experiences and concrete proposals for continuing consideration'.[41] Important to the style of engagement of the consultation and of the report was that the group had been requested to speak *to* the World Council and not *for* it. *VANV* in this respect bears comparison with *BITL*, though the former is more direct and emotive. *VANV* is in eight chapters. Chapter one sees the world community of humankind as a given. 'Violence therefore can be understood as any breach of the community of mankind as we are led to understand it in the light of Christ.'[42] Chapters two and three especially address themselves to the theme of *structural violence*; the church has a ministry in respect of personal, structural and strategic levels of violence. Chapters five, six and seven deal with 'challenging structural violence' – by empowerment strategies some of which accept, and some of which reject, the option of violence – and with the grounds of choice. Chapter eight is entitled 'Mobilizing the Churches'.

The crucial paradigm to which the actual engagement of the report bears witness is of two 'sides', violent and non-violent – admittedly an over-simplification – being constrained to try to hear and to understand each others' position, in the light of their own and others' long-held, deeply-pondered, and often existentially tested, convictions. A member of the consultation has communicated with me concerning the importance, pain and difficulty of that attempt for the participants. Notable about the Report is the desire always to come as close as possible to particulars, and to explore the many fine distinctions which must be made between, and the many questions which must be asked in respect of, individual strategies both of violence and of non-violence. Both strategies are, or ought to be, deeply reflective and self-critical. In the final analysis there are not 'everywhere and forever two categories, violence and non-violence, which move in separate worlds and remain only as rivals'.[43] This leads to what some may find an inconsistent conclusion: 'our greatest problem is not that some Christians are acting non-violently for justice and peace while others are resorting to violence. The great problem is simply that most of our fellow Christians are not consciously acting on such matters at all. Thus we must ensure that this widespread concern about violence and non-violence will highlight rather than obscure the larger challenge to which the ecumenical movement in recent years has given increasingly clear expression: the challenge to all Christians to become wiser and more courageous at translating the generalities of faith into the specifics of social and political engagement'.[44] The style of engagement of *VANV* points beyond itself to a style for Christian engagement at large.

On the other hand *VANV* bears witness as do, in their own way, the other three documents discussed in this chapter, to the profound and conscientiously held differences between people about responses to peace and war, and to the futility of too easily won reconciliations. The Heidelberg Theses of 1959 anticipate, and provide a possible amplification of, *VANV* in this respect. 'Thesis 6: We must try to understand the different conscientious decisions taken about nuclear arms in this dilemma as complementary actions . . . So far it has not been possible to reconcile these views, nor does it appear that this will happen in the near future . . . Nevertheless, their experience of two years of continual discussion has led [the authors of this report] to believe that the statement "we remain together under the Gospel" has a more profound meaning than merely tolerating the irreconcilable at the present time . . . The common basis must be the aim of avoiding nuclear warfare and the establishing world peace (*sic*). . . . But in our threatened world, with its lack of examples to follow, people with different background and insights can be led to this goal along different paths. It may be that the one can only follow his path because there is someone following another path.'[45]

I bring this chapter to a close with three more general reflections on the documents whose styles of engagement I have analysed and commented upon.

First, the four documents give the clear impression that the theology, ethics and practice of nuclear disarmament is for the most part a male preserve. So much is this the case, and apparently so much is it taken for granted, that the documents do not comment upon it in any significant way. No account is taken of the various feminist critiques of war and politics which raise searching questions about the psychological sources of warmaking. Nowhere in the four documents does the theological discussion engage with the psychological dimension. Yet it seems so obvious that the debate is myopic and impoverished if it does not allow itself to be challenged by the feminist critiques with their alternative readings of cultural history in the West. For example, Nancy Harstock has argued that war and the masculine role of the warrior-hero have been central to the conceptualization of politics for the last 2500 years. Moreover, this political community constructed by the warrior-heroes and the political philosophers has been a particular type of male community, whose 'most extreme form is represented by the military barracks of Sparta where . . . military capacity, civic personality, and masculinity were co-terminous'.[46] Seen in this perspective, it seems that women, who were excluded from that community, have represented dangerous, disorderly and irrational forces which threaten the very existence of the political community – threats with which the political community has had to deal in one way or another. Out of this retreat to the well-defended Sparta barracks when faced by the symbolic female threats, have emerged distinctions between the public and the private realms, between masculine and feminine worlds, which have deep roots in present-day culture. The 'world' is a battleground on which 'manliness' is tested. If there is any truth at all in these arguments, then Harstock is right to observe that to effect significant changes would 'require a re-understanding of the shape of the political community itself'.[47]

Jean Bethke Elshtain looks at arguments, and specifically the just war arguments, which can be used to challenge the realist account of politics where struggle is endemic to the system, where wars must and will occur because there is nothing to prevent them. Just war theory has emerged as a challenge to the 'no exit' character of realism. It begins as a 'pacific ontology' but changes its nature in e.g. Augustine. Just war discourse comes down to us as 'a gerrymandered edifice scarred by social transformation and moral crisis'.[48] Its strength is that from time to time it has offered 'a critical discursive edge'.[49] But one major criticism of just war discourse concerns the cultural images of males and females which are rooted in it. 'Men were constituted as just Christian warriors, fighters and defenders of righteous causes. Women . . . got solidified into a culturally sanctioned vision of virtuous, non-violent womanhood that I call the "beautiful soul" . . . '[50] 'In matters of war and peace, the female beautiful soul cannot put a stop to suffering, cannot effectively fight the mortal wounding of sons, brothers, husbands, fathers. She continues the long tradition of women as weepers, occasions for war, and keepers of the flame of nonwarlike values.'[51] On the other hand, the image of the just warrior moralizes collective male violence. But times have changed; just warriors and beautiful souls 'are vulnerable in the face of nuclear realities'.[52] But the just war theory is continually stretched to breaking point. Though we are 'faced with historic transformations' of the nature of political bodies, of the context of international life, and of the totalistic deadliness of weapons, 'just war thinkers seek valiantly to apply the appropriate rules to cover increasingly horrific situations'. A greater evil to excuse warmaking can somehow always be found. Elshtain commends that kind of feminism which rejects the frames of 'beautiful souls' and 'just warriors' as features of inherited discourse, yet finds worth in the just war discourse. The female subject insists that politics must come under moral scrutiny, insists that 'ways of knowing flow from ways of being in the world and that hers have vitality and validity in ways private and public'.[53]

Whether or not one buys into Harstock's and Elshtain's arguments in detail (and there are plenty of feminists and non-feminists who would not), I am of the opinion that a sufficient overall case has been made out to justify much more detailed historical and contemporary exploration of the set of ideas men-women-war-politics-feminism by the Christian community. Theologians in particular are herein obligated to lift their sights from that feminist theology that is preoccupied (perfectly properly) with questions of gender and ministry also to bring into their range of vision this (not of course unconnected) set of ideas.

Second, as we have seen, the four documents, in different ways, pick up and begin to develop the theological and ethical implications of the growing democratization of the nuclear disarmament debate which was chiefly the work of the secular peace-movements. One of the principal features of this democratization has been the partial willingness of the historic mainline churches to begin to allow the *concerns* (in the Quaker sense) of the historic peace churches and of the modern peace-movements into the debate. A major challenge to nuclear-debate elites flowing from this democratization is to the ready acceptance that living under the nuclear threat is normal and inevitable.

In this connection, all four texts, in differing degrees, bring together into closer relationship what have often been, and often are, held apart, namely *thinking about* nuclear disarmament and the presence or absence of *human resources* to bring this about. This may be put in the form of an extended question. *Does reduction of the nuclear threat depend upon the continued, albeit more skilled and sophisticated, use of traditional human resources, deeply flawed as the history of human conflict shows them to be: or is the natural human inheritance so malign and the nuclear threat more serious, not only in degree but in kind, than previous threats to the humanum that only the presence and activity of a 'new person', a 'new being', a 'converted self', will suffice successfully to carry the weight of responsibility?* There is some evidence in the four texts – most clearly in *BITL* and *VANV*, but also in *TCOP*, though perhaps less in *TCATB* – that they would haltingly answer 'no' to the first and 'yes' to the second part of that question. This evidence is most visible in the theological portions of the texts which are severally concerned to question static and externalist views of human nature as incapable of change in this world. I have already noted that the several appeals to eschatological and apocalyptic strands of biblical thought are especially pertinent and provocative. For their use signals a deep religious conviction that, first, we live in a special *kairos* and that, second, in that *kairos*, human selfhood can somehow be transformed and enabled by God. (Does GS 542's comment on *TCATB*'s neglect of apocalyptic in part reflect this concern?)[54]

Third, George Weigel's recent far-ranging and suspectful study *Tranquillitas Ordinis: The Present Failure and Future Promise of American Catholic Thought on War and Peace* devotes chapter nine to "'The

Challenge of Peace", American Catholicism and the New Nuclear
Debate'.[55] He concludes that 'the bishops were quite right in their
sense that the times required a powerful statement of the Catholic
heritage of moral reason and political vision on the central problem
of war and peace. What they delivered, though, was a document
that, for all its soundness of intention, summed up the abandonment
of the heritage which had been underway in the American Church
for fifteen years'.[56] It did not pay sufficient attention to 'the peace
that was possible in this world'.[57] TCOP manifested a 'virtual detach-
ment of the problem of nuclear weapons from the political context in
which they are best analyzed, morally and strategically'. The claim
that the threat of nuclear weapons was unique and absolute (argues
Weigel) made the bishops vulnerable to external intellectual currents
and emotional passions. Their choice of the word 'terror' to describe
responses to the signs of the times was not the way to begin. 'Did it
reflect a renascent, New Testament-based apocalypticism within the
NCCB? Was it an attempt to bring the eschatological teachings of the
Judaeo-Christian tradition to bear on contemporary issues (no small
task, given the complexity of that tradition)? Or, much more likely,
was it a reflection of those survivalist currents in American political
culture that had played a notable role in shaping the nuclear debate
of the late 1970s and early 1980s?'[58] There is no need to take Weigel's
critical analysis further, since what has been summarized captures
the main thrust of his thinking. In broad terms, Weigel would side
with a positive answer to the first part of my question formulated in
the preceding paragraph. But on what presuppositions does his
standpoint rest? Weigel's title *Tranquillitas Ordinis*, drawn from
Augustine, provides a clue. Weigel keeps the two cities well apart.
The earthly city is in a profound sense external to the Christian
believer who has on earth no abiding home. True, the believer shares
with the earthly rulers a divinely-commanded concern for human
order, not least to serve the well-being of the church, but an order
whose values remain earthly and ephemeral. By contrast the style of
engagement of our four documents – documents which manifest
differences from each other – have tentatively in common a vision of
a more closely bonded heaven and earth, a bonding whose foundation is laid in the action of grace in the created order and whose
greater fulfilment in *this* world is obliquely adumbrated in eschatology. In that vision, women and men are called to take on substantive responsibility for a world to which they are not external, but to
which they belong – by God's mandate.

8

Reflections on Love, Power and Justice

RONALD PRESTON

Modern technological developments in military weapons have focussed attention on the most difficult issue that has perennially confronted the Christian ethical tradition, the relation of love to power and justice. Those who follow contemporary work in theological ethics are well aware of numerous discussions related to the theme in general and the particular problems raised by the invention of nuclear weapons. Many of them have come from churches at the highest level, such as the Vatican or the World Council of Churches; or from national councils of churches, or particular church synods; whilst some have come from specially convened groups or from individual authors. One of the most weighty in recent years has been the Pastoral Letter of the Roman Catholic bishops of the USA, on War and Peace in the Nuclear Age, *The Challenge of Peace : God's Promise and Our Response.*[1] A notable Scottish effort was *Ethics and Defence: Power and Responsibility in the Nuclear Age* edited by Howard Davis.[2] Whatever degree of authority they carry, they have been the means by which many Christians have become somewhat detached from following the cruder militaristic and nationalistic attitudes in their respective countries which has been a standard Christian response since the rise of national sovereign states. However, there has always been a minority attitude within the churches, notably within historic peace churches, of which in the United Kingdom the Quakers have been the chief, which has never agreed with the majority on the use of force. It represents an attitude which has existed within Christianity since its earliest days, and which has adopted a pacifist stance, though on different grounds in different centuries. Its persistence leaves an unease in the majority. How to do justice to a view of coercion whose roots are in a radical attitude to power in the ministry of Jesus and at the same time to the role of the state, also acknowledged in the ministry of Jesus (Mark 12.17),

which includes the securing of an order in human life without which
it would fall into anarchy, and no humane possibility of living would
exist? This chapter makes no claim to originality, nor does space
allow a review of the varied approaches to this theme. It merely
charts what seems to me the most cogent way of drawing upon key
elements in the Christian tradition from the New Testament onwards
to relate love, power and justice, and then bringing it to bear on
the horrendous situation created by the invention of large scale,
indiscriminate, weapons of destruction, mainly but not exclusively
nuclear.

I

First of all, what content is to be given to the terms love, power and
justice? By love is meant that New Testament virtue which is referred
to by Jesus in the synoptic gospels in his summary of the meaning of
the Old Testament Torah (Mark 12.28 ff.), by his injunction to the
disciples in the fourth gospel to 'love as I have loved you' (John
13.34), and by St Paul in Rom. 13.8 and in his picture of love in I Cor.
13. It is a virtue which is adumbrated in the Old Testament, elements
of which are found in human life the world over, but which Jesus
radicalized by his teaching and his death, not least by the injunction
to love our enemies (Matt. 5.44). To denote it the New Testament
uses the hitherto comparatively colourless Greek word *agape*.[3] If we
ask what it means in practice, what is its 'cash value', in the homely
terms sometimes used by moral philosophers to stress the need for
precision in the use of terms and the avoidance of vague abstractions,
the reply would be that first of all it involves an active concern for
the well being of all within our capacity to serve them. The stress is
on the *need* of the neighbour (not his or her *wants*), as we can best
understand it. It is not in the first instance on the sacrifice of the self.
Christian love is not concerned so much with self-abnegation as with
the good of the neighbour. A proper self affirmation, a proper self
love, is necessary if we are to respond to our God-given status, and
before we can have a self to sacrifice when neighbour love requires
it.

The next reply would be that *agape* in Christian thought is non-
reciprocal. It hopes, of course, for a response. But it does not depend
on one. It is not based on doing good to those who do good to you.
One of Jesus' most radical teachings is that anyone can do that (Matt.
5.45). Citizens of the kingdom of God, as taught and lived by
Jesus, are to follow God's overflowing love to the deserving and
undeserving alike.

Justice, whether corrective or distributive, as a norm for human
society has had a complex history in the Christian tradition. Perhaps
because of apocalyptic expectations there is no stress on it in the New

Testament, and because of this biblically minded Protestants have not been at ease with it. In the Old Testament it is related to God's saving work, focussed in his love towards his covenant people. The radicalization of this in the New Testament led Paul into arguments as to whether God is just if he forgives the guilty. However, the Old Testament enjoins even-handed corrective justice in dealing with punishable offences, and this is a moral law which rulers of other states should also obey (Amos 1). Protestant Christians have for the most part had no difficulty with corrective as distinct from distributive justice, though moving uncertainly when it comes to questions of punishment. The Catholic tradition has had a different problem. When Christianity moved so rapidly into the Gentile world it encountered the Greek philosophical legacy and took over a concept of natural law; and in distributive justice it took from Aristotle the phrase *reddere suum cuique*, give to each his due. Hence the notion of justice as fairness. But of course what is due to each remains to be worked out. Aristotle, for instance, excluded slaves from citizenship. At times the Catholic tradition has held that while justice is a precept binding on every Christian, love is a work of supererogation to which some are called on occasion; but this is not so today, when the more authentic Catholic tradition holds that justice is to be shaped and directed by *agape*, which while it requires more than justice can never require less. Protestants should agree. Justice as fairness arises as soon as more than two people are involved; for instance as between children who are loved dearly by their parents who must none the less still strive to be fair between them. The Protestant who ignores questions of justice either sentimentalizes love in assuming it can be realized in principle without difficulty in collective relationships, or separates love sharply from the kingdom of this world in favour of a pietistic otherworldliness.

Power at first seems remote from love. Yet it is basic to the corporate life of human beings. Questions of nuclear warfare merely highlight it at its sharpest. Power can be defined as the ability to control the behaviour of others and to bring about intended results. Without the possession of such power the body politic could not function. It is needed to make ordered human life possible. And it implies the reality of coercion. Coercion cannot be removed from human life. It ranges from various levels of non-violent pressure to various levels of the use of force. States use coercive power at many levels; our present concern is with the threat or use of coercive force in international disputes. However, force is not the same as violence. Violence is the term we use to denote the use of force which we consider illegitimate, just as murder is the kind of killing which we will not permit. This is a distinction of fundamental importance. It causes only confusion if those who talk of violence as against non-violence, mean coercion as against the absence of it, whether in domestic affairs (as in strikes), or in war between states; or in the case of civil war and guerrilla strife. It assumes that any death caused by coercion must be condemned as an illegitimate use of it. It obscures the distinctions which must be made when the need is to derive the kind of institutions and conventions which will mitigate the inevitable evils involved in the use of force, and increase the chance of their being held to, and not ignored, when tensions lead to hostilities.

It is the habit of established authorities and those who support them to ignore the coercive force involved in the structures of power, or else to approve any use of it as necessary in enforcing law and order; and if political and social tension rises to such an extent that force is used by those authorities they habitually denounce the use of force by their opponents as violence and call upon them to renounce it (often calling them terrorists), without considering within what parameters the use of force against a *de facto* authority might be justified. Examples from Southern Africa and Northern Ireland come at once to mind. Indeed when white Christians urge black ones to abjure violence, black Christians ask in reply why this should be so when, to take the European heartland of Christianity as an example, Christians have almost always supported 'violence' used by their respective states in conflicts with one another. Many instances of this in the past now seem dubious to us, to say the least, but not all. Most of us think the use of 'violence' against Hitler's Germany was justified. Is South Africa's institutionalized racism to be condoned when Hitler's was not?

However, such distinctions are very far from the way the most radical strain in the Bible understands the way God himself used his power. It is this which crystallizes the problem of relating love, power and justice. If the larger nuclear weapons are the most extreme examples of the use of power, and if a theology of power is a necessity for Christians, we must examine the roots of this in the Bible, and its subsequent development in Christian tradition, and then bring it to bear on power relations between states today.

II

The Bible is not a book of systematic theology, whether in doctrine or morals, nor of sociology nor political theory. It is important, therefore, to notice what it presupposes. Three presuppositions are fundamental; they are not argued but must be assumed if the Bible is to make sense. The first is the reality of Yahweh himself (and/or herself). The second is the reality of human persons who are made in God's image (Gen. 1.26) and to respond to their creator it is assumed are able and called in the realm of moral judgment, distinguishing what they judge to be right and should follow from what they judge to be wrong and should shun, and are able to exercise this judgment in particular cases (of which the ethical problems raised by nuclear war are examples). Thirdly, the Bible presupposes structures of society in which human persons find themselves living willy nilly; structures of family, economic life and state authority and – less clearly demarcated because all pervasive – culture. These provide the boundaries and constraints within which at any given time human life has to be lived and which potentially encourage or discourage finer levels of personal moral discernment. Issues of war arise especially within the sphere of the state. In addition there is an explicit presupposition which has controlled the selection and interpretation of the varied material found in the Bible, the election or call of Israel as Yahweh's Covenant people as the means of implementing his purpose as Redeemer of *all* peoples. Christians accept this in respect of the Old Testament, and its re-interpretation controlled their selection of the New Testament canon.

Within these presuppositions the Old Testament speaks of Yahweh as Creator, Sustainer and Disturber. Yahweh is Creator because the world is an order and not a chaos. Science also rests upon this presupposition, whether it holds that it is fortuitous that it is so, or that it is due to God's creative intention. As Sustainer Yahweh is not like the deistic watchmaker who sets the universe going and then leaves it to continue on the basis of the original creative act. There are different understandings in the Old Testament of *how* Yahweh uses his sustaining power; sometimes the emphasis is on his direct use of his power as evidenced in natural phenomena like a thunderstorm; sometimes on his quiet inspiration of humankind as a sustainer of basic moral order, as in most of the Wisdom literature. As Disturber Yahweh is thought of as overshadowing the movements of history, challenging and shaping his covenant people, and involving other earthly authorities in this process, whilst also requiring of them a certain basic morality, even though they do not acknowledge him but only a pseudo-God of their own. There is for instance a graphic picture of the state entry of the ruler of Babylon into Sheol in Isaiah 14, a passage full of heavy irony. Yahweh, however, is especially the Disturber of his covenant people who were tempted to think of him as being obliged to be solely their Sustainer. This is expressed in the ambiguous attitude to the establishment of the monarchy in I Sam. 8 and 12, and continues throughout the history of the Kingdom of Israel and Judah until the time of Jeremiah, who is convinced that monarchy, temple and priesthood must be swept away and the people go into exile before the Covenant people will give up an idolatrous trust in Yahweh as of necessity a Sustainer; so their moral insight is corrupted and Yahweh flagrantly disobeyed. Yahweh's concern for righteousness was flouted by corrupt corrective justice, and his concern for the poor and weak was flouted by lack of distributive justice.

Yahweh as a Disturber is particularly characteristic of the prophetic tradition. Furthermore the prophets wanted to detach Israel from political alliances in favour of trusting in Yahweh's power alone. But this is not possible for a collective entity if it wishes to sustain itself in the world as an independent self-directing unit. Those in the Maccabean revolt who began by refusing to fight on the sabbath had to abandon this stance, for they were slaughtered (I Macc. 2). It is possible for an individual to do so, but he or she will suffer the consequences. Jesus did. And he was crucified. His death expresses in a radical way the most paradoxical understanding of Yahweh's power adumbrated in the Old Testament; he expresses it by self-limitation, thus calling into question all usual concepts of power. Looking back on the Old Testament with Christian eyes, and with the ministry of Jesus in mind, it perhaps stands out more clearly. As already mentioned both Jews and Christians agree that in so far as there is a unifying thread binding together the very varied types of literature found in the Old Testament over many centuries, that of the Covenant people is the key one. And it is in relation to the Covenant people that Yahweh's direct use of his power by self-limitation is most clearly brought out.

Let us consider three ways in which Yahweh expresses his power directly.

1. He establishes a covenant with Noah, with Abraham and with Moses. He intends it to be the means, through Israel, by which all peoples will be blessed. By this covenant Yahweh binds himself and will not go back on it. The prophet Hosea learned this from Yahweh through his unhappy marriage with Gomer. On the human side the covenant is to be fulfilled by a joyful response expressed both in worship and in conduct which conscience judges to be right. God's people needed to refine their own moral judgment and obey it. This is the theme of the classic confrontation of Nathan and David in II Sam. 12. They are to refine it not by dreams, nor oracles, nor by examining the entrails of birds, but by moral reflection on the nature of Yahweh.

2. What does Yahweh do when his people fail to fulfil their side of the covenant? He renews it. At the time of the exile both Jeremiah and Ezekiel held that Yahweh would make a new start with his covenant people since the people itself was unable to do so. He would give his people a new heart and a new spirit, reaching to each individual Israelite.[4] But, again, the reality after the return from exile was far from this expectation.

3. The Christian understanding is that Jesus was the one Israelite who was able to appropriate these gifts and establish the new

covenant people as a leaven in the world. This belief is based on traditions of Jesus' ministry orally transmitted in the early church and edited and interpreted by the gospel writers. In the first three there are his parables and pithy sayings concerned with the paradoxical rule, or reign, or kingdom of God in the world and the appropriate human response to it. Accepted standards are turned upside down. The fourth gospel contains extensive meditations on the same theme. All four concentrate on how Jesus met his death. Jesus saw his ministry as intimately linked with Yahweh's covenant purposes. He studied the scriptures of Israel and applied them in a new and creative way to himself. He understood that Yahweh as Redeemer used his power in the world created, sustained and disturbed by him not directly by overthrowing and punishing the wrongdoer but by himself suffering the effects of the wrongdoing. This is the supreme witness to the self-limitation of his use of power. In ethical terms the corollary is a non-reciprocal ethic, not based on doing good turns to those who do good turns to you but on the boundless love of God, who continues his blessing on humankind, always seeking a response but not giving up when he does not get one after seven times but even to four hundred and ninety times, which is to say without limit.[5] St Paul gets to the root of the matter when he says that God commended his own love towards us in that while we were yet sinners Christ died for us (Rom. 5.8). Because of this radical overturning of accepted standards the people of God are not to behave to one another as those in the structures of society do. In particular Gentile rulers lord it over their subjects and make them feel the weight of their authority. Among the people of God power is not to be exercised in this way; those who are first among them are to be the servants of all (Mark 10.42ff.).

But Jesus was crucified. The parties in Judaism in his day could not cope with him (and he made the Roman authorities nervous). In different ways they all hoped that Yahweh would use his power to punish the wicked and vindicate his covenant people. However, St Paul can speak of Christ as the power as well as the wisdom of God (I Cor. 1.24); and the general theme of the New Testament is that whatever principalities and powers there may be in the universe, and the ancient world thought there were many, Jesus Christ is Lord over them – the earliest Christian confession – because of the power of the cross.[6] He had won a victory over sin, death and every adverse power. However, the victory is not yet evident terrestrially (Heb. 2.8). Christians are called to live in the strength of it and to await its final consummation. In doing so they live in two kingdoms, not one. In the Old Testament there was one kingdom, Israel, the covenant people which was both church and state. In the New Testament there

are two. The church as witness to and agent of the kingdom of God
found itself under a separate earthly authority, the Roman Empire.

On the whole the New Testament takes a very favourable view of
the pagan Roman Empire (Rom. 13.1–7); also of the moral perception
of the pagan neighbours of Christians (I Peter 2.12). But it can be
fiercely critical, as in apocalyptic literature, especially in Revelation.
Of course it takes on the whole a very favourable view of the church,
though it can be critical of that as well (I Cor. passim; I Peter 3.15f.).
Later the church was to spread widely and live within many different
kingdoms of the world. So it was that the doctrine of the Two
Kingdoms or Realms developed, particularly in the Lutheran tradition: the Kingdom of this world (the state) and the Realm of the
church (often mistakenly equated with the kingdom of God instead
of being seen as its agent). In this understanding *both* are God's
kingdoms.[7] How life in the two has to be related is a perennial
problem. The ethical issues raised have been sharp. Those arising
from nuclear weapons are the most acute.

Before dealing with them we need to look briefly at the biblical
witness to Yahweh's indirect use of his power. First, if the covenant
people flout his moral order they suffer disasters. The prophetic
tradition is a tale of disasters proclaimed and suffered, so much so
that any prophet proclaiming smooth things was regarded as a false
one.[8] The element of disaster was later to be intensified in apocalyptic
writings, though usually as a judgment on the rest of the world rather
than the people of God. But the Old Testament witness is that no
states can succeed if they flout the basic moral order established by
Yahweh's kingly rule over all peoples, not only the covenant people
(Amos 1). The mills of God may grind slowly or quickly but they do
grind. Pagan Rome, on which some New Testament passages pass
judgment, lasted centuries but in the end the Christians ironically
found themselves heirs to its ramshackle structure. In this century
Hitler thought he was settling affairs in Europe for a thousand years.
In twelve he was gone. If humanity should wickedly allow an all-out
nuclear war to develop it will destroy a large part of itself and produce
a ruin from which it will take generations, perhaps centuries, to
recover, and from which some think there can be no recovery.
Secondly, as far as the people of God is concerned, the Old Testament
witness is that pagan rulers can be unwitting servants of Yahweh,
permitted by him to prosper in order to bring the people of God to
their senses. This is the view taken of the rulers of Assyria, Babylon
and Persia.[9] If the movements of history are interpreted from this
point of view, Marxism should surely be put in the same category,
so long as it is also included within the spectrum of God's ceaseless
care for all peoples.

The upshot of this understanding of human history is that humans have the responsibility in each generation under God of relating love, power and justice. There are no guaranteed permanent historical gains; there is no immanent divine process driving human history inexorably towards the fulfilment of human hopes and divine intentions. But neither are there limits laid down by God to human possibilities if humans are faithful. He does not say 'here shall you come but no further and here shall your proud waves be stayed', as he says to nature in the poem in Job 38.11. Even so, gains made by one generation have to be made their own by subsequent ones. If they fail to secure their moral inheritance the fall will be all the greater than if they had started from a lower base. Nazi Germany is the great instance of this in the twentieth century. Its synthetic barbarism was so much worse than savage barbarism. The fulness of the reign of God transcends historical possibilities. But the fact of having a celestial hope in no way diminishes the challenge to pursue a terrestrial one in terms of the opportunities of our own day. This has to be worked out in the kingdom of this world from the perspective of life in the kingdom of God.[10]

III

How is the radically non-reciprocal ethic of the kingdom of God related to the kingdom of this world? We should note that there are other elements in the gospel ethic, which are not distinctive to it, such as the Golden Rule (Matt. 7.12); this enjoins impartiality between oneself and others at whatever depth one chooses to take it. But it is not these other elements which focus the problem of love, power and justice. Jesus did not give any detailed guidance as to how this task was to be accomplished. This is true even in the question of marriage and divorce, which is the only exception which might occur to a reader of the gospels. However, apart from the intrinsic unlikelihood that of all the detailed pressing ethical questions Jesus gave guidance on only one, modern study of the gospels and the way the traditions about Jesus were preserved prior to their being incorporated by the gospel writers within the distinctive theological concern of each of the four, suggests that it is a mistake to interpret the sayings on marriage and divorce as a detailed rule.[11] Moreover, it is fortunate that he did not teach such rules, for if he had they would be relative to the context of his time and ingenious exegesis would be needed to bring them to bear on the vastly different situations in subsequent centuries.

The detailed ethical guidance in the rest of the New Testament has to be seen in this light. Viewed in this way it provides valuable examples of how the first Christians set about relating the radical eschatological ethic of the kingdom of God to the issues arising for them in the first-century Roman Empire. In the earlier epistles this guidance is largely conditioned by the apocalyptic expectation of an imminent *parousia*, or return of Christ, and the end of the present time series. This is the case, for instance, in the replies given by St Paul to six questions about marriage presented to him by a deputation from the church at Corinth (I Cor. 7.29). As apocalyptic expectations lost their intensity, and as an indefinite ongoing life in the world seemed likely, the radical ethic was domesticated. The church, quickly in a predominantly Hellenic environment, took over Stoic Household Codes and gave them a setting within a Judaeo-Christian framework. Examples can be seen in Colossians, Ephesians, I Peter, the Pastoral Epistles, and I Clement (this last outside the New Testament canon).[12] These show a marked deference to authorities, with stress on the duties of the inferior to the superior, children to parents, wives to husbands, slaves to owners, and all to the state authorities. This trait has had an unhappy legacy in Christian history, and it is only since the Enlightenment that Christians have begun to emancipate themselves from it, and the process is far from complete. For instance since then Christians have become much more sensitive to toleration as a virtue, and to the necessity of 'natural justice', especially within the church itself. The Enlightenment certainly had its superficialities, but it produced cogent criticisms of Christian practice. Apocalyptic thought has also left an unhappy ethical legacy. I am not thinking so much of its propensity for predicting the date of the *parousia* (though that is distracting enough), but of (1) the quietism on the one hand or fanaticism on the other to which it tends; (2) its assurance of its own rightness with God and of the wickedness of, and its hatred for, its enemies and rejoicings over their expected punishments and sufferings; (3) its preoccupation with the visions of battles between supernatural powers; (4) the tendency of those influenced by it to concentrate on extreme interpretations of empirical evidence on contemporary situations where they pay any attention to empirical evidence at all. (Other attitudes to apocalyptic can be found in the chapters by Richard Bauckham and John Riches.)

As far as the state is concerned there is another attitude to the Roman Empire; the book of Revelation is startlingly different from St Paul in Romans 13.1–7. But interesting as these various texts are – I Corinthians, the Household Codes, Revelation – as examples of problems arising from life in the two kingdoms, no fixed detailed rules can be derived from them. The perennial problem remains: how to maintain the eschatological rigour of the kingdom of God in the absence of apocalyptic expectations of an imminent *parousia*, as we deal with contemporary issues such as those of nuclear weapons?

Christians today in the UK and many other countries have much more responsibility than those of the first century, and more complex problems to face. The 'pacifism' of the church in the first three centuries was in a different situation for different reasons from that of Christian pacifists today. Nor was it consistent.[13] Rapid social changes, following upon the technological innovations since the industrial revolution are undermining traditional authorities. Any ethical guidance by the churches must be based on as accurate an understanding as possible of the empirical data. In the case of military issues these can be of considerable technical complexity. It is not responsible for churches and Christians to keep piously silent. Usually churches can best give guidance on domestic and international social and political questions at a middle level of generality, which falls short of detailed policy implementation;[14] but individual Christians as citizens cannot stop there, and they need help in making more discerning individual judgments on detailed policies which as citizens they cannot avoid.

At this point we need to take up the nature of the structures in the kingdoms of this world which the Bible presupposes and which have already been mentioned. They are those of sex and the family, the economic order, political authority, and culture. It is the third that concerns us, the realm of the state. It is not that of the nation, which is best subsumed under culture, though the identification of state and nation is often thoughtlessly made in the modern world, not least by nationalistically minded Christians.

There are six points to notice about these structures. (1) The Bible assumes them. Without their reality it makes no sense. But since it is not a textbook of systematic theology or sociology it contains no ordered treatment of them. (2) Their reality is arrived at by rational reflection, even as the result of a moral order in the world is arrived at by rational reflection on the existence of moral judgments. In the Nazi period some German Protestant theologians attempted to add nation and race to these four basic structures, and revulsion at this led for a time to the attempt to avoid any use at all of the concept. But it is not possible on sociological or political grounds to make the concept of nation so basic, or on genetical grounds to do it with race. The Nazi attempt to do so was witness to its basic irrationalism. (3) These structures vary enormously in their empirical manifestation, and as experienced they fall short of what human insight sees they might be. (4) Human persons do not choose to live in these structures; they are born into them and are profoundly influenced by them as they grow to maturity, when they have an ability to stand outside them to some extent, to evaluate their good and bad features, and to resolve to work to strengthen the good ones. (5) Because of their belief in God as Creator, Christians believe that these structures are part of his creation and intended for human fulfilment; humans are not born into them on account of their potential faith in God but on the grounds of their common humanity, and they find themselves cheek by jowl in them with men and women of different faiths and ideologies, with whom they must work, so that the structures encourage justice and humanity and discourage what hinders human fulfilment. That is why, for example, Christians are basically concerned with the structure of marriage as such and not only with the adjective Christian attached to it. (6) There are different names given by different theologians to these structures but within their differences of approach the basis point is the same. I have so far deliberately used the term 'structures', as being the easiest one to introduce the concept, but I think the classical name, Orders of Creation, is the best.[15]

It is the order of the state which is the focus of our theme. Anyone writing on that theme today cannot fail to bear in mind the classic discussion by Paul Tillich in *Love, Power and Justice*, where he says 'constructive social ethics is impossible as long as power is looked at with distrust and love is reduced to its emotional and ethical quality . . . constructive social ethics presuppose that one is aware of the element of love in the structures of power without which love becomes chaotic surrender'.[16] Power is necessary, with coercion latent if not necessarily explicit; but the use of power has always to be under scrutiny lest it be abused. There is no human activity which is not liable to abuse. Love of power is a human trait which demands constant vigilance. Checks are needed on power, but not to the extent to make it unusable. It is true that power corrupts but so does unwillingness to use it. Force does not necessarily breed force; it may contain it. It is too simple to say there is *no* arms based security. Its use is a duty. God does not rule primarily by the 'powerlessness' of the cross in the kingdom of this world. But that does not mean that distinctively Christian perceptions should not be brought to bear on it as far as they will go. For instance Sydney Bailey has reminded me that the Geneva (Red Cross) Conventions are non-reciprocal. No state is forced to become a party to them, but any state which does so agrees to implement them even if the other side is in violation.

What should the Samaritan have done if he had arrived on the road from Jerusalem to Jericho at the very moment when the man was being robbed by the thieves? Or what should his attitude have been if the state proposed a tax or toll to police the road and so prevent travellers being beaten up in the first place? It is considerations such as these which led St Thomas Aquinas in his brief treatment of war in the *Summa Theologiae* to set his discussion of it within the setting of the consequences of love, or charity.[17] Force is the strange work of love if it works towards human fulfilment by preserving what love would unite.

The thought of St Thomas on the just war has been further developed.[18] Conflicts of power and interest are endemic in human life and the task is to devise structures to contain them as far as possible, or to lead to a tolerable resolution of them if they do break out into overt strife. That is why, as Sydney Bailey says, international law and conventions in this area, however liable to violation, should not be undervalued by Christians. War, including civil and guerrilla war, is the hardest of all issues of power to contain. The just war doctrine embodies what Christian wisdom has so far arrived at in tackling it. It involves criteria of discrimination and proportion; and prudence in bringing them to bear on particular issues. Prudence is the key intellectual and moral virtue in Christian moral reflection on particular cases. Prudence is required to recognize authentic human limitations as distinct from self-made ones. It is also required to assess both alternative visions of the future and current empirical evidence as it bears on the making of decisions.

The doctrine applies both to the justification of war and the manner of waging it. It is a mistake to say that the development of nuclear weapons has made the doctrine irrelevant.[19] The fact that it is all too easily ignored, especially in the heat of conflict, is no argument against it. It is rather witness not merely to the monstrous dimensions of human collective sin, but also to the lack of serious and continued reflection on the doctrine in the modern world in peace time. When war breaks out an 'all or nothing' attitude quickly develops, with a minority of pacifists on one side, and a large majority on the other who advocate any means to defeat the enemy, assuming that morals can be put in cold storage in war and picked up again afterwards without seriously damaging the end achieved by the means adopted to achieve it. Public reflection on the just war tradition is all the more important because while appropriate to Christian thinking it is not dependent upon it. Originating in a Graeco-Christian context it can be commended to all in a plural society of the 'secular', 'western' type or, for example, to the sacred societies of the Muslim world. Geoffrey Price refers to the virtual abandonment of public discussion of just war issues in recent centuries dominated by a romantic nationalist idealism, but while his analysis of the ideological elements in contemporary attitudes of, and to, the state throws some light on the roots of the totalitarianism which darkened the 1920s, 1930s and 1940s, it seems much less relevant to the 1980s. Nor does it do justice to the 'international civil war' aspect of the 1939–45 conflict, nor to the 'sceptic crusader' attitude of many combatants among the allies to whom I refer in the penultimate paragraph of this chapter. The need is to relate just war analysis to our present situation.

Pacifism on principle is not a corollary of the Christian gospel for life in the kingdom of this world. As a matter of tactics it may well be judged in particular situations to be the best course. Some advocate nuclear pacifism on these grounds. As a matter of principle, however, it is impossible to defend in terms of just war categories the use of large scale nuclear weapons, either in the first instance or in retaliation. They are inherently indiscriminate and disproportionate. Nothing justifies their use. The possession of thousands of them by the two great nuclear powers is an affront. How to get states who possess quantities of nuclear weapons which it would never be morally justifiable to use out of this situation is the key question for diplomacy. It will be hard to solve, not least because nuclear weapons cannot be disinvented. Many less than satisfactory stages will be needed on the way. It is unlikely that Christians will have a 'solution' to this problem so distinctive that no others can share it; but they may well have resources which they must contribute to combined efforts to deal with it. Two aspects of it are (1) how to reduce, or eliminate, morally unjustifiable weapons without increasing international instability, and, (2) whether, or how far, conventional forces need strengthening. But the same does not so clearly apply to battlefield nuclear weapons.[20] (Happily it looks as if some land-based intermediate ones will be phased out.) Decisions about them involve estimates of risk in their use. How far would their use lead inevitably to an escalation involving the 'blockbuster' large scale nuclear weapons. It may well be, as Hugh Beach argues, that the risks are so incalculable that their first use is ruled out by the criterion of proportion, as has been the case with chemical weapons since 1925. Then the issue becomes whether they would have any role in a second strike or whether a certain ambiguity as to their use should remain.

These and many other decisions in warfare, including nuclear warfare, remain to be made after the non-permissible use of indiscriminate and disproportionate weapons is accepted. These decisions are examples in a more hazardous area of moral decision we are constantly called to make in every sphere of life. Changing circumstances throw up issues which cannot be settled purely on principle, but involve a balancing of values in the light of the estimates of the probable consequences of possible lines of action. One can decide that on principle policies of deterrence are morally legitimate and necessary, but how to exercise them is a further question. Again the military rightly aim at stability in terms of fighting power, but political control of them is necessary, otherwise their desire to guard against every conceivable eventuality leads to a perpetual proliferation of arms, and the pursuit of the mirage of absolute deterrence. Or again, we can decide that an ethic of bluff may on occasion be legitimate, but it requires great prudence in operating it, on grounds of practicability and because of the danger of bluffing oneself. We can also decide that stability in power relationships is desirable. If deterrence secures this it may be judged successful. On the other hand prudence is needed lest it become an immobility which stores up trouble and provokes an explosion. Risk taking is central to these issues. Risk is endemic in human life, personal and corporate. Christians should have the confidence to live a life of risk taking, not because they will always prove to have estimated the risks rightly but because they are held in the security of God's graciousness. Aristotle (followed by Aquinas) was right, as John Elford points out, to say that in ethical issues we can only achieve the certainty the subject permits; the nearer we get from generalities to particular decisions the more uncertainties are likely. What the just war doctrines do not do is to proclaim a clear rule, like 'the inviolability of innocent human life', from which a direct deduction to military policy can be made *without* reference to other values or particular circumstances. Here I differ from John Haldane.

If love, power and justice go together the greatest of the three is love, for God is love (I John 4.8). So we need to keep our heads. The use of apocalyptic language in connection with all nuclear weapons is in danger of spreading the idea that all out nuclear war is inevitable, and precluding the making of careful analyses of the military situation. Moreover if a conflict should break out (which God forbid) it would not mean that the sovereignty of God had collapsed. His fate is not tied up with ours.[21] His gracious purpose of love and fulfilment for those made in his 'image' would remain. We would do better to weigh carefully the parameters of a constrained freedom with which we must resist evil in *both* kingdoms, and do it without the self-righteousness which forgets that we are all involved in a tangle of evil in the world. Here are the elements of a theology of responsibility of which Simon Maimela writes. I know this is possible because I owe much to Christian friends who fought against Nazi Germany because they judged that the evil of Hitlerism must be stopped, but they did so without any hatred of Germany. Indeed they loved their enemies whilst fighting them. Nor had they any illusion that if they succeeded the post-war world would be some kind of utopia. Better still it would have been, in their judgment, if the allies had had enough prudence to check Hitler earlier in the decade and prevent the drift to war.

In this whole area Christians should strive to keep public discussion alert. As Donald MacKinnon points out, an interrogative attitude is needed in the dangerous situation produced by nuclear weapons. They should exercise a critical function in exposing short sighted and blinkered attitudes, ambiguities and deceptions; they should aim to defuse ideological confrontations, not least by relativizing overweening claims by states, and still more by nations. Accurate understanding of what is going on and an accurate understanding of the hazards we face are both needed. All the resources of the Christian tradition are to be called on, not least to kindle our imagination and deepen the perceptions of our moral reasoning. Here the dramatic and symbolic aspects of that faith can come into their own and be used to kindle public awareness of the issues. Only a small number of people can make crucial decisions involving nuclear warfare. We of 'civil society' must create a climate of opinion which minimizes the danger of their moral vision being corrupted. Above all we need to make the most of our sources of hopefulness to liberate us from a sense of powerlessness.

9

Defence, Deterrence and the Taking of Life[1]

JOHN HALDANE

It can happen that even when war is declared by legitimate authority and there is just cause, it is, nevertheless, made unjust through evil intention.

St Thomas Aquinas (*Summa Theologiae* 2a, 2ae, q. 40, art 1)

1 Introduction

Perhaps the most important development in recent analytical moral philosophy is the trend to engage in discussion of particular questions of value and conduct. It is now common to address matters of practical concern beginning, where appropriate, with established opinions and then attempting to confirm or refute them. This pattern of argument is in fact very old. It originates in the *quaestio* technique developed in the thirteenth century and can be seen employed to great effect by Aquinas, such as in his discussion of the morality of war from which I have quoted. From the second half of the seventeenth century until the latter third of the present one, however, philosophers have preferred to operate within the narrower compass defined by purely abstract questions about the metaphysics and epistemology of morals. The feeling that this was an undue restriction neglectful of important issues in the resolution of which philosophy could be effective was perhaps first expressed by Bishop Berkeley[2] but went largely unheeded until about twenty years ago. Since then the modern orthodoxy, that in their professional writings thinkers should only concern themselves with the *logic* of moral discourse, has happily lapsed. This is generally apparent given the common situation of philosophers engaging in public debate of moral and social issues. It is also indicated by the less well known but institutionally important fact of the establishment within universities in Britain and America of centres for the study of philosophy, social values and public policy.

Christian moral theologians, by contrast, have never felt restrained by the theoretical aspects of their subject from engaging in debate about questions of conduct. However, the separation of philosophy and theology in this century (when the former has advanced in its analytical methods and the latter has often been willing to abandon systematic argument and the idea of absolute requirements in favour of act utilitarianism and/or historical relativism) has meant that the Christian contribution to contemporary debates too often lacks vigour and logic, for all that it is passionate and well-intentioned. In this respect post-enlightenment theology compares badly with its scholastic counterpart. Recently, however, there have been signs of a resurgence of systematic moral thinking among Christian writers. Three names come to mind in this connection: those of John Finnis, Germain Grisez and Gerard J. Hughes.[3] Significantly, each draws upon the traditions of scholastic natural-law theory and analytic philosophy, and passes to and fro without discomfort between meta-ethical and first-order issues. Of more particular interest here is the fact that they all have addressed themselves to the question of the morality of nuclear deterrence, though they come to rather different conclusions concerning it.[4]

In consequence of these developments within secular and Christian thinking matters of public policy are now discussed to an extent and at a level not previously seen. In this context the Christian moral philosopher enjoys mixed blessings. On the one hand he may feel satisfaction that academic philosophy has returned to questions of conduct from which his own tradition has never departed and to the resolution of which it has much to offer. On the other hand, however, he has to demonstrate more clearly than his secular colleagues the general cogency of his arguments. First, because he may find himself proposing solutions calling for sacrifices which the world regards as unnecessary. And second, because it is likely to be thought, if not said, that his views are not so much reasoned judgments as rationalized prejudices. However, this latter liability to attempted *argumentum ad hominem* should encourage great care and thereby may be to advantage in the effort to arrive at secure conclusions.

I have sketched this background in part for its general interest and also because it is my own. That is, I write as a Christian and as a moral philosopher educated and working in the analytical tradition at a time when it has broadened the range of its concerns to include the morality of war and peace. In what follows I present a line of argument which draws its inspiration from scholastic moral theology and its methods from analytical philosophy. Whatever the fate of the particular argument, I believe this combination is one which could prove fruitful in many other areas of current difficulty.[5]

2 Counterforce and the just war

The nuclear weapons policy of NATO has traditionally been based upon the assumption that the aims of a response would be to destroy the enemy's capacity and willingness to wage war by attacking his nuclear and conventional forces and his centres of command, control and logistic support. This strategy is, therefore, properly speaking a counter*force* one, i.e., directed against military resources, and as such its employment may satisfy the long-established conditions of just war, those being as follows:

1. The war must be made by a lawful authority.
2. The war must be waged for a morally just cause, e.g. self defence.
3. The warring state must have a rightful intention, i.e. to pursue the just cause.
4. The war must be the only means of achieving the just end.
5. There must be a reasonable prospect of victory.
6. The goods to be achieved must be greater than the probable evil effects of waging war.
7. The means of war must not themselves be evil: either by being such as to cause gratuitous injuries or deaths, or by involving the intentional killing of innocent civilians.[6]

Of course a counterforce response might be unjust and it is clear enough where the threat of its being so is most likely to arise. For while any of the above conditions could be breached the destructive power of nuclear weapons is such that even a well-intentioned, lawful authority waging war in pursuit of a just cause may easily violate conditions 5, 6 and 7.

It should be obvious that the liability to injustice is a function of the targeting policy and the destructive power of the weapons involved and is not a matter of their physical constitution as such. However, in the long running debate about the morality of nuclear defence policy there has been a tendency for all parties, but in particular for opponents of such policies, to become obsessed with the *nuclear* aspect of the matter and thereby to lose sight of the central philosophical arguments which are instances of quite general ones concerning the ethics of violence. Principal among these is the following:

1. It is always wrong intentionally to kill innocent human beings.
2. A nuclear weapons strategy involves intentionally killing innocent human beings, either directly or indirectly.

3. Therefore, a nuclear weapons strategy is always wrong.

Assuming the truth of 1, the conclusion 3 can yet be avoided by denying premise 2. And, indeed, as a universal claim 2 is surely false. For example, the counterforce use of tactical weapons at sea and even on land *may* pose no threat to innocent parties. Accordingly, the blanket condemnation of nuclear defence policy based on just war principles is contentious given the (probable) non-moral, empirical facts about the power of certain weapons and about the targeting strategies involving them.[7]

Furthermore, the nuclear obsession blinds many (on *both* sides of current debates about the ethics of modern warfare) to the important fact that not all unjust defence policies are nuclear ones. For, as before, a lawful authority engaged in war as a means of last resort and in pursuit of a just cause may yet act wrongly by employing evil means; for example, by using weapons of mass destruction against civilian populations.[8] Injustices of this sort are familiar from recent history and include, most shamefully for the former Allied forces and in particular for Great Britain, the deliberate area bombing of German centres of population during World War II.

3   Countervalue and morality

In short and in general, therefore, the use of nuclear weapons is neither sufficient nor necessary for violation of the conditions of *just war*. There are, however, certain nuclear strategies which if employed would be unjust. Among these are *some* counterforce policies, e.g. first strike without declaration of war, acts of aggression, use of disproportionate force, etc.; and *all* counter*value* strategies, i.e., ones directed against non-combatants and non-military resources. Such as the latter cannot ever be just since they violate (at least) condition 7 of those listed and are condemned by the argument set out above.[9]

Since 1945 the defence policies of western nuclear powers as individual nations and in association with NATO have drifted from the tradition of counterforce, with which I began, to countervalue. And from the late 1950s onwards, talk of 'mass destruction of Soviet cities' and of 'annihilating an enemy society' has featured in official policy reports and in research analyses of national and NATO targeting strategies.[10] The clear implication of the foregoing, therefore, is that inasmuch as it includes a countervalue component, current western defence policy is immoral.

In reply, advocates of such policies have tended to argue in one of two ways: claiming either that the ethics of violence and warfare have been changed by the development of weapons of mass destruction and that the *just war* doctrine in particular is anachronistic; or else,

that while the enactment of currently held strategies would certainly
be immoral it is not wrong to *threaten* to enact them with the intention
of thereby deterring hostility from potential aggressors.

The first line of reply can itself be interpreted in one or other of
two ways. Either it is being asserted that the moral claim set out as
premise 1 in the earlier argument and those others implicit in the
conditions of *just war* are false; or alternatively the suggestion is that
somehow a countervalue attack is not at odds with them. The
historical drift from counterforce to countervalue defence strategies
does, I believe, mark a movement away from general acceptance of
these moral claims. But this is no argument against their truth and it
is difficult even to conceive of a plausible moral view according to
which it is permissible intentionally to kill innocent human beings.
The prohibition against doing so is a familiar and prominent tenet of
the Judaeo-Christian ethical tradition and persists in secular moral
theories. Certainly adherents of this tradition and of its non-theologi-
cal rivals have not always practised as their theories preached, but
the prohibition has never been thought to be less than absolute for
being violated. Even offenders pay tribute to it by attempting to
represent the victims of their killings as being in some way culpable,
or otherwise legitimate targets.

In the Judaeo-Christian tradition murder is an absolute evil – a
course of action that can never be justified by weighing the taking of
innocent life against the achievement of some material or social
benefit. Caiaphas, the high priest, went wrong in counselling the
judicial murder of Christ claiming that 'it is expedient that one
man should die for the people'.[11] But his error did not consist in
misidentifying the man in question – if he did – or not in that alone.
His mistake was in believing that murder could be justified if it
produced an otherwise beneficial outcome – in this case 'the saving
of the nation'. He ought to have known better, for Judaism (and, of
course, Christianity) take a firmly anti-consequentialist line in such
matters. As St Paul was later to remind the Romans, it would be
slanderous to say that what Christians believe is that one can do evil
if good may come of it.[12]

The inviolability of human life can be argued for in different ways.
One line of thought connects the idea of rational agency with that of
universality. The potential killer requires that his own life not be
threatened by others in order that he may pursue his goals. But if
these goals include causing the death of another person then he is
simultaneously affirming and denying the requirement that an agent
should not have his life threatened. The pattern of argument can be
reworked in a variety of ways but the basic idea remains the same,
i.e. that murder involves inconsistency and is thus irrational.

A second, related approach involves the notion of reciprocity in claiming that one ought not to act towards an individual in a way that you would not want them to act towards you. This – a version of the 'golden rule' – is more restricted in scope than the previous reasoning. It cannot rationally bind those who are prepared to be 'done unto as they would do unto others'. However, it is not likely that any sane person would assent to being killed so as to legitimize his killing another. Certainly, it has been known for murderers to seek execution as retribution for their actions and this is intelligible, but not because it is thought to make the first killing acceptable. On the contrary, it is because the murderer sees the enormity of what he has done, and the impossibility of nullifying it, that he volunteers his own life. One may perhaps question the coherence of his attitude inasmuch as it may seem to compound the evil of taking life. But it is crucially important to note that *this* is the direction in which our thoughts move in search of consistency, and *not* towards the view that murder is acceptable so long as the murderer is willing to be killed in turn.

A third line of argument in favour of respect for human life rests not on appeals to general rationality but instead focusses attention on the particular value of our lives. The sort of worth in question is obviously meant to be intrinsic to human beings as such. It does not attach to them in virtue of capacities or other valuable features which may be possessed to a greater or lesser degree by different individuals. Within the moral theology in which the just war theory originates, the notion of an inalienable right to life is derived from the claim that we are all alike in being children of a loving God. However, even accepting general religious doctrines it is difficult to give sense to this metaphor and then to see how particular moral claims can be derived from it.[13] It is not simply obvious (even if it is true) that the fact that two men are related as brothers makes the killing of one by the other wicked – as if it otherwise would not be. Certainly, we do think that *fratricide* is evil but this is partly because we already think that *homicide* is bad.

The difficulties in the theological approach notwithstanding, it is not implausible to argue that the instrinsic value of human life is a brute fact such that to destroy it intentionally is always bad no matter what goods are achieved by doing so. This possibility would serve to explain the 'phenomenology' of moral experience. For the idea of innocent life presents itself to thought as that of something to be respected whether or not the sorts of arguments against murder outlined previously are found compelling. Of course, the moral nihilist is not likely to be troubled by this or any other response since he denies that *any* moral claim can be true. Nonetheless, national governments, international military codes and the thought and practice of most people presuppose morality, and more precisely acknowledge such claims as that one may not deliberately slaughter the innocent (in the sense of those who present no aggressive threat) – which is what countervalue attacks intend. Even if murder could not be shown to be irrational, blasphemous or contrary to the natural order, its being anathema according to common judgment and positive national and international law is sufficient ground to discount the denial of the moral claim set out as premise 1. Furthermore, the belief that one may intentionally kill the innocent, for whatever reason, is not only repugnant but also self-defeating with respect to whatever other human value or end is given priority. Anyone who urges that it is acceptable to act in this way in order, for example, to advance a political ideal, is unlikely to live to see the kind of society he wants. Nor could such a society be expected to survive. Since from the very moment of its conception it would be vulnerable to the activities of those who, like its architects, adhere to a doctrine of justified murder.

On the second interpretation of the first reply to the charge that current western defence policy is immoral, the response is that contrary to initial appearances such attacks escape moral condemnation. This follows, it is said, because the *just war* doctrine and the earlier argument both presuppose a distinction between the innocent and the non-innocent which is no longer applicable in the modern context. Thus, countervalue would be evil if the target populations were innocent but they are not.

This line of thought has recently gained support, particularly in the United States. Yet, as before, acceptance is no argument in its favour. All it betokens is woeful ignorance or neglect of the moral dimension of war. From the middle-ages onwards the principle of the immunity of the innocent has been the primary rule governing the conduct of hostilities and it is no objection to it that it has been neglected in recent times any more than that it was often ignored in the mediaeval and intervening periods. Certainly the scale of likely hostilities has increased and this encourages the idea that we now face 'total war' in which the distinction can no longer be made. The latter claim, however, though familiar, is either false or question-begging. If it means that every member of the community wages war it is clearly incorrect. And if it is interpreted as saying that modern warfare is often (and henceforth always will be) directed against entire populations, then while this may be true it remains to be determined whether such a practice is acceptable. That it is done is no proof of the claim that it is legitimate to do it. There can be no serious doubt that there is a difference between those who are engaged in threatening one (either as combatants or as suppliers to them of the means of waging war) and those who are not. Indeed, the strategists' language of 'counterforce and countervalue policies' and of 'hard and soft targets' is intended in large part to mark just this distinction.

4   Threats and bluff

It is principally in recognition of the collapse of the previous response to the moral arguments that other defenders of current nuclear policy have adopted the second line of reply, arguing that although it would be immoral to attack centres of population it is not wrong to threaten to do so. Moreover, the reply continues, the manufacture and deployment of strategic weapons is justified because it is a way of avoiding nuclear warfare. Thus, not only is it not evil to threaten with sincere intention an action which it would be evil to perform, but where the formation and expression of this conditional intention (to retaliate if attacked) is designed to serve the purpose of ensuring that one never has to act upon it, such a policy may actually be morally virtuous.

Before turning to consider something of the ethics of intention it is appropriate to address the issue of a deterrence policy based upon the mere threat of retaliation in circumstances in which there is no actual intention by government to do so – either because the authorities are committed never to using nuclear weapons, or else because they do not possess them. Policies of these sorts obviously involve deception and it might be argued that this fact alone is sufficient to condemn them. To mislead a person into holding false ideas and planning his life on the basis of them is to deprive him doubly of the truth – once as the proper object of belief and again as the correct foundation for practical reasoning. This consideration does show that lying (or otherwise deliberately misleading someone) is bad, and if all one knew about an action was that it was a case of deception this would be reason to refrain from doing it. However, the matter is not so simple.

Actions can be described in (indefinitely) many different ways. For example, moving my hand is also an instance of writing, a case of making a philosophical point and a contribution to earning my living as an academic. To determine the moral value of a particular piece of behaviour, therefore, one has to bring it under a relevant description. Sometimes this can be difficult but the real problems for moral assessment arise when an action instantiates two or more act-types which merit conflicting evaluations, e.g. to withhold the truth from someone about their partner's infidelity may be bad because dishonest, yet good because compassionate. Fortunately, not all moral conflicts of this sort are irresolvable. It may be that one of the types which the behaviour instantiates is such as ought never to be performed whatever other values it realizes.[14] The infliction of gratuitous suffering on a child against its will is a clear case of an action-type every instance of which is prohibited. No matter that some of them may also be cases of gaining pleasure or relieving frustration, which considered in themselves are valuable activities.

A less obvious resolution of conflict in practical deliberation can be achieved even when none of the action-types to which the proposed behaviour belongs is morally prohibited though one or more of them is nonetheless bad. Intentionally depriving someone of his property without his consent, for example, is a bad sort of action but in some circumstances it may be that this is the only available way of maintaining one's life. Here then a single piece of behaviour is bad *qua* theft, yet good *qua* act of self-preservation. However, assuming what will generally be the case in such circumstances, that the good to be achieved is greater than the likely bad effects, it will be permissible to steal. Indeed, it may even be that in a particular case one has a duty to do so.

It is important to note that the moral view invoked above is *not* a version of utilitarianism. The difference emerges in two ways. First, unlike the latter which claims that the moral value of an action derives entirely from its consequences, and which therefore cannot reconcile the idea that a *type* of action is bad though an instance of it may be morally right, the former view allows that the bad aspects of an act are not nullified by its valuable ones. Hence, it requires that, where possible, subsequent recompense should be made. Secondly, and relatedly, this view makes sense of feelings of regret and even of remorse generally experienced in such circumstances. For again, it does not deny that the right thing to have done may have been bad in some other respect.

I have elaborated this line of thought because it has often been too quickly assumed by opponents of deterrence policy that the deception involved in a strategy of bluff is clearly morally wrong. And also assumed by the defenders of deception that so long as it delivers the goods there is nothing whatsoever wrong about it. Both assumptions rest on a shallow conception of the structure of morality. The fact that a threat to retaliate if attacked is insincere is reason to judge it bad, but this alone is not sufficient to condemn it. For it may be that the threat succeeds in deterring an otherwise certain lethal onslaught, in which case it also instantiates a good sort of action – one which may even be obligatory; viz: saving life.

If current or likely future defence policies were of this form I should not oppose them. However, various aspects of the strategy of bluff imply that it is either practically impossible or else morally unacceptable. To this point the supposition has been that the powers issuing the threat lack the will or the means of executing it. But without both it is not clear how an aggressor is to be deterred.

Certainly for a threat to be effective it may be enough that an opponent believes in one's willingness and ability to carry it out and this belief may be false. However, he is hardly likely to hold it without very good evidence and in the modern world it is impossible to succeed in pretending that one has an effective, nuclear, counterstrike capacity if in fact one does not. Without this ability, therefore, there can be no successful policy of bluff.

Similarly, an enemy will not be deterred unless the threat appears to be backed by sincere intentions to carry it out. Of course, it is logically compatible with creating this appearance that the authors of defence policy and those at the top of the ladder of command lack such intentions, but the vast majority of those in government, in the civil and military services and in the population at large must be deceived into believing that their nation is willing to retaliate. The problem this presents is not simply that of justifying large-scale deception for the sake of a greater good which I allowed may be done. The moral difficulty arises from the practical policies which this deception requires. For in addition to commissioning the design, manufacture and deployment of adequate weaponry, government must also secure that those charged with those tasks are willing to have the weapons used and, in the case of the military, intend to use them if commanded to do so.[15]

In this context, therefore, there can be no deception without corruption. The weapons must be deployed and the services must maintain them with the intention of retaliating if attacked. Such retaliation is likely to be murderous because directed against soft targets, or because of collateral environmental effects or through initiating countervalue exchanges. The only practical form of dissuasion by bluff thus involves murderous dispositions. In this respect it does not differ from direct deterrence policies incorporating sincere intentions on the part of government to order retaliatory strikes. Only real military power can deter and a nuclear arsenal only constitutes real power if it is in the hands of persons trained and willing to use it.

This state of affairs directly raises issues concerning the ethics of deterrent intentions. Before turning to consider these, however, it should be noted that, aims and attitudes apart, practical policies of bluff may already be morally culpable inasmuch as the production of the weapons required to sustain them creates risks of accidental and deliberate exchanges. Given the destructive power of these devices, therefore, policies which depend upon them can be challenged by appeal to principles of *just defence* modelled on the conditions necessary for *just war*. In particular the following are of immediate relevance:

1. The weapons must be deployed for a morally just cause.
2. Their deployment must be the only means of deterring aggression.
3. There must be a reasonable prospect of success of the policy.
4. The goods to be achieved must be greater than the probably evil effects of deployment.
5. The means of deterrence must not themselves be evil.

It is not obvious whether the mere possession of nuclear weapons without the intention to use them must, or is likely to, offend against these conditions. The issue seems to be an *a posteriori* one and to depend upon contingent facts of deployment. Nonetheless, in present circumstances even if it were the case that NATO and Warsaw Pact policies did not involve countervalue retaliatory intentions (and they do), the contingencies of deployment would seem to bring them into opposition to the idea of just defence as defined by principles 1–5.[16]

5 The intention to deter

Attempts to provide a morally acceptable deterrent strategy by securing the benefits of threats while not relying upon sincere intentions fail, because without effective weapons and a genuine willingness on the part of the military and many others to use them such threats are not credible. If the conditions for credibility are supplied, however, the resulting strategy is open to the objection that it involves evil intentions.

The latter objection is the one replied to by the counter-claim that while it may be wrong to use certain weapons it is not thereby wrong to intend to use them if attacked. Furthermore, if the purpose of forming this conditional intention is to deter an aggressor, and therefore to ensure that the circumstances for which retaliation is designed never actually occur, the policy is morally virtuous. This argument is subtle and admits of further refinements which there is not the space to detail and examine here.[17] Nonetheless, I believe they, and it, can be shown to rest upon several false assumptions. The first of these is the belief that intentions are not in themselves liable for moral assessment. The intuitive idea supporting this claim is the thought that right and wrong, permissible and obligatory etc., are properties of *behaviour* and that while there is a conceptual connection between intention and action it is not such as to allow the transmission of moral properties from the latter to the former. No piece of behaviour is an action unless it embodies an intention but not every intention is acted upon. Given this direction of independence the moral character of actions does not extend to prior intentions. Hence, whatever may be true of an act of violence the mere intention to perform it is not liable to assessment, and *a fortiori* it cannot be morally wrong.

Certainly merely intending to kill someone but never actually doing so lacks the evil of carrying out this policy. However, it is not on this account immune to criticism. Intentions are psychological states whose content is given by a description of the circumstances they aim to produce and therefore they cannot be divorced entirely from the moral assessment of their intended states of affairs. One who countenances the evil acts of others or prepares himself to perform such acts reflects in his moral character the quality of that behaviour. The intensity of this reflected image is perhaps less than that of the state of affairs it mirrors but nonetheless it shares its moral quality. Thus, intentions to do evil are themselves bad. Independent evidence for this conclusion is provided by the familiar fact that we regard someone who harbours evil intentions of being of bad character no matter that for whatever reasons he never succeeds in achieving his ends. Correspondingly, we regard him as morally improved if he comes to recognize the evil of his intentions and disavows them. Virtue and vice are essentially traits of character relating not only to what one does but to what one intends to do, or is willing to do or is prepared to countenance in others.

Following from the recognition that intentions involve dispositions to action it becomes clear that even in advance of their enactment mental attitudes of this sort make a practical difference to the state of the world. To have a genuine intention to perform in a particular fashion in certain circumstances, one must believe that it is possible for one to act in the prescribed way and often this will involve making preparations in advance. In the context of seeking deterrence through sincere threats to retaliate, this means establishing a counterstrike capacity and appropriate command structure with the implication, considered above, of creating a probability of an actual exchange initiated either by accident or design. In this case, because of the general presence of sincere intentions, the probability is greater than that attaching to the mere possession of nuclear weapons.

To this point, then, it has been argued that threats and bluff will either be ineffective or else must involve genuine violent intentions and that these latter are liable to moral assessment in respect of both their intrinsic character and their likely consequences. The final reply to be considered acknowledges both conclusions but insists that nonetheless a policy of nuclear deterrence may be morally acceptable. The core of this response is the claim that the complex of intentions involved is not evil.

One version of this reply invokes the *principle of double effect*, claiming that an agent is only morally responsible for the foreseen and intended consequences of his actions and not for those which though foreseen are not intended. Thus, while it may be the case that a disposition to wage-nuclear-war-if-attacked is bad, the content of the agent's intention is not this but rather the avoidance of war. This will not do, however, for it misconstructs the circumstances of deterrence. The disposition to retaliate is not a merely foreseen consequence of the policy. It is an essential constituent of it. Relatedly the intention to deter war is more fully described as the intention to avoid-it-by-intending-to-wage-it-if-attacked. The concept of deterrence by sincere threat simply does not admit of the separation of means and end in the manner required by the principle of double effect. One may speak intelligibly of 'primary' and 'secondary' intentions in this context but then the waging of war in relevant circumstances is both a foreseen and intended component of the policy. Accordingly, the latter cannot escape from the challenge that it involves a murderous intention and as such may not be justified by the (valuable) end it is employed to serve. As was seen earlier, an action or intention may be good and bad in different respects. If, however, it instantiates a type which it is absolutely wrong to realize, then whatever may be good about it or its consequences one is morally prohibited from employing it. Put simply and familiarly: one may not be or do evil in order to achieve good.

The last twist in the attempt to justify the policy of nuclear deterrence again begins with a concession. It allows that the policy involves both war-making and war-preventing intentions but observes that the former is a conditional intention and secondary to the unconditional aim of avoiding war. Accordingly, the agent in these circumstances is importantly different from an aggressor. For, unlike the latter, he does not have a categorical intention to commit mass murder but rather is unconditionally intending to prevent war, albeit by making preparations to wage it and intending to do so if attacked. The proper object of moral evaluation in these circumstances, therefore, is not the latter conditional intention in isolation but the complex of which it is a part, viz: the intention to-deter-war-by-intending-to-wage-it-if-attacked. And this, it is claimed, is morally acceptable and perhaps even obligatory.[18]

Once more, however, the defence of deterrence is vulnerable to the objection that it involves murderous intentions. In the circumstances described the agent has a complex intention including a genuine one to use weapons of mass destruction. Certainly, he is not merely and unconditionally intending to make war but aims to wage it in the belief that by having this intention war is less likely to break out. Clearly the structure of this complex psychological state is central to the argument and what matter most at this point, therefore, are the agent's understanding and intention.

In leaving behind the bluff interpretation of deterrence we must take it that the subject believes that if attacked he will retaliate. Otherwise we cannot ascribe to him a sincere intention to wage war. Certainly, should the day arrive when the enemy launch an attack he may correctly say: 'I did not believe that this would happen. I thought that my intention to counterstrike would prevent it and I would not have formed that intention unless I hoped and sincerely believed that I would never be brought to act upon it.' At that point he may even change his mind and disavow retaliation. For the intention to perform a certain action in given circumstances does not *logically* commit one to acting in that way should the circumstances come to pass.

All of this allowed, however, it remains the case that the pre-war policy in question (which is that presently employed by NATO and the Warsaw pact) involves a genuine intention to wage nuclear war. To form this *intention* – not just to go around saying 'I intend to retaliate', or to build bombs – it is necessary to believe that in some circumstances one would launch an attack. Otherwise, whatever one's mental state it is not that of *intending to retaliate*. On the most charitable interpretation of his policy the agent believes that only by being able, willing and disposed to strike back if attacked can he prevent aggression and for this reason brings himself to intend to counterstrike. But this last move goes morally wrong. It is the formation of a murderous intention.

6   Unjust defence

The argument of the preceding section can be put in the form of a dilemma to the defender of deterrence. Does the agent have a genuine intention to wage war, be it that he hopes that thereby war is made less likely? or is it that he has absolutely no war-waging intentions but seeks to deceive the enemy and in this way to deter him? If the latter, then the objections to bluff present themselves. If the former, then he is countenancing evil and thereby is himself corrupted. The final response was to claim that the genuine war-waging intention is embedded in an intention to prevent hostilities. But once one considers the relation between intending to perform an action and believing that one would do so, it becomes clear that any attempt to disconnect the intention to wage war from the belief that one really would, has the effect that the former ceases to be a genuine intention. And it thus fails to meet the condition which the defender of deterrence takes to be necessary for avoiding war.

None of this is to claim that if an agent intends to act in a certain manner then he will. The point is simply that if a military power believes that intending to wage war is the only way of preventing it, and so makes whatever preparations are necessary, then *ipso facto* it believes that in a given circumstance it would retaliate. Given the murderous nature of the retaliation in question, those states of mind are morally bad ones and the states of the world they bring about involve danger and further corruption.

A power thus condemned may ask: what else are we to do? For, in the circumstances we face, this policy is the only means of avoiding war or nuclear blackmail. Two replies now suggest themselves. The first is as previously given, that some means are such as may not be employed and hence some goods must be denied us if the only route to them is an evil one. In saying this, however, let me make it clear that nothing argued for above is intended to suggest that we should disavow military policy, including threats of retaliation against aggressors – even ones involving restricted uses of nuclear weapons targetted upon combatants.

The second reply concerns not morality but empirical fact. What good reason is there to believe that unless they are deterred the great world powers will attack or invade other nations? And even if the image of them as waiting to pounce were accurate, what good reason is there for supposing that the only deterrent is a nuclear one? Some current Western (and Eastern European) defence strategies are immoral. They probably also rest upon faulty empirical assumptions. These suggestions can hardly be matters of indifference to those concerned with strategy, design and enactment; or if they are then our problems are even greater. No less should they concern theorists and analysts of defence policy. For if the arguments presented above are correct it follows that the most significant feature of the policies of the world's greatest military powers is that they must be abandoned and replaced with just forms of defence. In thinking about possible alternatives one must, of course, acknowledge that modern political and technological circumstances add difficulties and complications not conceived of in traditional just war theory. However, the resources of this tradition are, I believe, sufficient to develop a modern military ethic which, like its scholastic predecessor, conceives of virtue as both *warranting and constraining* the use of lethal violence in defence of one's country.

10

Risk Decisions and Moral Values

JOHN ELFORD

1 Introduction

Human welfare is risk laden. We may either ignore this fact or
become so obsessed with it that neurosis dominates over rationality.
Somewhere between these extremes lies a balanced approach. It will
require, among other things, responsible decision-making about
alternative courses of action, all of which can be expected to entail
risks. A considerable, if diverse, literature on risk analysis of this kind
now exists and is growing rapidly. Risk decisions are complicated by
the fact that they are, for the most part, political ones. Pre-political
decisions concerning private and family life are no less important,
but they will not concern us here. Features of such politics do not
always congeal. The established political will may be at odds with
wider public perceptions and both may be out of step with technical
opinion. The latter will be more likely when, in an age like ours,
most of our decisions about risk embrace questions about advanced
technology; its beneficial and other effects on human welfare. The
speed at which new advanced technologies now present themselves,
and at which they may be expected to continue to do so, requires us
to make rapid decisions in the hope that they eliminate or minimize
the risks of harmful effects and maximize beneficial ones. Only in
such a way can technology be subject to responsible social policy.
What we can never do, however, is to eliminate all risk whatsoever
and it is undoubtedly and uncomfortably true that we are inescapably
committed to living with higher levels of risk than once might have
been the case or we would prefer. Risk itself is part of nature: 'man's
history is part of natural history: and he is part of nature still. His
increased complexity has brought him no immunity: rather he is
more vulnerable because of it.'[1] How, then, do we discover the risks
which it is in our best interest to take, as well as those which it is not?

This question is now, for reasons explained, vitally relevant to innumerable areas of human activity and interest. At least five different stages of enquiry may be necessary before it can be answered. They are; (1) Risk Identification (RI), (2) Risk Evaluation (RE), (3) Risk Decision (RD), (4) Risk Implementation (RIm) and (5) Risk Review (RR). We will later examine each of these in detail but first some wider remarks are necessary.

Religion has been, and still is, one major way in which many people cope with risk. Beliefs in destiny, such as that exercised by 'guardian angels', have enabled believers to cope with often very high levels of risk such as that incurred by war. Making ritual sacrifice is another religious way of coping with risk. What is unknown but feared is propitiated with the aim of securing a desirable outcome. More generally, religion has enabled the insecure, which is most people for some of the time, to accept their insecurity by placing it within a wider understanding of life, its nature and purpose. In very general historical terms, following the Enlightenment, the security formally provided by religion was replaced, for some, by a security based on the powers of human rationality. This is exemplified, for example, by Jeremy Bentham and others in the Reform Movement. In this, area after area of human need was subjected to rational examination and calculation. The political, not to mention the philosophical, success of this movement generated a not unwarranted self-confidence. This laid the foundation for the liberal optimism of the nineteenth century. It was liberal in the sense that it inculcated an openness to observation, experiment and innovation and optimistic in the sense that it came to trust in the beneficial prowess of its own inventiveness. Such is something like the general mood in which the modern sciences developed. It met with much opposition which often came from some exponents who represented religions, the authority of which was apparently being challenged. The nineteenth century, as is well known, abounds with such incidents and curious, even comic though some of them may seem to us, they displayed fundamental differences in understanding.

Things have changed dramatically and continue to do so. The older sciences are now spawning innumerable advanced technologies which are applied and made available in rapid succession. It is, perhaps, instinctive for us to treat these new technologies with the older liberal optimistic confidence. But we equally instinctively know that this cannot be done. There are at least two reasons for this. The first is our knowledge of the total collapse of that optimism in international relations in 1914 and in the conflicts which have followed it. The inevitability of the improvement of the human condition by dint of human effort is something we can no longer take for granted. The second is the important empirical fact that our optimism is often ill-founded because so many of our technologies are harbingers of harm as well as, or instead of, bearers of good. The difficulty is that we cannot always be sure which they are in the necessary advance. But it is imperative that we find out. It is important that we set our modern understanding of technology and the risks that it presents in this wider historical understanding. It is an understanding which is clearly relevant to questions about the acceptability or otherwise of risks which attach to the deployment and possible use of nuclear weapons. As it attaches, also, to their disavowal. Countless uncertainties arise whenever the effectiveness or otherwise of nuclear weapons is discussed. These are not always given the careful and critical attention they require. Quite the reverse usually happens. Sweeping claims are made both in support and opposition to them as sloganizing becomes a substitute for analysis. Risk decisions are endemic in the nuclear technologies in general and in the nuclear weapons ones in particular. In this sense those technologies are not unique since their infinite capacity for both good and evil is equally reflected in some other technologies. It is now widely recognized that approaching nuclear weapons from the point of view of risk analysis is one useful way of trying to discover whether their deployment or disavowal is beneficial or otherwise.

Nuclear weapons are developed, deployed and their possible use contemplated, because it is desired to bring about a certain state of affairs. Namely: security, freedom from hostility, and the peace of the deploying agents; either a nation or an alliance. Those who wish to justify all such deployments invariably do so by pointing to the alleged success those already made have had in achieving freedom from hostility. 'Nuclear weapons have kept the peace in Europe for forty years.' There are at least two presuppositions being made here which need to be questioned. The presupposition that the absence of hostility in Europe for the last forty years has been effected by a single cause as claimed. The second presupposition is that what has worked, if it has done so, in the past will continue to do so in the future. Indeed, even if it has so worked it does not necessarily follow from that that it is morally acceptable. We need not detain on these questions unduly beyond the fact of noting them as illustrations of the sort of way that the risk factors in nuclear weapons deployments are commonly discussed. This illustrates something we shall later note; the assimilation of technical questions under general political slogans. Historically, it is generally true to say that risk has been minimized by using knowledge of the past as a prologue to the future. Such a view has been central to claims that there are 'traditions of wisdom' which are handed down from one generation to another. A common feature of many systems of morality including the Judaeo-Christian one. The sheer novelty of our technology itself threatens the effectiveness of this tradition, simply because the risks we face are so often unique ones. Even the denial of that itself entails risks.

2 The nature of risk

Risks are empirical facts in the sense that they either exist or they do not and as such they can be observed and analysed. RI is a comparatively straightforward exercise which is carried out whenever risk is expected to occur. There are some which are well-known; for example, in pharmacy, in aviation, and in chemical processes. Comparatively little is still known about why there is public concern for some risks and not for others.[2] Public arousal is part of a complex process of social psychology out of which certain risks become politicized and given priority over others. Enmeshed in this process is the arousal of moral opinion and this gives rise to questions about the relationship of the facts of risk to our systems of value. Risk analyses contain inextricable moral elements. The nature of this inextricability is, of course, hotly debated. Some deny that values are in any way contingent upon facts, so called ethical non-naturalists, and others claim that values are contingent upon facts; so called ethical naturalists, though these may disagree among themselves about the precise way in which they do so. One recent claim suggests that some facts are 'brute relative' to values in a way which others, 'brute facts', are not.[3] Some such distinction enables us, in risk analysis, to identify some facts which are 'brute relative' to risks we are trying to identify. In this process, facts, risk factors and values are interrelated in a manner which is familiar in every day life, if not entirely clarified in philosophical opinion. This mention of the moral aspects of risk analysis raises a central question: has morality anything to do with risk analysis or is the latter simply a matter of rational calculation?

It is important to recall, particularly from the point of view of a theological engagement with the analysis of risk, that the modern discussion about it relates to a much older one. We have been discussing the ethics of risk as something like a rational guide to self-interested action and taken 'self' here in its widest social and political setting. Such an attempt does not strictly need to relate the analysis of risk to moral virtue. Indeed, Kant, influentially, took a view in support of the separation of risk analysis from moral virtue when he wrote 'Now skill in the choice of means to one's own greatest well-being can be called prudence in the narrowest sense. Thus an imperative concerned with the choice of means to one's own happiness – that is, a precept of prudence – still remains hypothetical: an action is commanded, not absolutely, but only as a means to a further purpose.'[4]

Such an understanding of prudence as the calculation of an interest which is separable from virtue was prefigured before Kant in the writings of Hume and Hutcheson on similar grounds; that prudence was the outcome of rational calculation in the service of self-interest. It needs to be asked whether such a framework for the discussion is adequate to the task of evaluating the risks attendant on nuclear weapons. Or to ask whether we should attempt, as can be done, to set the modern discussion of risk in the context of a much older discussion of prudence which considers it to include notions of moral virtue. Indeed, we should perhaps welcome such a move, especially when we doubt our ability to secure our well-being by rational calculation alone. We are faced, among other things, with the limitation of our knowledge of the consequences of our actions, a frequent inability to politicize real risks and not apparent ones, as well as with the fact that when we calculate technological risks we frequently need knowledge which is simply not available to us. Rational calculation is, of course, a necessary condition of responsible risk management but it is not a sufficient one.

A clear statement about the relationship of moral virtue to prudence is to be found in the writings of Thomas Aquinas, who argues that prudence is both an intellectual *and* a moral virtue. 'It is necessary', he writes, 'for the prudent man to know both the universal principles of reason, and the singulars about which actions are concerned.'[5] Such universal principles of reason are those expressing the moral virtues. The singulars, he observes, are infinite in number and cannot be comprehended by human reason, with the result that rational counsels are unavoidably uncertain; a mediaeval observation which has a remarkable relevance to the difficulties with calculating risks on a rational basis mentioned above. In the face of this difficulty Aquinas, perhaps optimistically, claimed that 'experience reduces the infinity of singulars to a certain finite number which occur as a general rule, and the knowledge of these suffice for human prudence'.[6]

In a sense this may be true of the modern debate about the risk of deploying and using nuclear weapons, since we do have a knowledge of a finite number of singulars, such as those concerning radiation. These might, as we shall see, suffice for our purpose. But argument about such singulars continues and there is no necessary widespread support for some opinions about them against others. Aquinas then importantly argues that right reason, concerning singulars, cannot be applied to action unless 'this is done with a right appetite'.[7] Using 'appetite' to mean something like 'disposition of virtue'.

Without prolonging this exposition of Aquinas we may take his claim that prudence comprises virtue as well as right reason and apply it to the modern discussion about risk analysis. Indeed, the very fact that debates about nuclear risks concern matters of life and death indicates, clearly, that to exclude considerations of morality would be an odd thing to do. The point being made is, simply, that risk analyses about nuclear weapons should be related to, and part of, discussions about the morality of them. Herbert McCabe makes the same point in a recent discussion of Aquinas's view of 'good sense' understood as practical decision making as a form of prudence, with the comment ' . . . good sense for Aquinas, is not mere cleverness but presupposes the moral virtues, the disposition that governs our appetites and intentions, for it is concerned not merely with what seems good to me but with what is in fact good for me: and is the lynch-pin of humane and responsible living because without it none of these goods will be attained'.[8]

Such a view implies, as we have seen, that post-Enlightenment rationalism is not capable of rendering a complete view of the relationship of rationality to morality. A view which has recently been argued by A. MacIntyre in *After Virtue*. See especially chapter 5 on 'Why the Enlightenment Project of Justifying Morality had to fail'.[9] The argument developed there claims that there can be no such thing as a morality without some account of the human *telos*. To the extent, therefore, that risk analyses embrace moral elements they too must embrace also some account of the human *telos*. There is no space to spell out here in detail what that might be like and those engaged in the debate about risk, doubtless, will bring many accounts of the human *telos* to bear. From a Christian point of view the *telos* employed will include beliefs about human beings being created in the image of God and about the responsibility they inculcate for respecting all human life. It will bring, also, beliefs about limiting death and violence in appropriate ways as they are expressed, for example, in the just war tradition. Such a *telos* has its essential place in risk analysis and Christians, as well as others, who share the view about the importance of human teleology, should protest against tendencies to conduct the debate as though it is only a matter of rational calculation, important though that may be.

3 Risk Identification (RI)

Recognition of the existence or non-existence of risks will depend, in the first instance, largely on *a priori* assumptions. For example, if we think that nuclear weapons are the best form of weapon ever invented we will either deny that deploying them is risky at all, or at least attempt to minimize the perceived risks by contrasting them with the benefits which can be had from so deploying them. Conversely, if we think that nuclear weapons are different in kind from all other weapons, and also that they are therefore totally unacceptable, we will tend to maximize the burdens of the risks entailed in their deployment. Clearly, the role of such *a priori* assumptions, when we attempt to identify risks, is a crucial one. This is not to say that they have no place in risk identification, they obviously do, but they should not be used as excuses for interpreting empirical evidence inadequately or incorrectly. Again, to argue that in the light of an *a priori* assumption that 'X' is the empirical case without proper examination is but to treat empirical questions, in the first instance, as though they were political ones which can be pre-judged. This would happen, in particular, of course, where such an *a priori* assumption was collectively held. Ultimately, the so-called politicization of knowledge and decision making is inevitable and not undesirable. What we have seen, repeatedly, is the undesirability of treating empirical questions in risk analyses as if they were nothing but political ones. When this happens serious empirical enquiry is either denied or at least curtailed as the political will pre-empts its outcome. A not unfamiliar state of affairs. Such a political will may, however, be expressive of considered moral values. These, for reasons explained above, may be vitally relevant and become, for that reason, a legitimate factor in the analysis and identification of risk. But not all political will is as morally virtuous and even if it is so it should not pre-empt empirical enquiry.

It has already been noted that the novelty of technology in general and of the nuclear ones in particular provides the first obstacle to the recognition of the risks they bear. Such experience of the use of nuclear weapons as we do have is itself minimal and for that reason largely discountable in relation to understanding the risks which would attach to the uses of presently deployed ones. The fact that life in Hiroshima and Nagasaki continues at all is not one which should bear directly on our estimates of the results of the further use of nuclear weapons. Indeed, it may wisely be feared that the recovery of life in those two cities at all could be taken as a dangerous precedent when we consider the acceptability of further nuclear explosions, notwithstanding the very real suffering and anguish that those explosions have left behind. When facing risks which attach to novelty we are, therefore, facing what is largely unknown and what will be, for that reason alone, in dispute. This, again, is where such debate is vulnerable to political takeover and sloganizing.

Dealing with the unknown as a gamble is not what responsible risk-taking is about. The gambler accepts the temporarily unknown as a situation which may be taken advantage of, a practice with potentially tragic and addictive associations. Making responsible decisions about risk-taking is not gambling. It requires that we attempt to get the unknown to reveal its secrets and in that we meet obvious difficulties. Establishing what is and is not the case in new technologies, like nuclear ones, is a specialized and professional business. It is, therefore, natural to claim that only those appraised of the technicalities are at all competent to judge them. This is why such technology often works against the principles of democracy, particularly so when technical information is popularly disseminated in an already politicized form. To a degree this is unavoidable, since the risk assessments which relate to nuclear deployments do not exist in a completely objective manner. Measurements of probability can never exclude human judgment. There is, in other words, no such thing as value-free information. What is at stake is whether such judgments can be exercized in a way which is not distorted by political intention to such an extent that relevant information is not properly considered.

Those who have argued that nuclear weapons are morally acceptable have usually done so on the grounds that their deployment as deterrents does not necessitate their actual use, and that the undesirability of such use should not be set against the desirability of so deploying them as deterrents. They would work as deterrents, it may be claimed, even if the threat to use them was a bluff. It would have to be, of course, an unprecedented one. On practical grounds such a bluff would have to be ruled out, since there is no way in which it could ever be guaranteed in advance that the bluff would work if deterrence failed. For this reason alone it is necessary to calculate the possible consequences of the bluff failing when the risks of deploying nuclear weapons as deterrents are considered. A popular version of the attempt to exclude the risks of the use of nuclear weapons from an evaluation of the risks engaged in their deployment as deterrents entails the claim that they are deployed for defensive purposes only and not for offensive ones at all. As is well known, this is met by the counter-claim that the defensive capacity embraces an offensive one, and that such a defensive capacity is vacuous unless a potential aggressor perceives the offensive capacity to be a real one. Some argue that, even then, such risks as do arise from the use of nuclear weapons can be minimized on the ground that they can be used in a limited way, limited, for example, to the use of tactical or battlefield nuclear weapons in strictly controlled circumstances. Such a limitation, however, again cannot be guaranteed in advance, since there will always remain a possibility that once nuclear war is engaged it will escalate up the so-called rungs of war, and there are only five of them, at an alarming speed. As has been pointed out ' . . . a conception of limited war remains fearsomely inadequate as long as it is unattached to a convincing political account of the purpose of a war of this kind.'[10] Such are the well-known practical difficulties of prognostications about whether or not the deployment of nuclear weapons as deterrents constitutes unacceptable risks. Curiously here the layman's intuitions often seem no less adequate than the specialist's prognostications, especially when those may be nothing more than disguised political opinions put forward to obscure the fact that they contain a large degree of subjective criteria. Identifying risks accurately without incontrovertible factual information remains extremely difficult.

We know that nuclear weapons kill from blast, heat and radiation, and the calculation of the collateral deaths and damage from the first two is comparatively straightforward compared with estimating them for the third. Radiation we know exists in at least three phases: initial, intermediate and residual. We also know that the proportion of these phases can be varied according to the type of weapon used and the manner of its detonation. Again, whilst it may be possible to estimate the collateral damage caused by the first two phases it is impossible to do this with the third, since we do not have sufficient empirical information on which to ground claims about what will or will not be the case about the effects of residual radiation on human life; radiation, that is, which at least for the purposes of calculation will exist indefinitely. Further, we do not know the truth, for example, about claims that nuclear explosions on any large scale will effect a 'nuclear winter' in which irradiated debris will blot out the sun's rays, or for how long it would do so. We simply do not know to what levels of what types of radiation human beings can safely be exposed, beyond knowing that there has recently been a tendency to revise previous estimates of these levels downwards.

A further well-known difficulty is that of estimating the probability of a nuclear war being started accidently, something which may be the more likely now that new systems are increasingly programmed to launch automatically on warning, e.g. those proposed in the emergent SDI systems. In these examples where hard empirical information is required it is not available. This is why even identifying the risks which attach to the development and deployment of nuclear weapons is so difficult. Does this mean that we can only despair of the failure to bring rationality to bear on the problem of identifying such risks? Not entirely. We do not live in total ignorance of the effects of using nuclear weapons. Nor do we live in total ignorance of the consequences which attach to their use, accidental or otherwise. Hence, the now widely acknowledged fact that a nuclear exchange on any scale would be counter-productive of the interests of all parties, including those who initiated it. This recognition is, doubtless, part of the reason why we may now, hopefully, be moving into an era when at least the Superpowers realize that they can disavow themselves of large parts of their nuclear arsenals without making themselves at all vulnerable to attack. Indeed, stockpiling nuclear weapons itself introduces a degree of instability which is counter-productive. Identifying the risks which attach to nuclear deployments and uses is not difficult. What is difficult is the evaluation of the nature of them.

A so-called cardinal principle of risk management is; 'avoid any (real) risk of catastrophe at any (ordinary) cost.'[11] This does not mean that catastrophe has to be avoided at all costs; it means, only, that the risk of catastrophe should be avoided *if possible*. But the obvious difficulty here is that the contemplated alternatives in nuclear dis-armament all attach to some catastrophic consequences. Estimates of what these may be will, as we have seen, vary according to the view taken. It is at this point that RI leads to Risk Evaluation.

4   Risk Evaluation (RE)

All risks, once identified, must be evaluated. Were it not for the fact that for the most part this is done by drawing on past experience, whenever risk is precedented, such evaluation would be an impossibly burdensome task. Even risks which are precedented, however, present a near impossible prospect.

For what purpose do we evaluate risks? Is it a normative one? That is, to find out what risks people are willing to take. Or is it a prescriptive one? That is, to find out what risks people ought, in our opinion, to take in their own interests. The former would be of interest, for example, to politicians in a democracy who are keen to establish whether or not the risks they advocate taking would be widely acceptable. It is the second question, however, which is more relevant to a consideration of the ethics of risk and its prescriptive tone introduces, yet again, the moral dimension to risk taking. Risk evaluation, in short, cannot be carried out exclusively on a democratic basis, for the simple reason that people cannot always be sure to have access to the technical information which is relevant to it. Again, we meet the uncomfortable juxtaposition of technology and politics.

Technological risk occurs whenever technology is applied to social need with a claim to success, but when burdensom as well as beneficial results occur. Risks, clearly, become unacceptable when the burdens outweigh the benefits. Calculating this would be a simple matter, and is, whenever such burdens and benefits are commensurable. In reality they seldom are and, at least, it is only possible to achieve fairly approximate agreements about how incom-mensurates can begin to be compared.

Consider, for example, the risks involved in nuclear deterrence. The burden of accidental or deliberate but limited use might well, to some, seem to be outweighed by the benefit of the absence of hostility, whereas, to others this might not be the case. Any hostility, even invasion, might be deemed beneficial to the burden of the risk of nuclear war. One way of proceeding in instances of unprecedented risks would be to effect controlled experiments. Partial disarmament is a good example. Such experiments would help us to find out if it is the deployment of nuclear weapons which is affecting the absence of hostilities. Of course, the knowledge which arose from such controlled experiments might itself be equivocal to the point that it was interpreted only in support of preconceived opinions. This raises, pointedly, the question about just what sort of information would be required for *a priori* assumptions of this kind to be over-turned. This difficulty, however, ought not to preclude attempts to set up controlled experiments in the hope of making progress. Such would have to be very limited, but hopefully they would provide sufficient information which could be used to extrapolate information about what would happen if nuclear war occurred on a larger scale. Another example of such an experiment would be that derived from military manoeuvres in which nuclear weapons were considered from the point of view of their tactical deployments and benefits. Yet another example of a controlled experiment can be found in the recommendation that nuclear weapons should be disavowed in a process of staged disarmament. Such a process allows adequate time for the evaluation of the changes to risks which will result.

5   Risk Decisions (RD)

To say that RD 'X' is acceptable is not necessarily to say that it will remain so forever. It would if 'X' were thought to be intrinsically right, for then no circumstances which were external to it could have any effect upon it. But 'X' is held to be morally acceptable because of an assessment of the acceptability, or otherwise, of contingent factors then moral acceptability will change if that assessment changes, at least at all substantially. In other words, to say that 'X' is morally acceptable, is in fact to say nothing more than that it is so for the time being or provisionally. We should not expect, after Aristotle, a thing such as morality to admit of more certainty than it is capable of, not expect moral decisions about 'X', that is, to admit of unconditional timeless certainty. This would not, of course, be strong enough for some, especially those who want their morality to have to do with incontravertible certainties. There are many such, not the least because moral certainty is often prematurely arrived at for chiefly psychological reasons which have largely to do with the insecurities of those who arrive at them. This is why it is always morally prudent to keep our most cherished moral certainties under review. They do not have to be suspended for that purpose. It is quite possible and proper to say of 'X'; I believe it to be morally acceptable but I will nevertheless review my belief. Such considerations bear obviously on decisions about risk. Here it is claimed that they must be provisional and subject to constant review. We will consider this below.

Even if we have identified and evaluated risks and come to a conclusion that they should be taken, how do we proceed? As we have seen, meeting this precondition itself presents formidable tasks which may well not be fulfilled with anything like the degree of certainty which is necessary for us to proceed to a risk decision. But suppose, for the purpose of argument, if not optimism, that we can so proceed.

Seeking democratic political agreement about which risks can be taken and which not, after they have been identified and evaluated, will raise issues which reach into the nature of democracy itself. We have already touched on some of these. The problem has been described as one which requires 'sensitivity analysis' which supposes that 'a best guess at the most acceptable option is derived from the best available estimates of the relevant facts and values'.[12] In other words, before agreement is sought in a democracy it is necessary to estimate the extent to which the electorate has identified and evaluated the contemplated risks. This itself, of course, cannot be known with certainty because votes are cast for many reasons including quite trivial ones, so the actual extent to which particular risks are identified and evaluated is difficult to ascertain. This simple fact throws much light on the role of pressure groups in modern democracies. These are, increasingly, the means whereby groups of individuals express their view on explicit risks. It is, of course, difficult if not impossible to estimate their effectiveness since governments rightly perceive it to be against their interests to acknowledge that changes of policy resulted from such pressure, even if they did so. To be at all effective, pressure groups have to be highly organized and ready to use sophisticated means of communication and protest, something which many of them are clearly able to do and which enables them often to exercise an influence which is out of proportion to their actual numerical strength. Membership of such pressure groups, however, remains small in comparison with the wider electorate. The majority remain content to leave even crucial decisions about their welfare to others, hence they become quiescent in the face of even fundamental questions about their own welfare. The obvious danger here is that this quiescence will be exploited by those who have the power to impose their own views about which risks should be taken.

This picture is considerably more complicated when we remember that actual RDs are usually taken in the light of previously and broadly agreed outlines of policy. This has clearly happened with nuclear weapons technology. For example, within NATO actual weapons systems have been deployed since the 1960s within the broad framework of 'flexible response' defence policy whereby it has been deemed necessary to deploy an escalating range of weapons so that any particular act of aggression could be responded to flexibly and proportionally, a doctrine which is now arguably threatened by the proposed removal of all land-based INF in Europe.[13] The point this raises is the obvious one about the democratic support for the broad policy as well as for its bearing on actual and relatively discrete decisions. Broad policy guides are often ephemeral and seemingly uncontentious. As a result they may attract widespread, but ill-informed support. When they are applied to actual decisions the situation changes as minds are focussed, perhaps by some arresting image or event. A comparatively recent example was the actual arrival of Cruise Missiles in the UK at Greenham Common and at Molesworth. Such vivid images and events usually have a greater effect on public perception than theoretical argument and discourse. Indeed, in a world where technology is so rapidly deployed it is likely that entirely unforeseen images and events will have a great effect on actual decision making. The obvious recent example is the effect of Chernobyl on public perceptions about the nature of radiation. This was prefigured in the response to the Three Mile Island accident in the US in March 1979. But that accident scarcely affected European perceptions as the Chernobyl one has obviously done. In democratic risk decision making there is, thus, a clear element of political coercion. But it can never ignore the emergence of unexpected relevant information and these are just some of the reasons why making RDs about technology is a volatile political business.

6   Risk Implementation (RIm)

The borderline between making RDs and implementing them is often a thin one. The reason for this is that it is frequently impossible to distinguish the research and testing of advanced technology from its actual deployment. This impossibility may lie behind the at least hitherto Soviet unwillingness to accept testing of SDI technology in the USA. The research and operation of advanced technology often goes hand in hand as it did, for example, in the NASA programmes, a fact for which they were criticized in the enquiry following the Challenger disaster. Hence, the implementation of new technology does not always follow neatly arrived at previous decisions to go ahead with it. The provinces of RD and RIm are frequently blurred. However, let us consider something of the significance for risk analysis of what happens when RIm does follow RD.

RIm often takes considerable time, up to several years and even decades after RDs are made. Indeed, embryonic RDs frequently have to be made largely in ignorance of what their implementation will entail. Although, as is well-known, the lead-time between the conception of a new technology and its implementation is always shortening there remains, especially in the case of sophisticated weapons technology, a significant lapse of time during which research is completed. This will be initiated by the claim that some new system is deemed to be desirable, and its research then has to be sustained by invariably high levels of funding from public expenditure. Such funding is seldom provided as the result of a single decision. Invariably, it is granted in phases up to and beyond a cut-off point where cancellation, short of exceptional circumstances, is impossible. In this way, a changing political will is often brought to bear on developing weapons systems. Such, for example, is the case in the USA where Congress cannot always be guaranteed to vote for the continued funding of unimaginably expensive research such as that involved in the SDI system. Even systems which are successfully implemented have a limited life-span simply because of the speed with which newer systems are initially researched. In nuclear weapons technology, as in advanced technological research in general, research into new systems, at initial stages, is largely carried out by private companies who operate quite beyond political control. This means that new weapons systems come into existence before any actual military or political reasons are found for their deployment. Making decisions about which initial research should receive extensive public funding will then require that the previous processes of identifying and evaluating risks have to take place with an inappropriate urgency.

7 Risk Review (RR)

Risk, as we have seen, can never be eliminated and because we have to live with levels of risk which make us uncomfortable, it is necessary to keep RDs under RR. This is the more necessary because the foregoing process may itself have taken place in ignorance of newly emerged information, as it may also have taken place under pressure of events which did not allow opportunity for the necessary thorough examinations to take place. Recognition of the importance of RR ensures that RE is on-going.

RR is now made imperative by the increasing public awareness that some technology has effects which are harmful to human well-being and that such harm cannot always be unequivocally identified before the technology is implemented, even where strict controls may already exist. But this presents problems. As we have seen, RI is politically and economically complex. In NATO for example, agreements are made about the implementation of decisions to deploy particular weapons systems which are effective for a number of years hence. Such implementations, therefore, cannot be rescinded easily, even if signatories to the agreements change their minds, on review, about their willingness to participate. This is why it is so difficult for a member of NATO such as the UK, to become nuclear-free even if it wishes to do so. It would take up to twelve to fifteen years for the UK to disengage honourably from its present NATO commitments, if it wished to do so and become nuclear-free. RR, like RI, RE, RD and RIm is politically complex. This undoubtedly explains the frequently apparent unwillingness of governments to review risks which they have already implemented.

RR on a responsible basis will require a number of things. First, the availability of easily comprehended and accurate information in a society which is educated partly for the purpose of knowing how to live responsibly with risks. This does not mean, of course, that individuals need to be appraised of the minutiae which attaches to all the risks they have to take. But they do want to be assured, at least, that those who are taking the risks on their behalf are continuing to do so responsibly. The example of air travel is sometimes used to illustrate this point: ' . . . the passenger does not want to participate in the split-second decisions of the pilot or air traffic controller, but he does want assurance that air and ground crews have been well-trained and are following correct procedures.'[14] The need for such assurance in a technological society is a growing one. It can only be met if our political institutions are able to maintain their accountability when they take RD, on behalf of others. But the sheer enormity of the task should not be underestimated.

8   Conclusion

The foregoing five stages of risk taking from Identification to Review are separable only for the purposes of analysis and argument, but as we have seen they are not always so easily separable in practice. Often they are confused by overlap to a surprising degree as might happen, for example, when in the extreme during RR it is decided that a risk no longer exists. In discussions about the ethics of risk there is a constant overlap of dialogue and perception between all five stages. As has been argued, however, this is no reason for not trying to unpack the process in the hope of throwing light on the whole of it. As yet we know comparatively little about how to handle complex risks in a technological society. All virtually remains to be done as has recently been argued in a proposal for International Risk Management Research.[15]

What is clear is that in assessing the acceptability of risks which attach to the deployment of nuclear weapons, moral considerations are central. RDs cannot be made on the basis of rational calculation alone. Moral perceptions have to be brought to bear. These moral perceptions will bring into play questions about whether or not specific technologies serve the best interests of humankind. Examination of such moral perceptions should itself be a prominent feature of RD research.

Initially, Christians engage in this process as they wrestle with decisions about whether the taking of particular risks is compatible with beliefs about human beings created in the image of God. Traditionally, of course, this has been carried out under the heading of the theory of just war and as that tradition has developed in the past it must continue to do so, if its mature wisdom is to be brought to bear in areas of nuclear weapons technology where rational calculation alone is perceived to be barely adequate to the political task of making decisions about the risks involved.

This is not to reject the post-Enlightenment tendency to transpose discussions of prudence into calculations of rational self interest. It is but to suggest that such a tendency needs to be tempered by an older one if we are to bring all our moral resources and rational wit to bear on the now rapidly developing discussion about the ethics of risk.

11

The Ethics of SDI

ROWAN WILLIAMS

I

In March 1983, President Reagan announced his commitment to furthering a research programme that had, in fact, already been in process for a couple of decades; he described his new commitment as a major shift in policy, from a nuclear strategy based on retaliatory capacity to one resting on defensive strength of such magnitude that nuclear weapons would be rendered 'impotent and obsolete'. The rhetoric of this celebrated speech[1] launching the Strategic Defence Initiative (SDI) is an intriguing study in itself. The President begins by commending the search for 'greater stability' in the nuclear calculus through negotiated arms reductions, but goes on to suggest that there is still an element of moral unsatisfactoriness in relying for stability upon the possibility of retaliation against an aggressor. Why not rather divert our energies to the development of the only possible guarantee of real stability, a full defensive system that 'could intercept and destroy strategic ballistic missiles before they reached our own soil or that of our allies'? This is a long task, and meanwhile we must maintain our nuclear arsenal and our 'flexible response' policy. We must continue to negotiate arms reductions, but be sure we negotiate from strength – i.e. we must proceed with the modernization of existing weaponry – and we must increase our conventional resources at the same time, so that there is less risk of our being pressed into the first use of nuclear weapons by an escalating conventional struggle. The President recognizes that it is possible to 'pair' defensive with offensive systems, and that a defensive development *can* therefore be seen as potentially aggressive, 'and no one wants that' (what? an offensive system or the perception of aggressive intentions?). The action envisaged is supposed to be consistent with the Anti-Ballistic Missiles Treaty of 1972 (and, presumably, the agreed definitions annexed to the treaty and the further protocol of 1974, operative from 1976); and the elimination of the menace of strategic nuclear weapons will, it is hoped, 'prove the way for arms control measures to eliminate the weapons themselves'. 'We are', the President concludes, 'launching an effort which holds the promise of changing the course of human history.'[2]

Public awareness of the 'Star Wars' research programme dates from this speech, though, as we have noted, it simply signalled a higher level of official backing for an already existing programme. The speech itself is a muddle, which does little except announce this backing while reassuring its audience that this will not mean any reduction in actual armaments or in modernization programmes. It assumes that American nuclear capacity is fundamentally retaliatory (i.e. that a first strike is bound to come from elsewhere than Washington), yet reiterates the policy of 'flexible response' (as held in NATO), which, of course involves the first use option (and so cannot be said to rule out 'first strike'). It describes the defensive policy envisaged as a capacity to 'intercept and destroy strategic ballistic missiles', while claiming not to infringe the ABM Treaty (which defines an ABM system as *any* one designed 'to counter strategic ballistic missiles or their elements in flight trajectory'[3]). It looks to the new strategy as rendering weapons obsolete, yet also sees it as merely a moment in a longer process of arms control. But for all these (and other) confusions, the moral force of this speech is considerable, in that it appeals to its audience's concern not to be perceived as violent or vengeful, and presents SDI as – in the long term – a real alternative to deterrence. If such a claim is justifiable, it is at first sight more or less impossible for any critic of the morality of deterrence and retaliation to complain; this chapter will examine the coherence of the claim – but it will also raise some wider concerns as to whether the idea of a perfect system of national defence has any moral credibility anyway. The issues of actual feasibility involved in SDI research are far beyond my competence; but it is worth remembering occasionally that much of the energy put into the 'marketing' of SDI derives from the sense that unprecedented technological challenges are being posed to the scientific community. We shall be returning to the moral issues involved in this a little later.

President Reagan invoked the need for *stability* in the nuclear calculus; we could gloss this further and say that *predictability* is crucial for classical deterrence. The ideal deterrent situation would be something of this sort:

(*i*) an exact balance of forces sufficiently equipped to survive a first strike and deliver an unacceptably heavy retaliatory attack;

(*ii*) a clear shared understanding of the circumstances in which weapons would be used (retaliation against unprovoked attack) and of the existence of the will on both sides to use them;

(*iii*) sufficiently accurate information-gathering systems (satellite surveillance) to assure each side of the other's capacity.

Bracketing for the moment the ethics of the whole scheme of Mutually Assured Destruction, it should be clear that anything which made either military installations or information-gathering hardware more vulnerable would upset this stability. A vulnerable nuclear weapon (land-based, fixed or transportable by predictable routes) has diminished retaliatory capacity, since it is an obvious target for a first strike; therefore its own use is virtually limited to a first strike, and it becomes, *de facto*, an aggressive weapon. Vulnerable and highly accurate missiles intensify the problem still further, as it is impossible for an enemy not to construe the deployment of such a weapon as threatening. And increased vulnerability for information-gathering (by the development of anti-satellite devices) is destabilizing in that it makes it possible to interpret any malfunction or accident in a surveillance satellite as the result of a deliberate attack preliminary to a nuclear first strike. Dr Robert Bowman, one of the most important American critics of SDI, puts the problem starkly:

> Once the US has both a first strike capability and an ASAT (anti-satellite) capability, what happens if a Soviet warning satellite is struck by a meteor or suffers a catastrophic electrical failure? Might they not reasonably assume that we have just destroyed their satellite in order to prevent them from seeing the attack we are launching against them? Would they not then be likely to give the order to launch a 'retaliatory' attack?[4]

What is the relevance of this to SDI as such? Any imaginable space-based defence against ballistic missiles naturally possesses an offensive capacity, in that the technology required to destroy a missile will serve equally well to inflict damage on the earth's surface: there is no such thing as a 'purely defensive' anti-ballistic system,[5] despite the misleading language of a 'shield' or 'astrodome'.[6] While it is possible to have such a system operating with non-nuclear warheads, it remains true that it has an offensive capacity (and is likely to be – as they say – 'ambiguous', i.e. capable of working with both nuclear and conventional material). At the same time, any space system is massively vulnerable: 'They have soft spots, such as sensors and power supplies; they have vulnerable electronics; and you always know where they're going to be at any given time'.[7] To quote the assessment of another professional observer, 'a single pebble colliding with [a space system] at orbital velocity would have a good chance of putting it out of action' – and a pebble, he adds, can be aimed.[8] Taking into account the complexity of such a system – and Bowman details this at some length in his study [9] – the problems of fuelling and of electronic maintenance, as well as its openness to attack, we are bound to conclude that an SDI 'defence' is strategically on a footing with Cruise or the SS20: sophisticated, accurate, low in what strategists call 'survivability' (i.e. capacity to survive attack, not, as you might expect, ineffectiveness against a target!), and thus destabilizing, useful only as a first strike weapon. It is manifestly able to threaten satellites, and its deployment would certainly be seen in such terms. Further, it could effectively act as a *support* for a first strike aimed at low-survivability weapons on the other side: given the destruction of a high percentage of these, there would be a vastly increased chance of successful defence against a retaliatory strike by what was left of the enemy forces. In other words, either as an offensive or as a defensive operation, it fits most naturally into a first strike strategy, and can indeed, as the President allowed, 'be viewed as fostering an aggressive policy'.[10]

So *within the terms of classical deterrence*, SDI represents not a move towards a defensive alternative but an aspect of the same strategy as has produced the Multiple Independently-targetable Re-entry Vehicles (MIRV), and, more recently, Cruise and Pershing II – that is to say, it is part of the subversion of classical deterrence by way of technological advance, which is, in the present context, inherently destabilizing. And it is manifestly incoherent to do what the USA is now (1987) committed to doing – negotiating the abandonment of medium-range land-based missiles, while pursuing the SDI fantasy. Francesco Calogero, the Italian physicist, was able to say to the WCC Hearing on Nuclear Weapons and Disarmament in 1981 that the deployment of Cruise would render arms control impossible and negotiation futile, because the nature of these weapons made surveillance almost unmanageable. To this we can add the destabilizing effect of a 'first strike' type weapon, as explained already. Happily, Calogero seems to have been unduly pessimistic, in the light of the agreement of September 1987; the irony is that everything about Cruise that threatened arms limitation in 1981 is now true of SDI – on which we have as yet seen no movement towards agreement, and apparently no recognition of the connection between what it represents and the problems posed by Cruise, Pershing II and the SS20.

II

Two closely related moral issues emerge from all this. Grant, for the moment, that the idea of deterrence by MAD – what I've been calling 'classical' deterrence – is a morally credible notion; then SDI, in so far as it makes MAD impossible, is obviously at odds with a moral account of deterrence, and, if the preceding analysis is right, can only be seen as part of a quite different strategic world in which what 'deters' is the capacity of one side for unpunishable aggression – which is not, by any stretch of the imagination, a moral account of deterrence. But what has happened to make this possible? Primarily – as all the authorities I have so far cited, and many more, agree – it is that technological refinement has not been restrained by strategy. Strategy based on MAD *assumes* (we are regularly told) that hostilities will not break out: tensions between the major powers therefore must be resolved by means other than warfare. But developments in military technology which undermine MAD raise once again the spectre of actual war: in principle, tensions may be resolved through the possession of guaranteed technological superiority – not in the form of higher security ('survivability') for the megatonnage required for MAD, but in the form of greater accuracy and sophistication for the vulnerable installations required for a successful first strike.

Here, then, is our first moral problem. If technological refinement dictates military priorities, are we not assuming that relations between the superpowers are not capable of being handled by the processes of the ordinary dealings between societies – negotiation, diplomacy? The issue is to do with whether the conflicts that arise between groups of people can or cannot be handled by 'human' means; and the characteristic modern temptation is, it seems, to conclude that they can be translated into technical terms and made susceptible to technological solutions. In such terms, they are, of course, easier to handle: technology does not, in itself, involve courses of action that require us to move or be moved as persons or groups of persons. In more loaded language, it does not require conversion. Morally and relationally, we remain where we are, but our resources for maintaining that position are increased. Technology refines our *control* over our environment (personal, social, natural), and is thus a perennially attractive alternative to the uncertainty, the vulnerability, of human agreement – a long process, involving losses and risks. If all important problems are technical, they are in principle soluble without risk to our sense of ourselves, our moral self-perception.

The identification of a technical 'can' with a moral 'should' – or the blotting out by the former of questions about the latter – is endemic in our culture: it lies (often unrecognized) at the heart of our debates over embryo research, for instance, or even cable television. We are largely incapable of asking what human purpose technology in such areas serves, because we largely lack a shared language about what *is* significantly human. Thus if a technique is available, the onus is regularly placed on those who want to *wait* and see why it should be used. But the theological tradition that looks back to Augustine insists that skill or mastery, *scientia*, successful 'use' of what the environment provides, is both futile and dangerous divorced from the sense of what is a life well-lived, what is to be sought and delighted in, *sapientia*, intuitive and contemplative wisdom. When the classical-deterrence apologist laments the dominance of technology over strategy, s/he is, however remotely, echoing the warnings of the theological moralist about *scientia* cut loose from *sapientia*, the pursuit of control cut loose from the pursuit of 'enjoyment', an informed and coherent view of human flourishing. Because in secular and pluralist societies, and between societies of differing ideologies, there is no one focal vision of this, living together is uneasy and risky, full of caution, compromise, the acceptance of limits to aspiration; as a theologian might remark, *sapientia* in its fullness belongs in the kingdom of God. No wonder, then, if we take refuge in the sphere where the compromises and the limits have nothing to do with the sense of our humanity – and where, in any case, we are increasingly encouraged to believe that any compromises or limits in the matter we work with are only temporary. Technological sophistication in itself *cannot* define moral or political goals, and when we are frankly afraid of thinking about human and moral purpose in our social life (as the recent scramble for the votes of the newly affluent in supposedly radical political parties painfully shows), this political emptiness is a positive attraction. It is not a question of working up cheap denunciations of technological *hubris*, or supporting a kind of Luddite hostility to technological change, but of reviving the human and political question of why we should want to do what we can do, and accepting the consequence of this – that the aim of control over our destinies isn't necessarily the model we need, that we shall discover more of our humanness in the risks of encounter and the struggle for a shared language.

The SDI issue, then, raises questions of a more widely cultural kind than might at first appear. But the second major moral point to emerge takes us back to the matter which chiefly concerns all the contributors to this volume. Is the kidnapping of a moral politics by technology not in fact a flaw inherent in the whole deterrence system of the last forty years, so that SDI is both its consummation and its nemesis? The advent of thermo-nuclear weapons has in effect meant that the great powers can guarantee their stability by reliance on a technological triumph – the creation of weaponry with indeterminate destructive potential. That is to say, nuclear fission warheads represent not only the possibility of geographically enormous devastation [12] and the wholesale elimination of populations (that would be true of a good many large-scale conventional weapons), but also – though this is something we have only gradually come to recognize fully – an unpredictable 'scatter' of results in the form of radiation and atmospheric damage. 'Controllability in regard to modern thermo-nuclear weaponry is a deception', as Ronald Santoni has bluntly put it, [13] writing of the morality of a supposed 'discriminating' use of nuclear arms. The pro-deterrence theorist – as has already been indicated – will claim that precisely this is the moral *strength* of MAD: it has made the cost of war impossibly high, and so secured peace. The technological threat of nuclear devastation is thus deployed to frighten us into coexistence, so that, in the hands of Christian apologists for MAD, it can be seen as a providential dispensation.

But what kind of providential order is it that has immobilized the two superpowers in frozen postures of hostility for decades? What has been achieved is not peace but an uneasy stasis between two empires, whose conflicts, so far from being resolved, are prosecuted in other ways – wars, major and minor, in the Third World, fuelled by arms sales, propaganda, and the arms race itself, with the now quite often articulated American goal of 'spending the Soviets into the ground', forcing something like a war economy on a less economically developed adversary. The nuclear sanction has enabled some very risky and provocative actions to take place, consolidating the USSR's sovereignty in Eastern Europe: arguably, the invasion of Czechoslovakia in 1968 was made possible by MAD, insofar as intervention by the West *might* have provoked a full-scale conflict. Each side is now almost militarily impotent in a direct confrontation with the other, and so far from this meaning 'peace', it has meant an expensive, corrupting stagnation, an increasing polarization of the whole world into two camps defined by the two most impregnable powers.

It will be objected that this polarization rests on ideological conflict, not on military rivalry alone. This is quite true; but MAD takes it for granted not only that ideological conflict means (at least potentially) military conflict – which is reasonable and prudent – but that the military conflict can be resolved into a minimum-risk situation by the *nature* of the military arsenal deployed – i.e. by a technological refinement. Other kinds of collision and competition – economic, cultural, technological in a wider sense – have their uncertainties: it is possible to fail, to fall behind, to question one's own social system and priorities. But if all these areas are shadowed by a military policy aimed at ultimate invulnerability, the *political* life of the societies involved is liable to become uncritical, either complacent or oppressive (or both). Contrast and conflict between two societies *not* poised in a military deadlock of the kind now existing between East and West may generate unsettling political questions: could we succeed with that sort of social organization? Do we want to succeed in that way? The recent confused history of China shows how such questions arise, and how hard they are to live with; but at least there is some possibility of learning from another society, and of saying something to that other society by reworking or transforming what it has learned. If such mutual learning is made impossible, all we can hope for between societies is the durably hostile stand-off that presently exists between East and West. There are signs, of course, that the Soviet Union wishes to move, indeed is in an unprecedentedly self-critical mood, and appears to recognize the role of nuclear armaments in holding back such honesty and hope. Decades of deterrence have not actually extinguished the possibility of such recognition; but those decades are themselves the witness to the politically deadening effects of deterrence.

MAD was (and is) a technological answer to anxieties about the possibility of coexisting with a hostile rival, ideologically committed to undermining one's own policy. It requires an unambiguously, manifestly lethal capacity for annihilating an opponent – hence the fact that sensible and enlightened defenders of classical deterrence insist on the necessity of sophisticated surveillance and welcome agreed verification procedures. Ignorance and secrecy are destabilizing. But here is the paradox and the weakness of this position. Deterrence must be credible and 'robust'; therefore weapon systems must not be allowed to become non-functional. They require maintenance and modernization, and, because this means at least a measure of technological exploration, there can be no absolute stability for systems. 'It is totally unrealistic', according to Professor Jack Ruina, 'to believe that it is possible not to have technological changes . . . [E]ven if we should think that we are going to keep the equipment the same generation after generation, it would be impossible.'[14] The necessary research naturally produces more than merely answers to modernization problems; hence the anxiety to press ahead with one's own research, lest the other side come up with superior technical innovations. There are some such innovations (to do with improving 'weapons safety' and communications technology) that work in favour of stable deterrence; [15] and there are, as we have seen, rather a lot that don't, of which the incipient SDI technology is a dramatic example. If the strategic armouries of East and West were self-contained, self-renewing, self-regulating affairs, sealed off from the rest of military strategy, MAD would have rather more to be said for it (whatever one's final moral judgment on the basic idea of an annihilating retaliatory power); as it is, this is not the deterrence we know. 'De facto, deterrence requires the escalation of armaments'.[16] To confide our security to the technological solution of nuclear deterrence is in fact to overlook the nature of technology: it is not and cannot be static, and, if its development is governed only by the mixture of practical necessity and the anxious attempt to forestall the other side, it is not surprising that it is capable of producing something as strategically disastrous as the SDI conception.

What I am suggesting is that this conception should at last make clear to us the central contradiction in the nuclear standoff as we know it. So long as the ideals of 'absolute' deterrence for the sake of absolute security prevail, the question of relations between the superpowers and their satellites will be seen as, in some sense, a technological problem: what needs to be done is to guarantee the absoluteness of the threat. And so long as it is seen in this light, we are condemned by the very nature of technology to abiding instability and *insecurity*. The case for 'minimum deterrence' (i.e. no more than the capacity to inflict unacceptable collateral damage) is, as its most expert proponents allow, much complicated by the inevitability of scientific advance. 'No sooner had the ballistic missile seemed to put the belief that retaliation was the only defence beyond doubt than increasing accuracy and the early glimpses of anti-missile defences reopened the question';[17] so it has continued, and it is hard to see that any variation of minimum deterrence avoids this pitfall. It is entirely right that the notion of 'common security', recognizing that the security of both sides in the nuclear confrontation is interdependent, should increasingly be discussed and explored; but I cannot believe that any progress is likely to be made with this so long as it is not acknowledged that the presuppositions of our deterrent situation are fraught with the contradictions which the *history* of deterrence shows.

III

If this analysis is correct, SDI forces upon us some general reflections about ethics, politics and technology, and uncovers some fundamental flaws in the whole programme of nuclear deterrence; but what are the specifically Christian moral pressures here? I have already hinted at some of them, but it is time now to draw them out more fully. The Christian commitment is to a God whose 'power is made perfect in weakness': God possesses power, is able, that is to bring purposes to effect, to change the world – that is, in one sense, what makes us speak of God, the fact that the world changes into an environment for human growth and trust; and that power, that changing of the world, works in the history of a human being betrayed and helpless, stripped of defence, of speech and action, and killed. We understand the divine power to the degree that we enter into the same movement away from defence or security or mastery. This is not a commendation of 'resignation' or passivity, but a bare exegesis of how God is *seen* in the Christian story. If we are to have a secure identity, to be delivered from fear of the Other, fear of being destroyed or assimilated in what we are not, we must learn to know our identity as a gift, not an invention, not something laboriously perfected, precariously possessed and violently defended: our value rests on an unchanging act of creative love, on the fact that God *desires* that we shall be and that we shall share something of God's liberty, and become agents to others and to the whole world of the same generative love. Yet to know this gift is 'hard and bitter agony for us, like death', because the letting go of mastery, or at least the longing for mastery, painfully displaces the ego from its controlling position and overthrows its aspiration to make or generate itself constantly out of itself; and it involves plain, uncomplicated, unmetaphysical material vulnerability, accepting limits and risks.

Christian commitment, then, assumes that there is a 'shape' to the human project, discernible in a difficult and strange act of imagination that takes us outside the world of competitive and acquisitive egos – conversion, renewed in contemplation. And if there is a 'shape' of this kind, the Christian will or should resist the idea that the way in which human beings organize their corporate life is of no immediate concern. In other words, the Christian is, I believe, committed to the idea that the political life is inseparable from the moral or spiritual: an area in which *sapientia* is relevant and necessary. The nature of this wisdom is such that a 'theocratic' legal securing of the Christian vision would be a nonsense: it is worked out only in passionate and argumentative engagement in the uncertainties and limitations of human political action, and above all in resistance to the pseudo-politics which pretends that human goals are at best secondary to the supposed laws of the market, or are identical with the growth of the GNP. It appears too in suspicion of those who believe human flourishing can be elided into the solving of problems and the minimizing of frustration and discomfort and the prolongation of life at all costs in some kinds of advanced medical technology in the wealthy world. And it will naturally be hostile to any assumption that peace can be sought and guaranteed by the sophistication of hardware.

But all this the Christian rightly holds in common with anyone not completely in thrall to managerial notions of our relation to each other and the world or hypnotized by the sheer range and excellence of *scientia*. The specifically Christian element in the critique is the question about whether 'absolute' security is a goal that can be pursued without evacuating the *human* of content. How far is the search for impregnability a withdrawal from the risks of conflict and change, a longing to block out the possibility of political repentance, drastic social criticism and reconstruction? The Christian believes that the preoccupation of human beings with controlling their environment can, at its extreme, be fuelled by a dread, a refusal to make terms with what is obstinately *other*, that shows itself in destructive patterns of action; it is a refusal of the power of God for grace and the hope of re-creation, or rather of the rediscovery of one's createdness in the hand of God. To seek to control one's environment in the light of a humane vision, a sense of life well-lived, is not of course, morally and politically vacuous: it is part of the proper creativity of ethical life in community. There is no suggestion that the eradication of pain or disease, the more efficient meeting of practical needs, even the refinements of military defence are wicked or hubristic in themselves. But in such contexts, the environment is controlled or 'managed' for the sake of a broader sense of what is human, a sense which accepts that the characteristically human excellences lie in working *with*, not against, limits – in living in the body, aware of its mortality and fragility. To work with a vision of transcending all limits is to seek not to be human (Christianity has regularly so far lost sight of itself as to suggest very strongly that this is what it is commending); and the search for a technologically impregnable social structure is in danger of this aspiration not to be human. We seek to stave off evil or destructiveness by the exercise of technical power, a power which will threaten away what is strange and unpredictable. The Christian is bound to say, first, that this is to seek the kind of power renounced by the world's creator, and, second, that to seek to be more than human issues in a condition less than human, removed from the vivifying force of authentic political and cultural encounter, plurality and, yes, conflict. By threatening *total* violence, we risk blunting the positive force of honest conflict, within and between societies; not armed slaughter, but the inevitable confrontation, pressure and rivalry that will exist between profoundly divergent orders and may force them to develop, examine themselves, even move to new levels of relation – so long as the possibility of annihilation by the other does not hang over them.

Over forty years ago, Bishop George Bell said in a debate in the House of Lords about 'area bombing': 'The sufferings of Europe . . . are not to be healed by the use of power only, power unlimited and exclusive . . . It is of supreme importance that we . . . should so use power that it is always under the control of law. It is because the bombing of enemy towns – this area bombing – *raises this issue of power unlimited and exclusive* that such immense importance is bound to attach to the policy and action of His Majesty's Government.'[18] Power answerable to law is power in the service of a social and political vision that accepts limits to aspiration – that *might* even, though this is a wider and more controversial point, say that 'law' comes before survival or victory. I have tried to show that SDI is an extension (in one sense logical, in another nonsensical) of the principles of nuclear security; by seeking 'unlimited and exclusive' safety, it is likely to jeopardize further what safety we have, and it steps outside the concern for *common* security that is more and more shown by geniune realists in the pro-deterrence camp; its attitude to the ABM Treaty shows a disturbing contempt for the very idea of a lawful limitation on deterrence; and the rhetoric with which it is promoted is frankly dishonest in respect of its aggressive and destructive potential. Pragmatically it seems bizarrely dangerous; ethically, it has little to be said in its favour (with its first-strike bias); theologically, it represents a further stage in the divorce of the technical from the humane, and thus in the loss of a lively sense of the humane – the transfiguration, not the destruction, of the limits of time, death and matter.

There *is* a place for advanced research into space technology in this context. As Bowman points out, information-gathering satellites can increase the possibilities of co-operation and action against natural disaster, 'repeater' satellites could increase the safety of ordinary air traffic, and, above all, it would be possible to create an international surveillance system to monitor unauthorized military development throughout the world.[19] Dyson goes further, suggesting internationally controlled installations relaying information to ground-based non-nuclear ABM forces [20] – a geniunely effective *defence* system against surprise attacks of any nation against any other, because operating from bases scattered throughout the world, not concentrated in one nation or its forces.[21] But for any of this to happen, we should have to see a massive change in attitudes to national sovereignty, as well as a new level of responsibility required of the technological community (the two in fact go hand-in-hand). Barrie Paskins proposed a few years ago that both international bodies like the UN and professional associations of scientists should press for conventions regulating areas of research according to the law of war – in which soldiers are already educated. The scientist should be encouraged to 'accept a modicum of responsibility to contribute to extending the capacity of the law of war to regulate all aspects of the weapons cycle and not solely the intrinsically difficult stage of the cycle at which soldiers in danger have the new weapons in their hands.'[22] The scientist's freedom must be exercised in awareness of specific answerability to international law, not merely in the context of an ever-expanding seller's market in offensive technology.

But all this is simply to reiterate the point that we need to recover a politics, national and international, that insists on the priority of questions about the corporate life we want and work for over questions of how we most successfully continue as we are; because the aspiration to secure the continuance of what we are comfortable with commonly succeeds only in undermining what political good we possess. And this, as I have argued, is the problem running through the whole of our deterrence strategy. The issue starkly highlighted by SDI is how we *choose to be human* in an age when we are on every side encouraged to think that this is not really a problem.

Let me end with two further quotations from Freeman Dyson:

> The non-nuclear world is a worthy end for mankind to strive for. The means to reach it must be firstly moral, secondly political, thirdly technical. Moral means are peace movements and public campaigns arousing the conscience of mankind against weapons of mass destruction. Political means are treaties and military doctrines and deployment decisions [and, I would add, pressure for democratic accountability in such operations]. Technical means are precision-guided munitions, non-nuclear ABM systems, and other clever gadgets still to be invented. Technical means come last, but they still may be helpful.[23]

And, putting the whole matter decisively in its proper context:

> What the world needs in order to be saved is not technological magic but a rebirth of hope.[24]

The Christian perspective on SDI, as on the nuclear issue overall, has to do with how the 'moral means' to disarmament can be nourished by just such a rebirth of hope, of trust within the risky encounters of our human finitude, of resistance to that seductive urge to break out of the world into security – so aptly symbolized by the myth of a defensive wall in outer space, the corrupting myth of SDI.

12

International Society, International Law and the Common Good

GILLIAN WHITE

The other contributions to this volume focus almost exclusively upon nuclear weapons and the theological and ethical issues raised by their existence and, more crucially, by the intentions of those who lead the states which now possess and deploy them. The task suggested to me by the editors in early exchanges was to offer an international legal perspective on some of the underlying issues of international relations in the closing years of the twentieth century. My contribution was not to be yet another appraisal by an individual international lawyer of the international legality *vel non* of the use of nuclear weapons in various hypothetical situations, or of their possession and deployment in pursuit of policies of deterrence. The provisional theme for this chapter was simply 'Internationalism', to include an assessment of some of the issues raised by the Brandt Reports and the Palme Report, [1] and observations on 'the concept of world peace, with reference to justice and ideology'. It was suggested that this chapter might refer to Clements' contribution, 'Nationalism and Internationalism: A Theological Critique'.

Clearly, such an agenda is impossibly wide-ranging. Even minimally adequate discussion of these fundamental matters which concern one's understanding of the nature and function of international law in a society of independent sovereign states and which relate to their most basic need, national security, would require book-length treatment. What I have tried to do is to select certain aspects of this overarching theme of international society, international law and the peaceful or hostile relations of states in our time, and to stand back from the mass of analytical, descriptive or theoretical literature of international law and relations in an attempt to see and evaluate some of the trends which are developing, particularly in relations between the nuclear weapon states in the opposing power camps.

Rather than taking specific findings or recommendations of the Brandt and Palme Reports as starting points, I shall first look more widely at the overall international political context in which they were compiled and which remains the inescapable given for any progressive endeavours to improve the condition of mankind through 'better', more rational and less damaging ways of conducting international relations. As part of this overall context, I shall indicate some of the fundamental principles of international law as the juridical framework for such endeavours. Secondly, I shall review certain features of the relations between the two nuclear super-powers, the USA and the USSR, against the background of a conventional Western positivist theory of international law. Thirdly and finally, I shall try to offer a few, fairly basic thoughts on the directions and ways in which all nations, not merely these two states, might move from where they now stand to positions which approximate a little more to 'the common good' of humanity.[2]

1 International society and international politics

In his chapter, Clements warns us of the error of supposing that 'sovereignty' should somehow be made obsolete, as a precondition for the establishment 'of a safer and more sane world order in which "international law" or even "world government" becomes the order of the day'.[3] He reminds us that the sovereignty or independence of states is the presupposition of international law, law developed by states to serve their basic relational needs and to supply the conceptual and technical framework for their political intercourse by diplomacy. While it is too facile to blame the ills of international conflict and mistrust upon the sovereign nature of states, as distinct from the fraternal and potentially co-operative nature of men and women as individuals, there is a germ of truth in such aphorisms as 'all men are brothers, but all sovereign nations are enemies'.[4] For co-operation, trust and fraternal benevolence are features of relations of a community type among parties, whether individuals or groups, sharing common values and priorities, ethical standards, and expectations of the behaviour of other members. International relations fall largely into the contrasting sociological type of society relations in which the parties – states, international organizations, the large multinational corporations, even individuals to a limited extent – are in a much looser association. Schopenhauer used the simile of an assemblage of hedgehogs living in a cold climate: they needs must huddle together for warmth but remain subject to 'an instinct of repulsion which is based on their characteristic anatomical structure'.[5] Schwarzenberger summarized the differences between the pure types of 'society' and 'community' as being, in the former case, a means to an end, whereas a community is an end in itself, and as residing in the lack of trust found between members of a society based on interest and fear, and the presence of mutual trust in a community.[6]

As for international politics, the relations of the subjects of international society, probably most observers would agree with de Visscher's evaluation in his classic study, *Theory and Reality in Public International Law*. Whereas from a formal point of view 'politics may be defined as the pursuit of the common good, understood as that which in a community should ensure the good of each in the good of the collectivity' in the international sphere 'we find that the search for the common good has nowhere so small a place as in international relations'.[7] However, even prickly hedgehogs have to co-exist after a fashion. We can all observe that states find it necessary to engage in reciprocal exchanges on all kinds of subjects, increasingly so as national societies become more complex economically and technologically. De Visscher, representative of many writers on international relations and international law, perceives that these necessities of co-existence and reciprocity 'create solidarities' which can become common value judgments, develop a certain discipline and promote the formation of legal rules.[8] But, again in company with numerous others, he notes that states generally are unwilling to allow the law to govern their self-defined 'vital interests', namely, interests held to be intimately connected with the preservation or development of state power. He concludes that treaties on armaments, for example, spring from 'momentary convergences of policy and do not survive their passing'.[9] It may be that this last generalization needs qualifying in the particular context of the bilateral relations between the USA and the Soviet Union. What we seem to be seeing there is a slow but definite build-up of arrangements, understandings and some formal treaties, beginning perhaps with the (multilateral) Nuclear Test Ban Treaty of 1963, or earlier with resolution of the Cuban missile crisis in 1962. To this phenomenon, which must be a central thread of this chapter given the nuclear quasi-equilibrium which underlies these relations, [10] we shall return shortly. First, it is necessary to observe that this nuclear stalemate has produced a kind of international order and that, to this extent, there exists and has existed since the late 1950s the social basis for political relations between the two nuclear superpowers and their respective alliances, relations which come to be cast in juridical form, when this suits both parties' wishes.[11] Schwarzenberger, very much of the realist school, has gone so far as to say that while for the most part our world is a society, yet in one sense, the most elementary of all, 'it is already an indivisible world community: it is a community for life and death'.[12]

2   *International law in late twentieth century international society*

This chapter was written shortly after the exchange of ratifications of the INF Treaty by President Reagan and General Secretary Gorbachev in Moscow in May 1988,[13] an occasion for much euphoria in some quarters and for misgivings, apparently, in some NATO circles. For example, the House of Commons Foreign Affairs Committee in its Report on 'The Political Impact of the Process of Arms Control and Disarmament'[14] warned that NATO governments should be prepared for 'a long haul' and should not allow themselves to be carried away by the wave of optimism created by Mr Gorbachev. The Committee warned, as have numerous Western commentators, that after the INF arms reduction, the Soviet Union's superiority in conventional and chemical weapons would become 'the prime source of instability'. Problems of verifying any agreed cuts in such weapons would be of an entirely different magnitude to the verification required by the INF Treaty.

However, whatever may be one's assessment of the strategic and security implications of this historic agreement, it takes its place as a further exemplar of the existence of a sufficient minimal degree of mutual confidence in these two powers as to enable them to enter into a formal, legally binding and scrupulously detailed treaty on matters affecting their 'vital interests'. Fundamental differences in their economic systems, their political and social philosophies, and the gulf between their underlying concepts of the nature of humanity, in the theological sense, between the concept derived from the Judaeo-Christian tradition and that embodied in Marxist-Leninist doctrine remain unaffected by such negotiated consensual arrangements. These vast differences are revealed rather as boulders in the stream, around which the diverse currents can find their way and merge for a while, than as impenetrable dams stemming the flow and preventing any union of streams.[15]

The writer's perspective is that of a Western educated international lawyer, whose Christian faith strengthens her abhorrence of the inhumane, deterministic aspects of Marxism-Leninism, let alone its Stalinist distortions. Leaning more to the positivist than the policy-oriented school of international jurisprudence, with a conservative approach to the sources of international law, the writer is unable to follow the natural law tradition, once so influential in the doctrine of international law. However, certain fundamental values colour one's approach to international relations and, hence, to the view taken of the essentials of international law, to its bedrock principles. The following propositions are offered as a personal summary:

1. That national societies ought to respect each other's right to live in peace within established boundaries.

2. That this right is expressed in the fundamental principles of international law concerning the legal equality of states; the right of self-determination of peoples; the obligation of non-intervention; the obligation to settle international disputes by peaceful means and the prohibition of the unilateral use of armed force save in self-defence.[16]

3. That national societies retain the inherent right of defending themselves – their territory, independence and population – against external attack. Attack includes indirect forms of aggression, such as the use by states of irregular forces, armed bands or terrorist groups to further their national policies.

4. That this right of self-defence predated and (perhaps more controversially) subsists alongside the UN Charter provision on self-defence, the notoriously ambiguous Article 51. The right to use force in self-defence is open to abuse in any legal system, but claims invoking it as justification for any particular use of force are subject to scrutiny by other members of the international society, both within and outside UN fora. Very occasionally, such claims are subject to judicial determination by an international court, as in the International Military Tribunals of Nuremberg and Tokyo, and in the International Court of Justice in the case brought by Nicaragua against the United States.[17]

5. That international law, in specific treaties and in rules of customary law, prohibits certain means of exercising the right of self-defence. As stated earlier, it is not intended to enter the detailed argument, but the writer agrees with the numerous international lawyers who submit that the use of nuclear weapons is contrary to international law except in retaliation for the first use of such weapons by another.[18] Even in this situation the legality is doubtful, and the morality of retaliatory use cannot be defended to my satisfaction. However, from observation of state practice and the *opinio juris* (the legal conviction) of the states which possess nuclear weapons, the writer is unable to conclude that international law prohibits their possession of systems of deployment and preparation for their possible use, as the key element of a policy of deterrence.[19]

6. That treaties and international agreements validly concluded are binding and must be performed in good faith. *Pacta sunt servanda.* This basic norm is the most salient expression of good faith, a fundamental principle of international law[20] enshrined in Article 2(2) of the UN Charter and in the Friendly Relations Declaration of 1976.[21]

7. That general customary international law now recognizes certain basic human rights which all states must respect in all those subject to their jurisdiction, without distinction of nationality, race, creed, sex or economic or social status.

The theoretical debate on the philosophical foundation of human rights, and on their identification and content continues, but the practical working-out of international legal protection of many human rights is an increasingly pronounced feature of the international scene. This development plainly bears a particular significance for, and is of great sensitivity in East-West-relations.[22] It is easy to be over optimistic, as perhaps Meron was when he wrote that although political realities set the parameters for the legal action possible to protect human rights,

> those realities are also altered in the process, as the way people think about rights changes over time. It is the sign of our time that states are finding it harder to assert unlimited sovereignty and that an international community is evolving.[23]

Just prior to the Moscow summit of May 1988, *The Times* published a letter signed by five 'second generation refuseniks' in Moscow, grown-up children of people refused permission to emigrate to Israel on grounds of 'secrecy'.[24] The writers declared that the problem of emigration 'remains within the despotic realm of arbitrary bureaucratic power and closed to *glasnost*'. Nevertheless, some individuals are being allowed, finally, to emigrate, and others have been released from prison or labour camps in the Soviet Union.

8. That the law of armed conflict, comprising treaties and customary law, contains a detailed corpus of humanitarian law, formulated to protect non-combatants, the wounded and civilians, whether in battle zones or occupied territories. We may refer in this volume to Bailey's chapter on 'International Humanitarian Law and the Nürnberg Principles'. The influence upon this branch of international law of Christian ethics and teaching, albeit indirect and perhaps now of only historical importance, has been widely acknowledged.

A legal development provoked by the necessities of an ongoing, bitter conflict involves the interrelationship and combination of this body of law with the international law of human rights, traditionally conceived as law applying in peacetime. In the West Bank and Gaza, an area of acute territorial and political dispute, compounded by ethnic and religious antagonism, international humanitarian law is invoked by the occupied population, with varying success, before Israeli military and civil courts and in various UN bodies. A balanced study by an Israeli scholar has demonstrated that in such a case of prolonged belligerent occupation, the law of human rights as such can and should be used 'to fill in the gaps left by the law of belligerent occupation'.[25] Dr Cohen submitted that during the period she studied, 1967 to 1982, Israeli policy had sought to balance security measures with respect for the population's social and civil liberties. The controversial repressive measures taken to combat the unrest since December 1987 must be set against this earlier assessment.

The above list is not comprehensive, but was compiled to highlight those basic principles of international law which bear most closely on the themes of this book. As stated, the list is a subjective summary, founded upon a particular approach to international law, its function and the modes and processes of its development. Space precludes any attempt at drawing up a corresponding list of fundamentals as it might be put by a Soviet international lawyer, but there would be a high level of agreement between us, if only in the formulation of principles.[26] Questions of thēir interpretation and application in particular contexts, even where there is accord on the factual situations, are of a different order.

3 Relations between the nuclear superpowers

One caveat is needed at the outset. This section is limited to relations between the USA and the USSR. In common parlance these two states are referred to as the nuclear superpowers, reflecting undeniable realities, whereas China is not yet commonly included in this category, although a comprehensive assessment of US-Soviet relations could not leave out the influence of China and the increasingly tripolar nature of security and general power relationships. But the writer's lack of expertise on China's view of international law effectively precludes any attempt to tackle this dimension.[27]

(a) Treaties and agreements

Two aspects of this bilateral relationship will be treated here, aspects of intrinsic interest to the lawyer but also the subject of increasing attention by historians, international relations specialists and the strategic/security community. First, and more briefly, we should notice the series of formal treaties and agreements on their mutual relations, on arms limitation and, most recently, on limited disarmament.

An appropriate starting point is the group of agreements reached at the summit meetings in 1972, which included the ABM Treaty, the Interim Agreement on limitation of strategic offensive arms, agreed interpretations and unilateral statements relating to these two treaties, and the Agreement on Basic Principles of Relations.[28] Although we should not overestimate the significance for long-term, genuine improvement of bilateral relations of the rather theoretical language of this Agreement on Basic Principles, neither should we overlook the fact that these two states agreed to commit this consensual declaration of principles to a formal text concluded in inter-state form, although not a treaty with positive contractual obligations.

After preambular references to their obligations under the UN Charter, the first agreed principle is that the two states will proceed from the common determination that in the nuclear age there is no alternative to conducting their mutual relations on the basis of peaceful coexistence. Differences in ideology and in the social systems of the USA and the USSR are not obstacles to the bilateral development of normal relations based on the principles of sovereignty, equality, non-interference in internal affairs and mutual advantage.

The second principle includes a commitment always to exercise restraint in mutual relations and to be prepared to negotiate and settle differences by peaceful means. Mutual recognition of their security interests is spelled out as a prerequisite for maintaining and strengthening peaceful relations *inter se*.

There is also reference to what has become known as 'regional conflicts', now a recurrent agenda item for US/Soviet summits. The third agreed principle accepts the special responsibility of the two states and of the other permanent members of the Security Council (China, France and the United Kingdom) to do all in their power to prevent such conflicts arising which would increase international tensions.[29]

Together with the 'hot line' arrangements, and the various bilateral agreements on economic, scientific and cultural matters, and on the notification of certain nuclear-related incidents, this 1972 Agreement on Basic Principles deserve more attention than they often receive. Many international lawyers tend to neglect this body of state practice, perhaps because it is confined to two states,[30] and is regarded as of no interest to the development of general international law. In my view, these agreements not only form an essential historical background for more recent developments such as the INF Treaty; they are also significant for the linguistic and solemn adherence to some of the fundamental principles of international law, underscoring obligations accepted by both states when they ratified the UN Charter, an event which pre-dated the onset of the cold war. The obligation to adhere to and perform international agreements in good faith should not be forgotten.

In a similar way, albeit multilaterally, the Helsinki Final Act of 1975 confirms and re-emphasizes pre-existing obligations in the human rights area, as well as obligations of mutual respect for territory and independence.

Coming to the immediate past, the INF Treaty was preceded by the signature in September 1987 by the two Foreign Ministers of an Agreement on the Establishment of Nuclear Risk Reduction Centers[31] which reaffirms the obligations accepted in the 1971 'notification' agreement and the 1972 agreement concerning 'incidents on and over the high seas'.[32] The preamble to the 1987 Agreement contains, for what it is worth and I believe it to be not completely worthless, the formal statement of the Parties' belief 'that a nuclear war cannot be won and must never be fought'. The Agreement, with its essential Protocols on the establishment and operation of the risk reduction centres and the confidential satellite communications between them, is concluded for an indefinite duration, subject only to unilateral termination by either Party upon twelve months written notice. We have come a fair distance from the primitive personal telephone calls and the 'spy plane' overflights of the early 1960s and the days of the Cuban missiles crisis.

The INF Treaty merits a chapter solely devoted to it,[33] and surely will prompt some detailed analyses from international law generalists as well as from disarmament or US and Soviet relations specialists. In the focus of this chapter, we can note that once again the two Powers have recorded their awareness of the devastating consequences which nuclear war would have for all mankind. A significant change appears in the drafting of the 'supreme interests' withdrawal clause, when compared to the corresponding clause in the 1963 partial Test Ban Treaty. Such a clause is now standard in modern arms control agreements.[34] The new feature is the requirement that if either Party should give notice of withdrawal, which it is entitled to do[35] 'if it decides that extraordinary events' related to the Treaty's subject-matter 'have jeopardized its supreme interests', the notice must include a statement of the extraordinary events which the notifier regards as having jeopardized its supreme interests. Again, a small step perhaps, but a sign of increased mutual confidence in that the additional requirement to spell out the events relied upon must be intended as a further deterrent to arbitrary, unjustified unilateral withdrawal.

The large step taken in the INF Treaty, undoubtedly, is the agreement on specific on-site verification procedures; no less than five different types of inspection are provided for.[36] Governments in both Alliances and in non-aligned countries as well as individual commentators on defence and security will monitor closely the implementation of these provisions over the coming months and years. The possible precedential value of these Articles is obvious.[37]

(b) Tacit understandings or 'rules'

The second aspect of the bilateral relationship which merits attention here is the growth of tacit, unspoken understandings, even 'rules' or 'norms', to govern their relations. In the era before 'Big Bang' and the enactment of the Financial Services Act 1986, the maxim of the City of London used to be 'my word is my bond', or so we are led to believe. The hallmarks were avoidance of formal written contract and absence of statutory regulatory institutions. Mutual confidence and trust were deemed sufficient. In the superpower relationship, we can see analogous informal understandings, but reached even more indirectly than in the City. No direct conversations, face to face meeting or handshake to fix the bargain, but a slow growth of understanding based on expectations of conduct or abstention from action, on 'coded signals' of behaviour.

Already in the mid 1950s academics on both sides of the East-West divide were writing about 'peaceful coexistence' and the imperative need for the nuclear super powers to observe restraint and to pursue their competitive struggle by political and economic means.[38] In 1965 Raymond Aron referred to the 'statutory complicity' that linked the two states in their efforts to avoid 'a thermo-nuclear apocalypse'.[39] This common interest in avoiding nuclear war provided the soil in which grew the seeds of tacit understandings about their respective spheres of influence, the avoidance of direct military confrontation, and the commitment that nuclear weapons would be used only as an ultimate resort.

These three understandings are categorized by the American historian John Lewis Gaddis as implicit *rules* which have grown out of 'a mixture of custom, precedent and mutual interest that takes shape quite apart from the realm of public rhetoric, diplomacy, or international law'.[40] Gaddis' list of such rules includes two others: a preference for predictable anomaly in the territorial and political arrangements following World War II over unpredictable rationality; and an understanding that neither side should seek to undermine the other's leadership in times of apparent weakness or change of personnel. His thorough study contributes greatly to our comprehension of many of the crucial episodes in US-Soviet relations since the middle 1950s. Gaddis and others[41] enable us to see how tacit rules and understandings 'establish limits of acceptable behavior on the part of nations who acknowledge only themselves as the arbiters of behavior'.[42]

In a few instances these understandings have led to formal agreements giving the 'rules' the status of binding legal obligations or acknowledgement of rights. For example, after the signature of the Test Ban Treaty in August 1963, banning nuclear explosions in outer space, the UN Committee on the Peaceful Uses of Outer Space reconvened and the Soviet Union tabled new proposals which broke the deadlock. Previously, the Soviets had discussed space law with reference to the 'illegality' of 'military' uses of outer space, and early antisatellite plans involved detonation of a nuclear warhead in the vicinity of the enemy satellite. The ban on testing in space contributed to the tacit legitimation of so-called 'spy' satellites. By October 1963 the two states jointly resolved to refrain from placing nuclear weapons in orbit, and in December of that year the fundamental Declaration

of Legal Principles Governing the Activities of States in the Exploration and Use of Outer Space was adopted unanimously by the
General Assembly.[43] In the words of one historian of this development, this was the breakthrough. The Soviet campaign against
US espionage ceased, and observation from space became 'tacitly
legitimate'.[44]

Other 'rules' in Gaddis' list have remained tacit, untranslated into
juridical form, particularly the fundamental understanding about
respective spheres of influence. The preference for predictable anom-
alies, with all the injustice which these entail for the peoples affected
by the arbitrary division of countries such as Germany and Korea has
been partially crystallized in treaty form – the 1970 treaty between
the USSR and the Federal Republic of Germany, and the 1972 treaties
between the two Germanies, and between Poland and the Federal
Republic of .Germany. The 1972 Agreement on Basic Principles of
Relations between the USA and the USSR is also relevant in this
context.

Falk has argued that the unspoken understandings should be
made explicit and become recognized as juridical propositions. The
positivist tradition requires that international law take account of
state practice rather than set rules which are observed only, or mainly,
in the breach.[45] Among the powerful objections to Falk's argument
is the need to recall the basic principles of international law which
the writer attempted to summarize earlier. The formal structure of
the equality of sovereign states in the eyes of the law, the obligations
to respect territorial integrity and political independence, the recognition in this century of the principle of self-determination as a legal
right, all these represent and embody fundamental values which can
be respected across all political divides, even if their content and
application must remain controversial in many situations. In the
future, the major powers may reach a more secure state of mutual
confidence and then may be able to 'practise what they preach' more
often and consistently. They may actually come to respect the
sovereignty of 'lesser' states within their respective spheres.

If the international order based presently upon nuclear deterrence
could continue to be managed by the two superpowers with clear,
albeit tacit, mutual understandings, and if they succeed in greatly
reducing their stocks of weapons and delivery systems by consensual,
verifiable arms limitation or reduction agreements, the world may
enter an era of more normal international political relationships. In
such a setting, the fundamental principles of international law will
gain strength from a higher degree of compliance by the major
powers. In the meantime, which may be a long period of years, these
principles must not be eroded by the unwary, hasty arguments of
scholars overly anxious to remould 'the law' to fit 'the facts'.

4 Towards a closer approximation to the common good?

More than twenty years ago Schwarzenberger highlighted the lack of mutual trust between the USA and the USSR as a major obstacle to developing their relations in more positive ways. Leaders of both camps had publicly questioned the good faith of their opposite members.[46] The minimal constructive task for the two powers was then, and remains,

> to attain the greatest possible *détente* within the framework of the prevailing nuclear stalemate, and this is attainable in one way only: by enlarging, step by step, the area of mutual confidence between the World Powers.[47]

International law, in the form of principles, rules and legal techniques, has a relatively minor but nonetheless important role in this process. Butler makes the perceptive and, in my view, correct observation that in periods of confrontation analysts tend to categorize opposed positions in terms of compliance or non-compliance with international law. They will try to clarify areas of disagreement and reduce these areas 'to avert excessive responses arising out of misunderstanding'.[48] He goes on to point out that relations based upon increased co-operation between the two sides are equally challenging to international lawyers. As well as understanding opposed positions, they have the task of 'crafting or devising solutions to seemingly intractable institutional, juridical and attitudinal barriers deeply rooted in the infrastructure of the respective social and legal orders.'[49] Perhaps the INF Treaty may be seen as an example of such crafting, particularly in the verification provisions.

So far as the terrible armed conflicts being fought outside the North American/European 'zone of peace' are concerned, we may be glimpsing, in the late 1980s, some signs that the superpower leaders are beginning to comprehend the need to widen the focus of their vision when devising policies for their mutual relations in the short and medium term. Beneath the phraseology of 'regional conflicts' in bilateral intercourse there seems to be a growing awareness of the inescapable, if sometimes indirect, connections between the stability or instability of 'Third World' states and the predictability and order indispensable to the mutual security of the superpowers. Greater understanding of these connections should lead to clearer perception of the realities of contemporary international relations, and of their economic, cultural, sociological and ecological dimensions which underlie and mould the political and military superstructure.

The significance of the Christian gospel for all of this is epitomized for me in the parable of the good Samaritan:

> When he came where he (the wounded man) was, he went to him.

In the words of Trevor Huddleston,

> God in Christ comes where we are. Into a world created 'very good', but now 'lying in the evil one' . . . The Christian Gospel is simply the proclamation of this truth – not that the problem of evil is no problem, but that he who is the Lord has come where we are with power, to overcome it.[50]

Humankind, and especially those individuals entrusted with the fate of nations, have awesome responsibilities to bear in every age, but in our time they possess an unprecedented and fearful dimension. The prickles of hedgehogs can wound only each other; nuclear weapons could devastate huge areas of the world for centuries and kill or maim millions of people. We need all our rationality, skills and fortitude to live, to co-exist in this situation. We need to learn to be humble before almighty God, to accept the power and truth of his love and to offer love in turn to our human neighbours, continually searching for common interests and values on which to build greater mutual trust to progress a little nearer to the common good.

13

International Humanitarian Law and the Nürnberg Principles

SYDNEY D. BAILEY

The international humanitarian law applicable in armed conflict had its origin in two separate streams of law and practice. One was the Law of Geneva or Red Cross Law, which provides for the care of military non-combatants and civilians. The other was the Law of the Hague, which governs the conduct of military operations. These two streams can no longer be kept separate, since some humanitarian treaties, as well as some arms control agreements, can logically fit into either stream. The UN General Assembly from 1968 to 1977 dealt with both streams as a single subject under the heading 'Human Rights in Armed Conflict'.

1 Red Cross law

The Red Cross movement was launched by Henri Dunant, a citizen of Geneva, who was appalled by the carnage he witnessed at the battle of Solferino in 1859. Dunant launched a Swiss committee to care for wounded combatants, the precursor of the International Committee of the Red Cross. Being a man of vision, enthusiasm, and persistence – but often lacking in tact – Dunant next set about the task of internationalizing the movement by proposing the establishment of other national relief committees 'to compensate . . . for the inadequacies of the official medical services of armies'. This was too much for the British, who disliked the idea of foreigners drawing attention to official inadequacies. Indeed, the British view was that, since Florence Nightingale, the inadequacies had all been remedied. There might well be shortcomings in other countries, claimed British delegate William Rutherford: if so, they should copy Great Britain. Dunant was persuaded to change the draft statute of the new international movement to read 'to assist the army medical services . . . '.[1]

Dunant was one of those people who get things done by ignoring the collective advice of colleagues, and when he was found guilty of duplicity after a bank of which he was a director had collapsed in bankruptcy, the Geneva committee severed all ties with him, and he was forced to resign as secretary. He soon disappeared from view and his whereabouts were unknown for more than a quarter of a century, though he was in fact living in extreme poverty in a town hospital near St Gallen. In 1895, a passing journalist happened to get into conversation with him in a public park, and fame descended on him once again. In 1901, he was joint winner of the Nobel Peace Prize.[2]

The Law of Geneva began as a movement to prevent the unnecessary suffering of military personnel, but it is now concerned with the immunity from direct attack and care of all those not taking part in the fighting: wounded, shipwrecked, or sick members of the armed forces, military chaplains, medical and relief services, prisoners of war, and civilians. The law of the Red Cross has been codified in a series of instruments, beginning with the Geneva Convention of 1864 'for the Amelioration of the Condition of the Wounded in Armies in the Field', and most recently in the two Geneva Protocols of 1977 'Relating to the Protection of Victims of International [and Non-International] Armed Conflicts'.

2   The law of the Hague

The Law of the Hague also began as an attempt to avoid needless suffering of combatants. The first international agreement of the Hague Law was the St Petersburg Declaration of 1868, which tried to establish limits 'at which the necessities of war ought to yield to the requirements of humanity'. The Declaration stated that 'the only legitimate object' in war is 'to weaken the military forces of the enemy', and it went on to state principles to limit the suffering of combatants: in order to weaken the military forces of the enemy, it is sufficient to disable the greatest possible number of men; this object would be exceeded by the employment of arms which uselessly aggravate the suffering of disabled men or render their deaths inevitable; the employment of such arms would be contrary to the law of humanity.

The St Petersburg Declaration banned the use of certain projectiles, but its ongoing importance is that it contained three important principles which still form a basis of the Hague Law: that non-combatants should not be directly attacked; that it is forbidden to use weapons which cause unnecessary suffering; and that even when national survival is at stake, belligerents should respect the laws of humanity. These principles have been repeated in each instrument of the Hague Law, most recently in the 1981 Convention and Protocols banning or restricting the use of weapons which are indiscriminate or cause excessive injury.

Nobody did more to transform the general principles of the St Petersburg Declaration into binding rules than the Russian jurist Fedor Fedorovich Martens. He was present at the Brussels conference of 1874 on the law and customs of war and at the conferences of 1899 and 1907 in the Hague. The British War Office was as uneasy about these conferences as it had been about Dunant's Red Cross initiative. In preparation for the 1899 conference, the War Office sent a memorandum to the Foreign Office stating that three things were 'not desirable' at the Hague:

1. to give any undertaking restricting the numbers and cost of Her Majesty's military forces;
2. to agree to any restrictions on the development or use of new weapons;
3. to assent to any international code on the laws and customs of war.

As a sop to humanitarian opinion, the War Office was willing to 'consider' the question of issuing instructions on these subjects 'for the general guidance' of British forces.[3]

Martens chaired the commission at the 1899 Hague conference on the laws and customs of war. Discussion was based on three existing documents: the US code drawn up in 1863 by Francis Lieber, the Brussels Declaration of 1874 (which had been agreed at the conference but never entered into force because there were not enough ratifications), and the so-called Oxford Manual drawn up by the Institute of International Law under pressure from Martens. When the commission at the Hague came to consider the conditions for combatant status, Britain proposed an amendment to the Brussels text to the effect that the draft did not diminish or deny the right of people to repel an invader 'by the most energetic patriotic resistance, and by all permitted means'.[4]

A heated debate followed, and deadlock seemed inevitable until Martens put forward the compromise formula which is now associated with his name and which formed part of the preamble to the Hague Convention of 1899:

Until a more complete code of the laws of war is issued, the high contracting Parties think it right to declare that in cases not included in the Regulations adopted by them, populations and belligerents remain under the protection and empire of the principles of international law, as they result from the usages established between civilized nations, from the laws of humanity, and the requirements of the public conscience.

This was repeated with minor variations in 1907. The Nürnberg Tribunal found that the rules laid down at the Hague were, by 1939, 'recognized by all civilized nations, and were regarded as being declaratory of the laws and customs of war . . . '[5] The Martens Clause was included in the four Geneva Conventions of 1949, and the International Court of Justice declared in the Nicaragua case in 1986 that the Geneva Conventions are in certain respects the expression of fundamental general principles of humanitarian law.[6]

3 The Nürnberg principles

It has been clear since the Hague Law was first codified that it imposes duties on individuals as well as on states. A military commander is required to warn the authorities on the other side before commencing a bombardment, for example:[7] that is an individual responsibility. According to the Judge Advocate General of the US air force, the responsibility of individuals under the law of armed conflict is 'an important exception' to the general principle that international law creates rights and imposes obligations only on states.[8] This exception had been established at Nürnberg, and in particular by the decision that an individual may not shelter behind the plea of superior orders.

Nürnberg was a watershed. The idea that war criminals should be punished had been given effect after the First World War, but only following decisions of national courts. The indictment at Nürnberg was drawn up internationally, and the tribunal was internationally composed, but from the victors only. It is significant that the Nazi leaders were not indicted for bombing cities, for that was an offence which the Allies had committed as well. In dealing with crimes against peace and war crimes, the tribunal applied existing international law, but it was difficult in the immediate post-war period to find an existing basis in international law for dealing with crimes against humanity. The tribunal wavered between two concepts: that in law the treatment of nationals was a matter of domestic jurisdiction and, on the other hand, that inhumane treatment of human beings was morally outrageous, even if committed by the perpetrator against his own compatriots and in accordance with national law, and ought to be penalized on the international level. Unable to resolve the contradiction between these two concepts, the tribunal compromised by limiting crimes against humanity to acts committed in time of war and accessory to crimes against peace and war crimes.

The main achievement at Nürnberg, however, was to make it clear that a person who commits a crime under international law is personally responsible therefor and liable to punishment. The principles of international law underlying the Nürnberg Charter and judgment were unanimously affirmed by the UN General Assembly in 1946.[9]

4 Prevention of violations

All this has a bearing on how international standards for human rights may be enforced. The parties to the UN and regional treaties on human rights are states, but violations are committed by actual men and women, 'not by abstract entities,' as the Nürnberg judgment put it:[10] and in some cases the offences are committed beyond national jurisdictions. While I would not wish to weaken the responsibility which states have assumed for enforcing the international human rights code, I would like to buttress this with procedures by which individual men and women would be held responsible under international law for specified violations.

None of the elements of the Hague Law makes express provision for dealing with violations, except for the Hague Convention of 1954 for the protection of cultural property in the event of armed conflict. Article 28 requires the parties to take whatever steps are necessary, within the framework of their ordinary criminal jurisdiction, to prosecute and impose sanctions on those of whatever nationality who order or commit breaches of the Convention. The Genocide Convention (1948), which is not part of the Hague Law, also includes provisions by which the parties undertake to establish national procedures for the prosecution and punishment of violators.

The Geneva Law on the other hand, contains detailed provisions for the repression of abuses and infractions.[11] The parties are required to establish national procedures for the prosecution and punishment of those ordering or committing grave breaches, and there are also provisions for inquiry or fact-finding if a party alleges that there has been a violation by the other side. In the first Geneva Protocol of 1977, grave breaches of the Conventions and the Protocol are regarded as war crimes,[12] and military commanders are required to prevent and suppress breaches.[13] These provisions depend to a great extent on the good faith of the parties since the Red Cross movement disposes of no coercive power.

Christians should take care not to deride international humanitarian law just because it is so often violated. It is significant that the transgressor never questions the validity of the law, but simply maintains that the other side violated first. The very existence of the law provides a standard by which the national authorities may restrain and if necessary prosecute hot-heads, and it also provides a basis for the activities of the International Committee of the Red Cross and other humanitarian agencies.

5   Need for an international criminal court

In addition to the express provisions of the Geneva instruments, the judicial processes of the International Court of Justice are available to the states-parties. Indeed, Pakistan instituted proceedings in 1973 regarding 195 Pakistani prisoners of war from the Bangladesh conflict whom India proposed to hand over to Bangladesh for trial as war criminals.[14] There is, however, no international court or tribunal for dealing with *individuals* accused of breaches of international humanitarian law or violations of other international instruments for the protection of human rights.

At an early stage in the work of the International Law Commission, it was suggested that the Commission should codify the laws of armed conflict, but the majority was opposed to this: as war had been abolished by the UN Charter, public opinion might interpret a codification of the laws of war as showing lack of confidence in the efficacy of the United Nations for maintaining peace.[15] Instead, in 1950 the UN General Assembly appointed a committee to draft a statute for an international criminal court,[16] but progress has been abysmal. Initially work was hampered because it was believed that such a court could not be established until a definition of aggression had been agreed. That task was completed in 1974,[17] but by then the problem had become entangled with an attempt to prevent a statute of limitations applying to war crimes and crimes against humanity, and that in its turn was involved with the question whether crimes against humanity should cover only those mentioned in the Nürnberg Charter and the Genocide Convention, or whether they should also extend to inhuman acts resulting from apartheid and colonialism.

As the direct approach to the problem of an international criminal court or tribunal had apparently run into the sands, a different idea has been pursued since 1981. The General Assembly has asked the International Law Commission (ILC) to draft a Code of Offences against the Peace and Security of Mankind.[18] One wonders how the General Assembly was able to keep a straight face in 1981, for it had first entrusted this task to the ILC in 1947,[19] and the ILC had duly submitted its draft in 1954.[20] However, the ILC resumed the work with a will by appointing a working group chaired by a special rapporteur, Doudou Thiam of Senegal. Mr Thiam submitted reports to the ILC in 1983, 1984, 1985 and 1986,[21] and each annual report of the ILC to the General Assembly has included a detailed progress report.[22]

The ILC has decided to begin with the criminal responsibility of individuals, and it therefore set about codifying the offences to which the new system would apply, listing first the most serious international offences. These would comprise offences against the sovereignty and territorial integrity of a state, crimes against humanity, acts in violation of the laws or customs of war, and offences covered in twenty-four named international instruments concluded since its previous draft in 1954, including violation of diplomatic immunities, hostage-taking, hijacking of aircraft, other acts of international terrorism, and slavery and the slave trade. To these one might add torture and the traffic in narcotic drugs. The majority of members of the ILC favour including also the forcible establishment or maintenance of colonial domination, apartheid, serious damage to the human environment, and economic aggression, if appropriate legal formulations can be devised. The majority of members would also like to include the use of mercenary fighters who take part in foreign wars primarily for private financial gain.

Opinion has been divided on whether to include the use of nuclear weapons. The UN General Assembly has declared that the use of nuclear weapons would be 'contrary to the rules of international law',[23] and the UN Human Rights Committee has maintained that the production, testing, possession, deployment, or use of nuclear weapons 'should be' prohibited and recognized as a crime against humanity.[24] The US manual of military law states unequivocally that the use of nuclear weapons 'cannot as such be regarded as violative of international law',[25] but the British manual states more circumspectly that use 'is governed by the general principles' of international law.[26]

The UK and the USA have taken the line that the Geneva Protocols of 1977 do not govern the deployment or use of nuclear weapons. This has caused some of the medium and smaller powers to ask whether the laws of war apply only to weak states and little wars.

6   The problem of belligerent reprisals

It is sometimes argued that deterrence depends on the conditional intention to perform acts of unspeakable horror; indeed, that the more horrible the conditionally intended acts, the more effectively will the other side be deterred. I have seen no convincing defence of this position in Christian ethics. Indeed, my impression is that the consensus of Christian scholars is that if an act is wrong, to threaten to commit the act must also be wrong.

The fact is that the doctrine of belligerent reprisals is a potent mechanism for undermining international humanitarian law. The theory is that a belligerent should not be put at a disadvantage because the enemy breaks the rules: the sole purpose of reprisal action is to put an end to the other side's illegalities. In the heat of war, however, it is almost impossible to determine which side committed the first illegality – witness the inconsistent accounts by the United Kingdom and Nazi Germany on the bombing of civilians during the Second World War.

There has been an inconclusive debate in the International Law Commission on whether belligerent reprisals should be permitted if an adversary violates the laws and customs of war. The prohibition of particular acts of reprisal is so extensive in the Geneva Conventions and the first Geneva Protocol that it is probably now the case that the only lawful belligerent reprisal remaining is to use illegal weapons or methods of fighting against combatants or military targets. The author of the most perceptive study of belligerent reprisals in the modern world has concluded that they can no longer be regarded as even moderately effective sanctions of the laws of war, and that 'total abolition . . . is the only tenable proposition.'[27]

There are important aspects of international criminal jurisdiction which the ILC has hardly probed as yet – the prosecuting authority, composition of a court or courts, rules of competence and procedure, what justifying facts or extenuating circumstances would be taken into account, scale of penalties, enforcement of judgments, and so on.

In addition to the establishment of an international criminal court, it has been suggested that national manuals of military law should be standardized. This will no doubt seem visionary to those in the military services or ministries of defence responsible for drafting national manuals, but if it is possible to draw up an international treaty on incendiary weapons, booby traps, land mines, and weapons which disperse fragments which are not detectable by x-rays, it surely is not beyond the wit of humans to decide how the agreed restrictions or prohibitions should be conveyed to the armed forces. If wholly international formulations are not yet possible, a start could perhaps be made on an alliance basis.

7   The Christian perspective

The Hague, Geneva, and Nürnberg streams of law are of world-wide application, but it is clear from other essays in this symposium that international humanitarian law expresses the *jus in bello* principles of the Just War doctrine. It is true that some Christians have a pacifist vocation (I do myself) and fear that attempts to humanize war will have the undesired effect of making it more likely. Christian pacifists and non-pacifists alike can, however, unite in giving substance to the Law of Geneva, which is concerned with the care of war's victims. Like the work of the Red Cross movement itself, such humanitarian efforts can be seen as 'a protest against violence'.[28]

The International Committee of the Red Cross has resolutely opposed the just war doctrine, but it seems to me that it bases itself on a misconception of what the doctrine requires – or, more plausibly, on how the doctrine is abused in practice. The new president of the International Red Cross Committee, Cornelio Sommaruga, has written that the just war concept should be avoided because it is inclined to use different rules 'depending on the cause for which a war is fought.'[29] But the Christian version of the just war tradition does not have that effect: it insists on the same rules for all parties, irrespective of the justice of the cause.

Secondly, the Nürnberg principle that we are responsible for our own acts is a legal expression of a basic axiom of Christian ethics – and doubtless of other faiths, too. The Christian is a liberated person, and true liberty is to be responsible for one's own acts.

14

What if Deterrence Fails?

HUGH BEACH

The most perplexing issue in the debate over the Christian acceptability of nuclear deterrence is whether it is possible to fight a nuclear war with morally permissible means if deterrence should fail. There are four ways at least of dodging this issue, and since all of them find favour in one form or another with Christian authors it is worth disposing of them. The first way is to sweep the problem under the carpet with the comforting reflection that deterrence, provided that it is 'robust' enough and loudly proclaimed, will always in fact work. Provided that NATO, for example, keeps up its nerve and its guard no question of implementation need ever arise. A weaker form of this argument but more insidious, is to aver that the whole object of possessing a deterrent is to ensure that it shall never be used. A French view might be that since deterrence is a logically consistent doctrine it cannot fail: since the aim is dissuasion no question of immorality need arise. All founder on the rock of uncertainty; *how* can one be so sure? As is well known, this argument, if one is to take it seriously, has to assume that the actors in the drama are rational, that no question of miscalculation or overreaching can arise, and that the technical mastery of warheads missiles and so forth is such that the chance of technical accident leading to inadvertent war is negligible. If any were disposed to take this position, two recent misadventures should have been enough to dissuade them. The Chernobyl reactor disaster and the Challenger rocket debacle stand as suggestive surrogates for a nuclear warhead and its delivery means. At Chernobyl it seems that for no good reason technicians embarked upon an unauthorized and unnecessary experiment, with insufficient knowledge, and then when things went wrong bungled the recovery procedures. In the case of Challenger, it appears that a known point of technical difficulty (the O-ring joints in the booster casing) was never sufficiently acknowledged in the risk assessment, and in the particular conditions of the final launch the judgments of those best qualified were overridden for reasons of managerial expediency. The point is that in both these cases the stakes were high and known to be so; the best qualified persons in the Soviet Union and the United States were involved; and the type of accident which occurred had shortly beforehand been publicly and explicitly proclaimed to be 'impossible'. The conclusion is straightforward and clear. So long as nuclear weapons exist there must also be the risk that for whatever reason someone will loose one off. This need not of course lead to a nuclear war. But it would be a rash prophet who asserted that it could never do so. It simply will not do to assert that so long as it is in place deterrence is sure to work.

The second expedient is to rely on bluff. It is surprisingly popular. It takes the form of saying in effect that it is perfectly acceptable to possess nuclear weapons and thus to derive the benefits of deterrence, provided that it is recognized that in the event they would be unusable. A more dignified description of this position is 'existential' deterrence: which presumably means that so long as these things exist no question need ever arise of being prepared to use them, because the opposition could never be *sure* that one would not, and that fact alone would be sufficient to deter. But this is to overlook two crucial difficulties. The first is that these things are weapons, and it is as weapons that they exercise their deterrent effect; not simply as a reassuring context (like an impassable range of mountains) within which the normal traffic of diplomacy can be conducted safely. Since they are weapons there has to be a concept for their use. In the case of nuclear weapons this is a highly complex extensive and sophisticated concept. It embraces the technical experts who design, test, manufacture, store, service and repair the warheads and the vehicles for their delivery. It involves a huge apparatus of geodetic and terrain survey, intelligence gathering, surveillance, command and control, communications and the means for governmental decision making whether to fire or to forbear. It involves the service and civilian crews who operate all these facilities: their selection training management and motivation. It involves the development of doctrine, plans, policy and exercises covering every aspect of their possible deployment and use. If they are never *in fact* to be used how is all this to be handled? Who is in the secret? Who is supposed to be fooling whom? And so far as the West is concerned, running as it does a quasi-open society, and one that appears to be highly susceptible to espionage, is it not probable that the *real* but secret policy of non-use will be equally well known to any potential enemy? It must be obvious that one could not run an enterprise of this magnitude as a gigantic spoof. And the second objection is even more compelling. Bluff is appropriate enough in a poker game where the stakes are affordable; it is totally inappropriate where the survival of peoples and civilizations are concerned. Russian roulette is not an operation of war. Bluff may always be called.

The third way out is to accept that the possession of and conditional intention to use nuclear weapons on the part of the West is justified (and indeed necessary) as providing much the best guarantee of not being involved in war – and above all a nuclear war – with the Soviet Union; while also admitting that no morally acceptable use can be realistically envisaged. As a gloss upon this it might be said that while in theory acceptable uses can be foreseen – for example the use of a very few low yield airburst weapons in open heathland to stop a tank column or wreck a nuclear missile site – such a use would not in itself be sufficient to deter. It is precisely the threat of escalation to morally impermissible levels which constitutes the deterrent element in the existing NATO doctrine of flexible response. And this argument is the more compelling to the extent that the metaphor implicit in the term 'escalation' is taken seriously; once place one's foot on the lowest step of the moving staircase and there can be no turning back, no emergency stop button, one will be carried willy-nilly to the very top. To this point we return. For the moment it is sufficient that this way of looking at the problem appears to be logically nonsensical. How can it, at one and the same time, be right and necessary to form a conditional intention which if it came to carry it out would be impermissible? This way of thinking has been characterized understandably as incoherent. Another way of describing it is as an inescapable paradox. But sane people could hardly accept it as the basis for a Christian survival policy unless they could be assured that it is indeed inescapable. All the more reason, therefore, to attempt to think through the possibilities for morally permissible use; even if it is only ultimately to discard them.

The fourth, and arguably the only logical consequence of accepting that no morally acceptable use of nuclear weapons can be found is the path of despair. If we believe that the existence of nuclear weapons is bound to lead one day to their use, that bluff is not a moral option and that it could never be morally justified to use them, then the natural conclusion is that the West should give them up and submit to what might follow. It is an unwelcome conclusion. First, save in the unlikely event that all other nuclear weapon states (notably Russia and China, but with others possibly to follow) were shamed into following suit, this would be to put a monopoly of nuclear military power into hands less scrupulous than ours and sworn, at least until recently, to subvert both our values and our freedoms. Secondly, it would lay the West open to nuclear blackmail in ways that are impossible to foresee in detail but which could prove very painful in practice. Thirdly, it is far from self-evident that the existence of a nuclear monopoly is the best guarantee against eventual use. Historically it was only in the existence of a monopoly (by the Americans) that the actual use of nuclear weapons occurred. So this is a counsel of despair indeed; a renunciation that might render more likely the very contingency that it is designed to obviate.

Thus the presumption is very strong in favour of seeking some concept for the use of nuclear weapons in war which is consonant with the precepts of the just war. What if deterrence fails? The criteria of *jus ad bellum* imply both a just cause and a reasonable prospect of success. These should be, in theory, comparatively simple to fulfil. The requirement of a just cause implies first that the war should be one of self-defence. It is difficult even for the Russians to suppose that NATO would undertake any other. It is a truism that the correlation of conventional forces on the Central Front is such as to rule out absolutely any aggression by the West whatever the provocation. Neither plans, policies, training nor logistical preparations could possibly support it. Soviet commentators make much of the American plan called Dropshot, current in the early 1950s, whereby the strategic bombing of Russia with atomic weapons would have been followed up by a conventional invasion. This has absolutely no credibility today if indeed it ever did. One need not believe for its own sake the declaration by leaders of the NATO governments that none of their weapons will ever be used save in self-defence. The transparent fact is that political support in the West simply does not exist for any attempt to roll back the frontiers of the Soviet Empire by force of arms. This has interesting implications for the concept of proportionality, to which we shall return. It suffices, for the moment, to clinch the issue of just cause in the sense of ruling out absolutely the prospect of war of Western aggression. The other implication of just cause is that a defensive war would be undertaken not simply to prevent a change of ownership (say of Bornholm), but to prevent either the physical destruction of one or more of the countries of the West (say Western Germany), or their military occupation leading to the imposition of regimes alien to their preferred system of values, or their coercion or blackmail whereby the fundamental freedoms and values that constitute their just cause would be lost. The question of *how bad* the alien regimes imposed in the event of defeat or appeasement might be is another to which we must return.

The other criterion of a just cause ought also to be attainable at least in theory: it is that there should be a reasonable prospect of a successful outcome. It is fashionable and certainly true to say that in an all-out nuclear war between the superpowers there could be no winners. It is true because the term 'all-out' as things stand at present, must imply the use of a substantial proportion of the strategic nuclear arsenals of both sides. Each possesses a myriad in the literal sense of ten thousand of such warheads. It is not necessary to invoke the hypothesis of 'nuclear winter' to demonstrate that the use of nuclear warheads on anything approaching that scale could never be justified under any definition of success. Nor is this an outcome that either of the protagonists could rationally desire. The aim of the Soviet Union in going to war with the West could only be to bring about surrender – either to remove a threat judged to be intolerable or more improbably to subjugate, if it were foreseen that no substantial defence would be offered. The aims of the West could only be to compel the aggressor to cease and desist. It might be hoped on top of this to enforce a return to pre-war boundaries and a promise of future good conduct but these would not be of the essence. It would be a sufficient concept of success to have brought the war to an end as quickly and as economically as possible. It is by no means obvious *a priori* that a readiness to use or indeed an actual use of nuclear weapons by the West could not have these effects. In fact it has been persuasively argued, not least by Leonard Cheshire,[1] that the use of nuclear weapons by the Americans against the Japanese in 1945 had precisely that effect.

We move on then to the criteria of *jus in bello*, that any use of nuclear weapons should be both discriminate and proportional in senses that we now define. The principle of discrimination rules out the direct intentional attack of non-combatants and non-military targets. The principle of proportionality requires both that the damage resulting from any operation must be proportional to the military ends sought and, more demandingly, that the overall costs of the war be pro-portionate to the good accomplished by conducting it; that is by resisting rather than appeasing, surrendering, accepting defeat or suing for peace. Of these discrimination is the easier to discuss, though far from straightforward in itself. Clearly the principle forbids the attack upon non-combatants and non-military targets *as such*, and thus by extension rules out the type of attack variously described as counter-value or counter city and any doctrine of 'mutual assured destruction' or 'minimal deterrence' erected upon them. The extent to which the plans of NATO and Great Britain do in practice involve a counter-value element has been much discussed. Dr Haldane in an earlier chapter avers that 'of course they do'.[2] He may be right. But this is not a logical necessity. As David Fisher has argued:

There is no reason why a limited damage plan could not be devised which, while eschewing counterpopulation strikes and concentrating primarily on military and related targets, particularly an adversary's conventional forces and their supporting infrastruc-ture, was still prepared not to rule out damage levels sufficient to convince an aggressor that the costs of any aggression would amply outweigh the benefits.[3]

A far more difficult problem is that posed by the existence of targets unquestionably military and combatant in themselves whose collocation with centres of population virtually ensures that any attack upon them will result in extensive civilian casualties. It is not much help to say that such casualties are unintended if they are in fact highly foreseeable. It is, of course, helpful to develop weapons which, by virtue of their accuracy, focussed effects and comparative freedom from radio-active fall-out can be reckoned to reduce unintended casualties to a minimum. This has been precisely the trend in warhead missile and aircraft design for the past several decades. Perhaps the point has now been reached at which it is permissible to merge this principle with that of proportion and to say that just war doctrine would allow the use of nuclear weapons against military targets provided that collateral unintended damage to non-military people and things were held down to a proportional level. On this basis it might be possible to meet Fisher's criterion quoted above whereby sufficient legitimate targets could be found, in Russia and the Eastern bloc, whose destruction would do damage to the Soviet system out of all proportion to any benefit she could anticipate by going to war and would thus constitute a legitimate strategy of deterrence. While this may be true it gets us only part of the way. To be legitimate a strategy must not only offer to the Soviet Union damage that she could not accept. It must also satisfy the further condition that the total damage suffered, by the belligerents by neutrals and by the world at large must be proportional to the good that is achieved thereby.

Thus the whole trend of the argument to this point requires us to focus upon the issue of proportion. 'The *calculus of proportion* between the values of the policies to be defended and their just causes and the costs of such just defence, in the light of the probability of success, is the central moral exercise in just war analysis'.[4] Yet it seems seldom to be attempted. If it is it tends to be in some such simplistic terms as 'you cannot put a price on a principle', or 'better to be red than dead'. These are conspicuously unhelpful. Yet the reason for shying away from analysis is also clear enough. Who indeed is qualified to evaluate the goodness of the values to be defended, the badness of the regimes that would supervene if they were not, and the damage to be anticipated in the act of defending them; let alone to strike a balance between these essentially incommensurate entities? But if this is not done then the whole exercise fails.

How good are the values to be defended? The difficulties here speak for themselves. It is self-evidently nonsensical to contrast the

Christian West with the atheistic East, at a time when church life at some points in the Soviet bloc is thriving and when Britain is arguably the most highly secularized society on earth. And if recourse is had to *democratic* values it is worth recalling that NATO doctrine caters for members of an alliance not all of whom at all times have been wedded to the virtues of democracy. In defining what it is we seek to defend the simplest and most truthful thing to say is that we stand to defend our land from being overrun by foreigners. No one should under-rate this as a matter of practical politics. From the earliest recorded wars in history to the successful ejection of the Argentinians from the Falkland Islands this has proved to be a motive of the utmost potency. Men and women die willingly for their country and their flag. And it is the essential founding principle of NATO that an attack upon any member state, no matter by whom, will be treated as an attack upon all. This is simply to extend the concept of territorial integrity to embrace the alliance as a whole. But more is at stake here than simply land and nation. Again and again, in the literature and even more certainly in popular perception, the issue of values is seen as central.

The societies of the West are capitalist, plural and produce prosperity and liberty to a degree quite unprecedented. The martial virtues are at a discount. Based on ideals which are peaceful, law-abiding, commercial and libertarian we tend to play down the heroic. The spirit is one of small gains and losses, prudence and mutual regard, practical accomplishment and compromise. Self government is cherished and imperialism despised. With every one of these terms the Soviet system is seen to be at variance. Its spirit is collectivist and monolithic. Life liberty and the rule of law are all subordinate to state and party. The priorities in the provision of rights for Soviet citizens are intended to be education, jobs and leisure rather than freedom of movement and of expression or the right to express dissent. There is an aura of dogmatism ruthlessness and expansion; quick to take advantage of any weakness and ready to crush opposition. It may well be true that the worst excesses of the Communist system, the destruction of the *kulaks* and the regime of the *gulag*, have been mitigated if not wholly renounced. The Gorbachev reforms seem set to go even further, though no one knows how far. But this is not much comfort. The Soviet Union still seems both alien and hostile. It suffers from the propensity to expand its borders which afflicts any great empire, particularly at the point of its greatest over-extension. For all these reasons it is mistrusted. As a social economic and political system its power of attraction among the nations at large is negligible. Most of the influence that it exercises over other nations is the product of military strength.

This would perhaps be a sufficient statement of the issue if the

question were simply that of fighting to prevent this country or a
NATO ally from being incorporated into the Soviet Union; as it might
be Estonia. The reality is more complicated. One possible outcome
of a failure to go to war might be the conversion of West Germany
into satellite status like that of East Germany. In the case of the
United Kingdom a more plausible outcome of submission might be
acceptance of protected neutrality as in the case of Finland or Austria;
preserving democratic forms and a high degree of cultural autonomy
alongside some measure of compliance with Russian concerns over
the economy and political affiliations. How terrible would either of
these outcomes be? Before putting a price on them, in terms of the
death and destruction which it would be morally permissible to inflict
and to suffer in order to prevent them, it is worth pondering two
further questions. First, if one were to ask today what answer would
the East Germans or the Finns give to these questions? Secondly, if
these are indeed such dreadful fates, worth almost any price to turn
aside, how is it that no question arises of *going* to war in order to
liberate the existing victims. If nothing else, these questions serve to
disarm any absolutist approach to the problem along the lines that
liberty (or democracy or Christian values or whatever) are worth
paying *any* price to preserve. Even if the whole globe were on the
verge of succumbing to the Soviet empire there are some prices that
it would not be worth paying to prevent it.

One further awkward feature of this argument must be acknowledged before the central issue is confronted. If the defence of the free
world could not so far as anyone could judge be conducted within
the limits of justice – that is if the costs of defending were held to
exceed the damages that would be suffered by conceding – then to
appease, surrender or to sue for peace would become not simply a
despairing gesture *faute de mieux* but a moral duty. Herbert Butterfield
catches the essence of this thought precisely. In speaking of the
eighteenth century he says:

> They rejected the fanaticism which felt that God and all His angels
> would be thwarted if you failed to defeat the enemy; and they
> argued that it was better to say clearly that you were fighting for a
> province, fighting for Alsace for example, and then when you were
> tired of fighting you could divide the territory or arrange a system
> of compensation while in a 'war for righteousness' you could never
> compromise. Don't awaken the moral indignation of the masses,
> they said, because you may want to withdraw from the war and
> public opinion will be at fever heat and will not allow it. They even
> said that you must keep the moral element out of war since, like
> religion, it only multiplied the number of the atrocities.[5]

In the twentieth century this has become more difficult. In World

War II the moral element was inescapable and it has remained so ever since, or else we should not be arguing the ethics of nuclear deterrence. But the moral argument must be allowed to cut both ways. If at the moment of transition to war the prospective costs outweigh the expected benefits it is morally imperative to turn back. If during the conduct of war the same condition applies, it is morally necessary, and generally far more difficult, to cease and desist and to pay the price. And so far as deterrence is concerned it is not sufficient to assert that *some* morally acceptable uses of nuclear weapons can be envisaged (as plainly they can) and that this in itself suffices to justify their possession. The condition to be satisfied for just deterrence is a far stiffer one. It is that the possessor nations must be able to conceive of a war policy, involving the use of these weapons, which in its totality can satisfy the tenets both of discrimination and proportion; and one which within these limits is sufficient to deter. It is not of the essence that such a policy be published, least of all to potential opponents, but it clearly must exist. And in devising it there would be no justification for assuming an optimum outcome for any move that might be made without considering the down side also. Reverting to our earlier example, it is possible that the use of one single nuclear weapon to destroy a tank column might so horrify the invader that it would suffice to stop the war. Certainly this is possible, but it has also to be asked how likely it is; the issue of escalation again. One has to consider a range of possible outcomes and where damage assessment is concerned it would be wrong to weigh the odds with optimism.

So to restate the question, how much death and destruction is it morally licit to inflict and to sustain as the price of preventing a member nation of the North Atlantic Treaty from falling under Soviet sway? And note once again that this is quite a different question from that implied by past calculations on the American side that the destruction of X per cent of the Soviet population and Y per cent of its heavy industry would suffice in prospect to deter. Ours is in one sense a new question forced into the open by the possibility of suffering and inflicting almost literally infinite damage. In past wars exhaustion or the overrunning of one side by the other has brought an end normally well short of total destruction. So while just war criteria might well have dictated an earlier accommodation at least the ultimate damage was confined. This might be so no longer. How much is enough?

In getting at an answer to this question two approaches may be helpful. The first is to examine a number of historical instances where something approaching the scale of devastation that might be suffered in a nuclear war has been experienced. Four examples come to mind. The first, if somewhat obscure, episode occurred at the

Jewish fortress at Masada in the year AD 73. It seems that the garrison under seige preferred to commit suicide to a man and woman rather than surrender to the Romans. Was this a preference for death rather than dishonour or simply to prefer death at one's own hand to life imprisonment or death by torture? It is difficult to arrive at an ethical judgment; the more so that the miseries of the Jewish nation (against which Jesus so explicitly warned them) seem to have been so largely of their own making. No other nation within the Roman imperial system was so recalcitrant. Cicero spoke of them as a nation born to servitude, Seneca despised them as wretched and criminal, Tacitus said they had made themselves notorious by their hatred of the human race. Was their mass suicide a principled gesture in the face of intolerable oppression or a collective act of paranoia more akin to the episode at Jonesville? One can only suspend judgment.

A second instance is the Thirty Years War, fought between 1618 and 1648 in Germany. This war also had its origins in religious disputes, between the Catholic and Protestant branches of the Western Christian churches, but developed into a struggle for power between the Holy Roman Emperor supported by Bavaria and Spain, and France supported by various Protestant states as well as by the Pope. The details were immensely complicated, but when the War ended France had gained most; Sweden and Brandenburg emerged as major powers; and the Holy Roman Emperor became thereafter little more than the ruler of Austria. The price paid by the people of Germany was fearful. Because the armies involved were larger than their own administrative capacity could cope with, devastation was for thirty years a logistical necessity. Religious passion was not generally a civilizing influence and no moral sanctions appeared to prevail. At the sack of Magdeburg 30,000 people were burned to death. In Germany as a whole 8 million people perished. In Bohemia only 6,000 out of 35,000 villages survived. The richest areas suffered most. Protestantism was preserved but in most other respects German civilization suffered deeply, perhaps ruinously. The effects were felt for at least a hundred years. The political issues involved, including control of the Rhineland and the organization of Germany as a unitary state, continue to bedevil Europe to this day. Most historians would no doubt judge that the Thirty Years War went over the top. The damage suffered by Germany was out of all proportion to any benefit gained. It was, indeed, as a reaction to all this that the eighteenth-century views applauded by Butterfield, originated. The issues involved – as between Catholic and Protestant, between Hapsburg and Bourbon – though we can view them with dispassion, were as compelling to contemporaries as are the issues between East and West today and for much the same reasons. They were issues of faith, style and race. Can this history then afford some clue to our question? Even in disputes of this kind maybe the sacrifice of five places of civilization in every six is just too much.

Another episode worth citing is that of Paraguay, though the parallels here are less close. In 1865 the then President Francisco Solano López, by ill-judged declarations of war, succeeded in combining against himself the triple coalition of Argentina, Uruguay and Brazil. The war went on for five years, only to end with the death of López in an obscure skirmish and the virtual destruction of his country. The economy was in ruins, the population halved, nine out of every ten adult males killed. Women in despair were reduced to mating casually with any available sailor at the riverfront. Militarist groups fought each other for power, presidents were compelled to resign or deposed or assassinated. The Bill of Rights drawn up in reaction to dictatorship remained for forty years a dead letter. The country is still poor and underpopulated. Of course the war of the triple alliance was unjust by any canon, whether of cause or conduct. But it teaches one sad and salutary lesson. President Francisco Solano López, megalomaniac, is revered as a national hero to this day. So in assessing the limits of justifiable sacrifice in war it may not be much help to trust the people!

The last inescapable instance is World War II. It was fought to destroy the regime of Adolf Hitler, megalomaniac, over one of the most civilized countries on earth. That regime as now appears believed in obliterating people systematically and on racist grounds alone because they were Jews. It believed as was even then apparent in locking away people of whom it disapproved in Concentration Camps. It was determined as gradually became apparent on extending its own borders (whether by conquest or intimidation) without limit. For too long the French and British, with Somme and Passchendael at heart, failed to define even to themselves what it was worth paying that price again in order to defend. At last when there was plainly no other way of stopping Hitler they went to war to do so. The price is said to have been fifty million dead (fifty mega-deaths) of whom twenty million were Russian. If it had been known at the outset that this would be the price would it have been thought worth paying? And would it have been right to do so? One cannot interrogate the dead. But among the living, even among Germans and certainly among Russians, the consensus seems to be that it was. With hindsight it should have been even more right if the Allies had made their determination clear and acted upon it five years earlier. This is the case for deterrence. But what does this story tell about the just war and the fair price? To answer, one need not defend all that was done on the Allied side; indeed it is important that one should not. But on the central issue it seems to say that tens of megadeaths need not be a disproportionate price to pay if it is the only way of stopping in its tracks a regime as evil, arrogant and aggressive as that which staged the Holocaust.

The Russian empire is certainly much less evil, arrogant and aggressive today than Hitler's was then. But it is alien, feared and hated. If there should be no other way of stopping it, what would be a proportionate price for the world to pay, and how is one to decide? To simplify the argument we consider two cases only; one at the level of strategic interchange, one at the tactical. The strategic instance is that devised by General Hackett in his persuasive novel *The Third World War August 1985*.[6] In this tale the Russians, having failed to overrun Western Europe with conventional forces and run out of steam, stage a single attack by SS-17 missile airburst over Birmingham. The prompt casualties are 300,000 killed, 250,000 with blast or burn injuries of a very serious nature and another 500,000 with lighter injuries requiring no more than first aid. The radiological hazard is small. In retaliation the British and American governments, with the concurrence of the French, launch two missiles each from submarines to explode airburst over Minsk. The damage is as for Birmingham, 'only many times worse'. It brings about the dissolution of the Soviet Union and the end of the European war. Most people would have no difficulty in determining the moral propriety of this action. The allied nuclear strike though undoubtedly indiscriminate is redeemed by being proportionate, both in the sense of tit for tat but in the much more important sense that the good achieved (of stopping the war) far exceeds the damage inflicted horrifying though that is. Of course this story was made up to point certain morals: among them no doubt the ethical justification of the British and American submarine based nuclear deterrents. One cannot make too much of this. But if it has any plausibility it may perhaps be taken as an instance where use of nuclear weapons, at least in theory, could be both rational, in the sense of producing the effect intended, and moral in the sense of minimizing evil.

A far more difficult case is that in which the Allied governments are required to opt for a first use of nuclear weapons in response to a conventional assault which they have otherwise failed to stop. This supposition lies at the heart of the NATO strategy of flexible response; the official doctrine for the last twenty years. In defending this doctrine it is usual to propose that, at a point before the Allied defence breaks up and becomes incoherent, NATO commanders would apply for and NATO governments collectively accede to what is ghoulishly known as nuclear 'release'. What might follow is the detonation of a small number (say six or twelve) airburst weapons of low yield, designed to destroy military targets (airfields bridges tank concentrations missile launchers radars or headquarters) in Eastern Europe, with minimal collateral damage. The aim would be by shock/horror effect to stop the Warsaw Pact in its tracks and compel it to sue for peace. If it worked the same comments would apply as in the previous instance, all the more strongly in that the strike would have been discriminate. But in this case we are not writing the plot. If we were we could not overlook some of the well-known implausibilities in the story. The improbability, for instance, of getting agreement on the part of NATO governments to such a fraught undertaking. The objection that in the highly foreseeable event of Warsaw Pact retaliation the West would have obtained no military advantage; rather the reverse. Setting these on one side we have here to confront the moral issue. Bearing in mind the range of probable responses to first use by the West and their consequences what is the likelihood of good being done in proportion to the wrong inflicted? Here everything turns on the issue of escalation.

There is a very marked consensus not least among the military that in the circumstances outlined in the previous paragraph the likelihood of Warsaw Pact retaliation at least at the same level is very high. Perhaps we have all been brainwashed by the automaticity implied in the very term 'escalation'? Delving more deeply it is contended on the one hand that to pay us back at least like with like is the declared doctrine of the Soviet forces, set out in training manuals and practised on innumerable exercises. To which it may be replied that 'they would, wouldn't they?' On the other side it is said that it could not possibly be in the Soviet interest to raise the stakes since their only motive for invasion would be to annex one or more NATO nations as a going concern not as wasteland. But this is demonstrably false. Annexation as such is a most improbable motive for Soviet military adventurism so long as NATO keeps its nerve and keeps up its guard. Almost the only plausible circumstance for a Soviet incursion would be under grave duress when they had grounds for apprehending something much worse; such as the defection of a major satellite country or the imminence of nuclear attack upon themselves. If they went to war they must have faced from the outset the possibility that NATO would have recourse to nuclear weapons, and the probable necessity for a counter-move to avoid being checkmated. An equally worrying thought is the possibility of escalation by inadvertence, through panic or plain loss of control. At higher levels of nuclear exchange this danger is obvious and has been much discussed. At the levels we are now considering it is an equally cogent reason for misgiving.

The plain truth is both simple and unwelcome. Given the first use by NATO of nuclear weapons in the circumstances postulated by the strategy, no one can possibly know or even hazard a plausible guess what the consequences might be. That they would be full of danger is self-evident. Could such an action in prospect ever be deemed proportionate short of the most culpable wishful thinking? Many in NATO for obvious reasons either want it to be so or are indifferent. Moral theologians stand in greater doubt. It is interesting that William O'Brien, at the end of a long and rather hawkish defence of nuclear war fighting under just war credentials, nevertheless concludes that nuclear weapons must be reserved exclusively for countering threats and attacks with nuclear weapons. He opts categorically for an operational policy of no first use. 'Given the risks of nuclear war it is long overdue to sacrifice the "creative ambiguity" of a mixed Nuclear/conventional deterrence posture in NATO'.[7] His opinion is not definitive. No one's is. But the thought of Germany, east and west, reduced through escalation to the condition of Bavaria in 1648 or Paraguay in 1870 (not to say Masada) is to go so far beyond any conception of 'preserving Western values' or 'defending democracy' as to make mockery of these terms. The General Synod of the Church of England, debating this issue on 10 February 1983, left their collective opinion in no doubt. By a majority of 387 to 49 (with 29 abstaining) they carried a motion judging 'that even a small-scale first use of nuclear weapons could never be morally justified in view of the high risk that this would lead to full-scale nuclear warfare'.[8]

One further consideration is raised by this discussion: the issue of competent authority. Who is to decide whether the intended gain is worth the risk? In practical terms, given the existence of survivable command control communication and intelligence systems (a huge question in itself) the answer is simple. At the strategic level only the Presidents of France and the United States and the British Prime Minister have the capacity to make the nuclear decision. At the tactical level the owners of nuclear delivery means must clearly play their part. Decision making has to be centralized in this way or there can be no deterrent. But the responsibility thus conferred on these few human beings is the most awe inspiring that has ever existed. It should be no surprise if, by Arms Control or other measures, they seek to mitigate it. But in a democracy there is a further most cogent consideration. While the ultimate go/no-go decision can only be taken at the top, it remains of the utmost importance that populations at large should have confidence in the ability of these individuals to decide wisely. Whether or not this is true at present, it would be unforgivable not to seek consensus in advance as to *policy*; not to spell out at least in principle what types of threat might be held to justify so seemingly dire a response; how far we must be prepared to go. And yet O'Brien is surely wrong if he dismisses 'creative ambiguity' out of hand. If we in the West spell out in too much detail how far we are prepared to be pushed short of nuclear response, or worse still at what point we should judge the totality of damage to be out of proportion to the good secured by continuing to defend, this would be an invitation to opponents to go the further step and thus be sure to win.

And so we return to the 'central moral exercise': the *calculus of proportion* between the value of the polities defended and the costs of just defence. If it is believed that World War II was a just war on the Allied side but that the Thirty Years War was unjust on all sides where is one to draw the line? Specifically to repeat; how much death and destruction would it be morally licit to inflict and to sustain as the price of preventing one or more signatories of the North Atlantic Treaty from falling under Soviet sway? To essay a specific answer (say twenty megadeaths) is simply to expose the difficulty of attempting to measure the incommensurable. Yet this is the type of exercise with which humans are confronted daily and to evade it will not do. One approach to a consistent answer might run as follows.

In present circumstances possession of nuclear weapons by the West is a moral duty, for the deterrence of aggression, the avoidance of moral blackmail, and as the best available guarantee against any future use by either side. If deterrence were to fail it would be the duty of nations to resist aggression. Under what circumstances, if any, it could be legitimate for the West to use nuclear weapons is exceedingly difficult to foresee. Nevertheless, such a possibility cannot be ruled out *a priori*. In any assessment it would be prudent to view with equal realism the expected benefits and the prospective damages from prosecution of the war by whatever means. This calculation must give due weight to the criteria of discrimination and proportion as we have discussed them. A 'first use' of nuclear weapons by the West in response to conventional aggression seems most unlikely to satisfy these criteria. It must be the urgent aim of policy to reach a position where such use would not be relied upon and should not be needed. Use of these weapons in retaliation might be demanded on the grounds that, nuclear destruction having started, the only incentive likely to stop the carnage would be demonstrated willingness of the opponent to respond in kind. But it must be the last resort.

Meanwhile there is an urgent moral imperative to seek whatever other means may offer for the resolution of differences and to lessen the possibilities of war. Pope John Paul II, in his address to the United Nations General Assembly on 11 June 1982, laid out the current agenda with precision:

> In current conditions 'deterrence' based on balance, certainly not as an end in itself but as a step on the way towards a progressive disarmament, may still be judged morally acceptable . . . The only realistic response to the threat of war still is *negotiation* . . . Such negotiations demand patience and diligence and must notably lead

to a reduction of armaments that is balanced simultaneous and internationally controlled.[9]

For long this seemed an unattainable ideal. Now, by a seeming miracle it is exactly what we have.

In Place of a Conclusion

RICHARD BAUCKHAM

This volume is an open-ended one. Most of the essays have been produced in a collaborative process of mutual criticism, from which they have benefitted but which was never intended to produce agreed conclusions and has not done so. What follows can only be one person's concluding reflections. Had it been submitted like other chapters to the other contributors for comment and criticism, it would doubtless have been subject to a process of constant rewriting without conclusion.

The volume perhaps manifests different 'styles of engagement', to use Tony Dyson's phrase, more obviously than differing substantive conclusions, though there certainly are also some of the latter. It is necessarily pluralistic in strategy, drawing on many disciplines and approaching its common topic from many angles and in many respects. For its subject is one whose wide-ranging significance continually breaks through the narrow parameters of so much of the political and even ecclesiastical debate which purports to address it. The contributors to this volume are united at least in recognizing the extreme seriousness and the radical challenge of the nuclear situation. They recognize that nuclear weapons have in a variety of ways changed the world, and that this remains true whether or not they are ever used again, and whether or not the human world is ever obliterated by them, as it could be. The essays in this volume are therefore a many-sided attempt to confront a changed world: to confront Christian faith with this changed situation and to confront the situation with Christian faith.

To use a term which becomes increasingly necessary in Christian theology, this is an exercise in the *contextualization* of Christian theology and Christian faith. It does not allow the great 'generalities' of Christian faith – such as the love of one's neighbour as oneself – to remain abstract, but attempts to reappropriate them in the specific circumstances of the situation created by nuclear weapons. Without contextualization the central beliefs and demands of Christianity become ineffective platitudes. They may retain people's assent, but their discriminating vision and their critical power too easily dissipate along the way to concrete decisions and actions. Contextualized theology must learn from all the available data and disciplines to understand its context, while (since perceptions of a situation are never neutral) being critically aware of the need to understand the context in the light of Christian faith. From the mutual interaction of faith and context should emerge a form of Christian faith which is both enlightened and effective in its particular context.

The need for contextualization in the nuclear situation should not be misunderstood as simply the need to formulate or to support specific policy options in the political sphere – something which is rarely done in this volume. It is rather the need to engage with all that lies behind and is the context for the policies. It is the need to expose, criticize, reformulate, recommend fundamental attitudes and judgments. The poverty of the public, political debate on nuclear weapons in this country results from a failure to question underlying premises and attitudes. Far too much is accepted as given. The problem for Christian participation in this debate is that, out of a desire to be realistic and to deal with the concrete, available possibilities for political action, it is all too easy for Christians to accept the unquestioned premises and attitudes and to be confined by the limitations imposed by the political debate as it exists. For the critical insight of the gospel to come into its own, there is a need to stand back from the discussion of specific policy options, though not from the specific realities of the nuclear situation. The point is that these realities are so often trivialized by the limits of the political discussion: they need to be explored in all their daunting and uncertain dimensions if the political debate is to gain an appropriate perspective. Only out of an awareness and a questioning of the nuclear threat as a major, novel feature of the whole contemporary human situation will come the proper kind of questioning and formulation of political options.

Of course, the adoption of a radically critical perspective on the assumptions behind the debate may lead to difficulty in engaging with the immediate political issues and may risk being dismissed as irrelevant. In some of the essays and especially in the collection as a whole a tension is evident at this point. One could describe a spectrum between a radically critical perspective, which takes the existence of nuclear weapons to be a manifestation of fundamental flaws in modernity, and a much more accommodationist approach, which, accepting the situation as given, concerns itself with showing how a Christian viewpoint can affect the choice of policy options in the immediate situation. The essays in this volume would situate themselves at various points between these two poles, though perhaps a majority tend towards the former pole. These tend to speak of evil, repentance, the radical transformation of human selfhood, a qualitative leap in attitudes, as what the nuclear situation calls for in its full religious and cultural dimensions. Writers towards the other pole of the spectrum tend to be more interested in the calculation of risks, the maintenance of stability and the cautious minimalizing of the human potential for evil. Both groups aim to be realistic, but understand the demands of realism differently. Both are capable of optimism, but on different grounds. Yet it is not really a case of two groups so much as of a spectrum, and it may be that the kind of Christian approach which needs to emerge in the church at large as it slowly awakes to the nuclear context in which it must live and work will not be situated at one point on the spectrum but at several points at once and in response to different aspects of the context. The present volume could be a contribution to that approach.

Honest contextualization requires an awareness and acknowledgement of the socio-cultural context out of which one's work is done. Most, though not all, of the contributors to this volume write out of the British situation, and most, though not all, from an academic intellectual environment. But they also write as Christians committed to the church of Christ which is international in its mission to the whole world community. A Christian perspective dare not be, in this context of a conflict-ridden and confrontational world, a partisan perspective, nor should it indulge in idealist abstraction from the actual divisions of our world. But it is a perspective which requires one to transcend, in dialogue with others, the interest-dominated perspective of one's own group in favour of the common good of the whole world community and especially in favour of the victims of present power structures and of possible future power conflicts. If it is in a special sense partisan, it should be so not on behalf of one group of the powerful against other powerful groups, but in constantly reminding all the powerful of the rights of the potential victims of their policies. Thus its internationalism will seek more than that balance of power which the self-interest of the powers requires. Of course, it cannot dismiss the realities of nations, states, power blocs and their self-interest, but it must try to transcend the limited perspectives which these realities foster. Like a variety of other developments in the contemporary world, the nuclear situation obliges us to recognize our context as the whole contemporary world (and not even just the whole human world). Though we think and write and act out of a particular part of that world, we must do so in a way which is responsible to the whole. The inherent universalism of Christian faith, which has so often in Christian history been forgotten or abused, has never needed to come authentically into its own as much as it does today.

The debate over nuclear weapons will continue. Hopefully, it will deepen and broaden, involving academic rigour, spiritual insight and popular passion. It will certainly not be concluded until nuclear weapons have been abolished from our world.

Notes

Introduction

1. For an analysis of these and other more recent reports see, R. J. Elford, 'The Church and Nuclear Defence Policy' in G. Moyser (ed.), *Church and Politics Today*, T. & T. Clark 1985, pp. 176–200.

2. See, Francis Bridger (ed.), *The Cross and the Bomb*, Mowbray 1983; Robin Gill, *The Cross Against the Bomb*, Epworth 1984; Richard Harries, *Christianity and War in a Nuclear Age*, Mowbray 1986.

3. Paul Abrecht and Ninan Koshy (eds.), *Before it's too Late*, WCC 1983, p. ix.

4. Wilfred Cantwell Smith, *The Meaning and End of Religion*, SPCK 1978, p. 8.

1. On Comprehending the Threat

1. *The Fate of the Earth*, Picador Books 1982.

2. See especially his lecture given at Basel on 9 June 1985, and published in *Evangelische Theologie* for January 1987, entitled: *Die atomare Katastrophe: wo bleibt Gott?*

3. An English translation of this work (*The Principle of Hope*) was published in three volumes by Blackwell in 1986. I have discussed it in a review-article in the *Scottish Journal of Theology* 41, 1988, pp. 247–52.

4. See such works as – *Our Knowledge of the External World; Mysticism and Logic; The Analysis of Matter; Human Knowledge.*

5. Professor H. H. Farmer was Norris-Hulse Professor of Divinity in Cambridge from 1949–60. He was a most distinguished teacher of the philosophy of religion, and a preacher of exceptionally searching quality. He was an English Presbyterian minister.

6. Percy Hartill was a leading Anglican pacifist, and contributed an appendix in that sense to the 1948 Church of England report: *The Church and the Atom* (edited by E. G. Selwyn). Archdeacon of Stoke-on-Trent, and a pupil of Henry Scott Holland, he wrote an impressive essay on Trinitarian theology: *The Unity of God*, Mowbray 1952. Readers of the first volume of Nigel Hamilton's biography of Field Marshal Lord Montgomery of Alamein (*Montgomery: the Making of a General*) will recall also that in the grave personal crisis which 'Monty' faced in 1937 with the death of his beloved wife, he owed much to the pastoral care of the priest who took Mrs Montgomery's funeral. That priest was Canon H. R. L. (Dick) Sheppard, the passionately committed Anglican pacifist leader of the 1930s. (His wife's brother had been Mrs Montgomery's first husband, killed in the 1914–18 war.) It is surely significant that Dick Sheppard's pacifist commitment in no way inhibited his readiness to minister (it would seem effectively) to the needs of the greatest British field commander of World War II on the occasion of a personal loss

218   Notes

that might have completely unhinged him. Sheppard himself then was a
very sick man, dying indeed on 31 October 1937.

7. *The Social Function of Science*, Routledge & Kegan Paul 1939.
8. Gifford Lectures given at Aberdeen University in the 1950s: Routledge
& Kegan Paul 1958.
9. I borrow the title of Professor Freeman Dyson's well known book –
Disturbing the Universe, New York, Harper & Row 1979.

2. A Theological View from the Non-nuclear World

1. S. S. Maimela, *Proclaim Freedom to My People*, Braamfontein: Skotaville
1987, pp. 133–37.
2. G. Kaufman, *Theology for a Nuclear Age*, Manchester University Press
1985, pp. 30–31, 59. See also T. R. Miles, 'On the Limits to the Use of force',
Religious Studies 20, 1984, p. 120; and B. Goudzwaard, 'The Monstrous Idol:
The Ideology of Guaranteed Security', *Third Way* 7/4, Spring 1984, pp. 10–11.
3. Goudzwaard, op. cit., pp. 11–12.
4. S. S. Kim, 'Global Violence and a Just World Order', *Journal of Peace
Research* 21, 1984, pp. 182–183.
5. R. Barnet, 'Of Cables and Crisis', *Sojourners* 12/2, 1983, p. 16.
6. Goudzwaard, op. cit., 12–13.
7. H. Thielicke, *Theological Ethics II: Political Ethics*, Grand Rapids: Eerdmans
1969, p. 420. See also Kaufman, op. cit., pp. 5–7.
8. T. R. Lee, 'Peacemaking in a Nuclear Age: A Biblical Perspective', *Dialog*
23/3, 1984, p. 186.
9. Kaufman, op. cit., pp. 24–28.
10. Ibid. pp. 31–32. See also Lee, op. cit., pp. 186–187; Goudzwaard, op.
cit., pp. 12–13.
11. Kaufman, op. cit., pp. 3–4.
12. Ibid. p. 5, 51–52.
13. Ibid. p. 8.
14. P. D. Simmons, 'The New Testament basis of peacemaking', *Review
and Expositor*, 74, 1982, p. 604.
15. Kaufman, op. cit., pp. 7–8.
16. Ibid. pp. 4–6, 31–32.
17. E. Fromm, *You shall be as Gods*, Greenwich, Connecticut: Fawcett 1969,
p. 53.
18. S. S. Maimela, *God's Creative Activity through the Law*, Pretoria: University of South Africa 1984, pp. 145 ff.
19. Kaufman, op. cit., pp. 24–27.
20. Ibid. p. 27.
21. Maimela, op. cit., pp. 191–98.
22. Kaufman, op. cit., pp. 7–13, 16–19.
23. H. Falcke, 'Confronting threats to peace and survival', *Ecumenical
Review* 36, 1984, pp. 35–38.
24. Kaufman, op. cit., pp. 55–56.
25. W. Brueggemann, *In Man We Trust*, Richmond: John Knox 1972, pp.
20, 23, 25.
26. Ibid. pp. 20, 23, 61.
27. Kaufman, op. cit., p. 58. See also Maimela, op. cit., pp. 203–8.
28. Brueggemann, op. cit., p. 21.
29. Lee, op. cit., p. 190.

30. Kaufman, op. cit., pp. 44–45. See also Maimela, op. cit., pp. 144–48, 198–209.
31. Kaufman, op. cit., pp. 19–22, 25. See also Maimela, op. cit., pp. 212–13.
32. Brueggemann, op. cit., pp. 19, 61.
33. Ibid. pp. 22, 24.
34. Ibid. pp. 25–26, 33, 47, 61.
35. Barnet, op. cit., p. 18; Kaufman, op. cit., pp. 45–46.
36. Barnet, op. cit., p. 18.
37. Ibid. p. 18. See also Kaufman, op. cit., pp. 1–3.
38. Barnet, op. cit., p. 18. See also Lee, op. cit., p. 190.
39. Barnet, op. cit., p. 18.

3. Facing the Future

1. Quoted in Nicholas Humphrey and Robert Jay Lifton (eds.), *In a Dark Time*, Faber & Faber 1984, p. 7.
2. Ernst Bloch, *The Principle of Hope*, Blackwell 1986, p. 305.
3. Paul Goodman, *Little Prayers and Finite Experience*, Wildwood House 1973, p. 68.
4. See Ernst Bammel, 'Das Wort vom Apfelbäumchene', *Novum Testamentum* 5, 1962, pp. 219–228, reprinted in E. Bammel. *Judaica: Kleine Schriften I*, Wissenschaftliche Untersuchungen zum Neuen Testament 37, Tübingen: Mohr (Siebeck), 1986, pp. 140–147.
5. Quoted in Gwyn Prins (ed.), *Defended to Death: A study of the nuclear arms race from the Cambridge University Disarmament Seminar*, Penguin 1983, p. 28.
6. Jonathan Schell, *The Fate of the Earth*, Pan Books 1982, pp. 115.
7. Ibid., p. 169.
8. Ira Chernus, 'Mythologies of Nuclear War', *Journal of the American Academy of Religion*, 50, 1982, p. 261.
9. Ibid., p. 266.
10. On the probable consequences of nuclear war, see Jonathan Schell, *The Abolition*, Pan Books, 1984, pp. 13–23, which summarizes, updates and qualifies his earlier account in *The Fate of the Earth*.
11. Some evidence about children is cited in Michael Warren, 'Young People and the Nuclear Threat', *Concilium* 181 (5/1985) = *Youth Without a Future?*, ed. John Coleman and Gregory Baum, T. & T. Clark 1985, pp. 83–94, but he warns that research has not yet been rigorous enough to allow firm conclusions.
12. On the derivation of the western sense of history from the Christian tradition and its secularization through the Enlightenment, see the useful brief account in Willis B. Glover, *Biblical Origins of Modern Secular Culture*, Macon, Georgia: Mercer University Press 1984, pp. 118–124, (interacting with Carl Becker on the Enlightenment), 179–212 (defending the Christian origins of the modern view of history and the future).
13. Robert Nisbet, *History of the Idea of Progress*, Heinemann 1980, ch. 9, chronicles the decline of the idea of progress in the twentieth century, but his failure even to mention the Holocaust and the other great evils of twentieth-century history is amazing.
14. Christopher Lasch, *The Minimal Self: Psychic survival in troubled times*, Pan Books 1985, p. 42.
15. Credit for seeing this and its theological significance, to a remarkable

extent, already in 1947, must go to D. R. Davis, *Theology and the Atomic Age*, London: Latimer House 1947.

16. Quoted in *New Internationalist* 182, April 1988, p. 5.

17. Quoted from Anne O'Hare McCormick, 'The Promethean Role of the United States' (*New York Times*, 8 August 1945) in A. Hammond, 'God's Nation Interprets the Bomb: A Collage from the Early Years', *Northwest Review* 22/1–2 (1984) = *Warnings: An Anthology on the Nuclear Peril*, University of Oregon: Northwest Review Books 1984, p. 5. For the Promethean image, see also p. 4.

18. Cf. Ira Chernus, *Dr Strangegod: On the Symbolic Meaning of Nuclear Weapons*, Columbia, South Carolina: University of South Carolina Press 1986, pp. 30–31, 45.

19. Senator Brien M. McMahon, quoted in Humphrey and Lifton (eds.), *In a Dark Time*, p. 84.

20. Ronald Aronson, *Technological Madness: Towards a Theory of the Impending Nuclear Holocaust*, Menard Press 1983, p. 21.

21. Prins (ed.), *Defended to Death*, pp. 136–144.

22. Mircea Eliade, *The Myth of the Eternal Return*, New York: Pantheon Books 1954 (trans. from *Le Mythe de l'éternal retour*, Paris: Gallimard 1949), p. 156.

23. This is not just an ordinary case of decisions in time of war. The peculiar character of nuclear deterrence makes it impossible for real intentions to be openly discussed. A declared intention to retaliate, for example, might be intended as a bluff, but no democratic process can ascertain or ensure that it is.

24. For the sense of helplessness and victimization as more generally characteristic of contemporary technological culture, see Lasch, *The Minimal Self*, pp. 43–44.

25. Cf. Chernus, *Dr Strangegod*, p. 54; Jürgen Moltmann, 'Die atomare Katastrophe: wo bleibt Gott?', *Evangelische Theologie* 47, 1987, pp. 51–52.

26. Chernus, *Dr Strangegod*, pp. 27–28.

27. Lasch, *The Minimal Self*.

28. *Northwest Review* 22/1–2 (1984) = *Warnings: An Anthology on the Nuclear Peril*, p. 120.

29. Cf. Bob Goudzwaard, *Idols of our Time*, Downers Grove, Illinois: Inter-Varsity Press 1984, pp. 61–77, 94–96.

30. Cf. Chernus, *Dr Strangegod*, pp. 54–57.

31. William F. Lynch, *Images of Hope: Imagination as the Healer of the Hopeless*, Baltimore, Maryland: Helicon 1965, p. 196.

32. Ibid., pp. 199–200.

33. Ibid., pp. 199–200.

34. Another notable recent theological response to the nuclear threat is Jim Garrison, *The Darkness of God: Theology after Hiroshima*, SCM Press 1982. See my critical comments in 'Theology after Hiroshima', *Scottish Journal of Theology* 38, 1986, pp. 590–592.

35. See G. Clarke Chapman Jr., 'American Theology in the Shadow of the Bomb', *Union Seminary Quarterly Review* 41, 1987, pp. 27–30 (= 'Amerikanische Theologie im Schatten der Bomb', *Evangelische Theologie*, 1987, pp. 37–42); Larry Jones, 'Apocalyptic Eschatology in the Nuclear Arms Race', *Transformation* 5, 1988, pp. 25–27; Roger Ruston, 'Apocalyptic and the Peace Movement', *New Blackfriars* 67, 1986, pp. 209–212. But much the most illuminating aid to understanding the effect on ordinary Christian attitudes is Grace Mojtabai's

fascinating account of religious attitudes to the nuclear issue in Amarillo, Texas, where the final assembly plant for all American nuclear weapons is located: A. G. Mojtabai, *Blessèd Assurance: At Home with the Bomb in Amarillo, Texas*, Boston: Houghton Mifflin 1986.

36. 'It is said that at least eight million Americans accept it' (Ruston, 'Apocalyptic', p. 211), but this is certainly a conservative estimate.

37. Modern dispensationalists are divided into 'pre-tribulationists' (the majority: expect the rapture before the tribulation), 'mid-tribulationists' (rapture in the middle of the tribulation period), and 'post-tribulationists' (rapture at the end of the tribulation period).

38. See R. Bauckham, 'Chiliasmus IV: Reformation und Neuzeit', *Theologische Realenzyklopädie 7*, Berlin: de Gruyter 1981, pp. 741–743.

39. See Pat Robertson's disclaimer in *Transformation 5*, 1988, p. 27.

40. Especially Hal Lindsey, *The Late Great Planet Earth*, Grand Rapids: Zondervan 1970.

41. See, for example, among Mojtabai's interviewees, who share the same dispensationalist expectations, the very different political stances of the Rev. Jerry Bryan and H. M. Baggarly: *Blessèd Assurance*, pp. 133–137, 144–148.

42. See, for example, the interview with Warren G. Brown in Mojtabai, *Blessèd Assurance*, pp. 79–84.

43. Chapman, 'American Theology', pp. 29–30 (= 'Amerikanische Theologie', pp. 40–41) gives the now well-known quotations, along with some reason for caution in deducing Reagan's convictions.

44. Of course, dispensationalism can also be faulted at the level of exegesis.

45. Gordon D. Kaufman, *Theology for a Nuclear Age*, Manchester University Press and Philadelphia: Westminster Press 1985. This is his 1984 University of Manchester Ferguson Lectures. An initial outline of his views was given in his 1982 presidential address to the American Academy of Religion, printed in 'Nuclear Eschatology and the Study of Religion', *Journal of the American Academy of Religion 51*, 1983, pp. 3–14, and discussed in L. Shannon Jung, 'Nuclear Eschatology', *Theology Today 40*, 1983, pp. 184–194.

46. Kaufman, *Theology for a Nuclear Age*, pp. 3–4.

47. Ibid., pp. 7–8.

48. Ibid., p. 45.

49. Historians have often noticed that the Calvinist doctrine of providence did not at all discourage sixteenth- and seventeenth-century Calvinists from responsible action; if anything, the opposite. Critics of the nuclear dispensationalists often suggest *both* that the idea of the nuclear holocaust as God's predetermined judgment on the sinful world encourages fatalism *and* that it might encourage politicians to stockpile and even to use nuclear weapons in the belief they were preparing for or carrying out divine judgment.

50. Kaufman, *Theology for a Nuclear Age*, p. 8.

51. Cf. Chapman, 'American theology', pp. 31–32 (= 'Amerikanische Theologie', p. 43.)

52. This is the same criticism as Stanley Hauerwas makes of Jonathan Schell (since Kaufman's reinterpretation of theism makes it scarcely distinguishable from Schell's humanism): *Against the Nations: War and Survival in a Liberal Society*, Minneapolis, Minnesota: Winston Press, 1985, p. 161: 'Schell presents us . . . with a clear case of humanistic eschatology that attempts to secure the eternality of our existence through our ability to control and master our history – exactly the same eschatological presumption that leads to our having nuclear weapons in the first place.' Some of Hauerwas' and others' criticism

of Schell's 'survivalism' is rebutted by his *The Abolition*, pp. 3–6, but this particular criticism remains valid.

53. Kaufman, *Theology for a Nuclear Age*, pp. 11–12.

54. Ibid., p. 40.

55. Ibid., p. 41.

56. Ibid., p. 45.

57. The problem of understanding *how* divine activity relates to human cannot be discussed here. It is no more of a problem in the nuclear age than before, and is not raised in Kaufman's discussion. (Kaufman's notion of 'hidden creativity' in history certainly does not escape essentially the same problem). For a recent very useful discussion, see Vernon White, *The Fall of a Sparrow: A Concept of Special Divine Action*, Paternoster Press 1985; and cf. also E. Schroten, 'Providence and contingency', *Nederlands Theologisch Tijdschrift* 41, 1987, pp. 48–59.

58. The following paragraphs reveal my general indebtedness to Jürgen Moltmann's theology, especially *Theology of Hope* (SCM Press 1967) and *The Crucified God* (SCM Press 1974). See my account in *Moltmann: Messianic Theology in the Making* (Marshall Pickering 1987). My complaint, in 'Theology after Hiroshima', pp. 589–590, that Moltmann had not addressed the bearing of the nuclear threat on his theology of hope, is now at least partially met by his 'Die atomare Katastrophe'.

59. Dale Aukerman *Darkening Valley: A Biblical Perspective on Nuclear War*, New York: Seabury Press, 1981, p. 48 and cf. the whole of ch. 8 and 27. Cf. also Moltmann's idea that the nuclear catastrophe will be a catastrophe for God himself because of his fellow-suffering with his creation: 'Die atome Katastrophe', pp. 57–58.

60. The christological eschatology of this paragraph can be linked with the retrieval of the apocalyptic tradition – in a very different way from that of dispensationalism – which I have suggested in 'Theology after Hiroshima', pp. 597–599, and which Ruston, 'Apocalyptic', pp. 214–215, also wants, but for the further development of which there is no space here. The use of apocalyptic in Garrison, *The Darkness of God*, is unfortunately marred by his Jungian interpretation of it.

This chapter was given as a paper to the 1988 meeting of the Académie Internationale des Sciences Religienses, and will appear in the published proceedings of the 1987 and the 1988 meetings of the Académie on *Temps et eschaton*.

4. The Use of the Bible in the Nuclear Debate

1. *The Church and the Bomb: Nuclear Weapons and Christian Conscience*, Hodder & Stoughton/CIO Publishing 1982.

2. Ibid., p. 104. Cf. pp. 102f.: 'In this chapter we have examined our overall topic from the standpoint of law and ethics, points of view which we can share with any man or woman of good will.'

3. Chapter 6: 'Wider Theological and Ethical Considerations'.

4. Ibid., pp. 107–8. It should be noted that, with the notable exception of T. W. Manson in England, scholars have recently been cautious about seeing the Wisdom sayings in the Gospels as characteristic of, or indeed original to Jesus' teaching. See, classically, R. Bultmann, *Jesus and the Word*, New York:

Scribner's 1934. See also my *Jesus and the Transformation of Judaism*, Darton, Longman & Todd 1980, ch. 7.

5. *The Church and the Bomb*, p. 109.
6. Ibid., p. 115.
7. Ibid., p. 105.
8. Ibid., pp. 111 ff.
9. Ibid., pp. 119 ff.
10. Ibid., p. 115.
11. Ibid., p. 115.
12. Ibid., p. 120.
13. Ibid., p. 123.
14. Ibid., p. 123.
15. The Lutheran doctrine has been subjected to severe scrutiny, notably by Scandinavian scholars, in the light of the problems experienced by Lutheran churches under the Third Reich. Cf. especially G. Tornvall, *Geistliches und weltliches Regiment bei Luther*, Munich 1947; G. Hillerdal, *Gehorsam gegen Gott und Menschen: Luthers Lehre von Obrigkeit und die moderne evangelische Staatsethik*, Göttingen 1955.
16. See especially H. Frei, *The Eclipse of Biblical Narrative*, Yale University Press 1974.
17. G. E. Lessing, 'Eine Duplik', in *Werke*, ed. F. Fischer, Zurich 1965, vol. 6, p. 296: 'Wenn Gott in seiner Rechten alle Wahrheit und in seiner Linken den immer regen Trieb nach Wahrheit, obschon mit dem Zusatze, mich immer und ewig zu irren, verschlossen hielte und spräche zu mir: "Wähle!" ich fiele ihm mit Demut in seine Linke und sagte: "Vater, gib! die reine Wahrheit ist ja doch nur für dich allein!"' ('If God held out to me in his right hand all truth and in his left the ever active impulse for truth, albeit with the qualification that I would always and eternally err, and said to me: "Choose!", I would in humility fall on his left hand and say, "Father, give! the pure truth is for you alone."')
18. But see J. Bowker, *The Sense of God*, Oxford University Press 1973.
19. Among the vast number of books on the subject, E. P. Sanders, *Jesus and Judaism*, SCM Press 1985, is of particular importance.
20. V. Turner, *Dramas, Fields and Metaphors: Symbolic Action in Human Society*, Ithaca, New York 1974.
21. W. Meeks, 'Towards a Hermeneutic of Social Embodiment', *Harvard Theological Review* 79, 1986, 175–186.
22. J. Wallis, *Agenda for Biblical People*, San Francisco 1984.
23. D. Berrigan, 'Sanity in the Face of the Beast', in A. Kee ed., *Seeds of Liberation*, SCM Press 1973.
24. See the interesting discussion by C. Rowland, 'Discerning the "Abomination of Desolation"', in A. Race ed., *Theology against the Nuclear Horizon*, SCM Press 1988. But I cannot agree with him that distancing oneself from 'such extravagances' is altogether an abrogation of one's responsibilities as a biblical critic. It is, it seems to me, precisely the critic's role to distinguish between Büchner and popular conceptions of the Rapture. Nor will such a distanced stance necessarily be a means of self-protection from the social critical message of such works as *Woyzeck* or indeed of more popular movements.
25. Cf. A. Chester, 'The Apocalypse and the Nuclear Holocaust', in *In God We Trust*, CND Publications 1986, drawing freely on C. Rowland, *The Open Heaven*, SPCK 1982.

26. Ibid., p. 63.

27. *The Open Heaven*, passim.

28. C. Potok, *The Book of Lights*, Penguin Books 1983.

29. Cf. M. Hengel, *The Zealots*, T. & T. Clark 1989; *The Charismatic Leader and His Followers*, T. & T. Clark 1981.

30. But compare the stories of the Jews' 'baring their throats' to Roman forces when the Temple was threatened with desecration: Josephus, *Antiquities* XVIII. 59, 127.

31. *The Church and the Bomb*, p. 123.

32. Cf. Alan Paton's short story 'Sponono', in *Debbie Go Home*, Penguin Books 1961, pp. 97–117.

33. *The Church and the Bomb*, p. 76.

34. See note 30 above.

5.   Nationalism and Internationalism: A Theological Critique

1. Michael Hare-Duke, 'International Year of Peace in Great Britain – Success or Disappointment?', *Christian Peace Conference* 89–90 1–11/1987. p. 4.

2. Quoted in W. Shirer, *The Rise and Fall of the Third Reich*, Pan Books 1964, p. 114.

3. Reinhold Niebuhr, *Moral Man and Immoral Society*, SCM Press 1963, p. 91.

4. W. Pannenberg, 'The Nation and the Human Race', in *Faith and Reality*, Search Press 1977, p. 117.

5. Hare-Duke, op. cit., p. 4

6. K. W. Clements, *A Patriotism for Today, Love of Country in Dialogue with the Witness af Dietrich Bonhoeffer*, Collins Liturgical 1986.

7. Cf. Keith Robbins, 'Religion and Identity in Modern Britain', in S. Mews (ed.), *Religion and National Identity*, Blackwells 1982.

8. K. W. Clements, *Friedrich Schleiermacher Pioneer of Modern Theology*, Collins 1987, p. 240 (emphases mine).

9. Alan James, *Sovereign Statehood: The Basis of International Society*, Allen & Unwin 1986.

10. Ibid., p. 40.

11. K. N. Walz, quoted in James, op. cit., p. 212.

12. Michael Alison, 'The Christian in the World', in *The Christian and Conservatism Conference*, Conservative Party Central Office 1983, p. 21.

13. See Clements, *A Patriotism for Today*, Ch. 3. See also Ronald Preston's chapter in this volume, 'Reflections on Love, Power and Justice', pp. 115f.

14. D. Bonhoeffer, *No Rusty Swords, Letters, Lectures and Notes 1928–36*, ed. E. Robertson, Collins 1965, p. 180.

15. Ibid., p. 167.

16. See E. Busch, *Karl Barth. His Life from Letters and Autobiographical Texts*, SCM Press 1976, pp. 430ff.

17. Augustine, *City of God*, Book III, Chapter XIV, in Volume I of Everyman Edition (Trans. J. Healey), Dent 1945, p. 89.

18. Bonhoeffer, op. cit., p. 290f.

19. K. Barth, *Letters 1961–1968*, T. & T. Clark 1981, p. 106.

6. Confrontation and Peace in the Nuclear Age: An Analysis

1. Arthur D. Nock, *Conversion: The Old and the New in Religion from Alexander the Great to Augustine of Hippo*, Clarendon Press 1933.

2. John Helgeland, 'Christians and the Roman Army from Marcus Aurelius to Constantine', *Aufstieg und Niedergang der Römische Welt*, ed. Walter Haase, Berlin and New York: Walter de Gruyter, 1979, II.23.1, pp. 724–733; see also John F. Helgeland and Robert J. Daly, *Christians and the Military: The Early Experience*, Philadelphia, Pennsylvania: Fortress Press, 1985, and SCM Press 1987.

3. Roland H. Bainton, 'The Early Church and War', *Harvard Theological Review* XXXIX, 1946, pp. 189–212; *Christian Attitudes to War and Peace*, Nashville: Tennessee, Abingdon Press 1960.

4. Cecil J. Cadoux, *The Early Christian Attitude to War*, Headley Bros 1919.

5. Helgeland, 'Christians and the Roman Army', pp. 725–9.

6. Thomas Aquinas, *Summa Theologiae*, 2a, 2ae q.40 arts 1–3.

7. Fyodor Dostoyevsky, *The Brothers Karamazov*, Penguin 1982, book 6.

8. Quincy Wright, *A Study of War*, second edition, Chicago: University of Chicago Press 1965, pp. 297–300.

9. Albert E. Marrin, *The Last Crusade: The Church of England in the First World War*, Durham, North Carolina: Duke University Press 1973, pp. 166–176.

10. Marrin, *The Last Crusade*, pp. 124–5, 140–163, 251–2.

11. Alan Wilkinson, *The Church of England and the First World War*, SPCK 1978, pp. 248–261.

12. Robert Graves, *Goodbye to All That: An Autobiography*, Jonathan Cape 1929.

13. David Jones, *In Parenthesis*, Faber and Faber 1937.

14. Marrin, *The Last Crusade*, p. 253.

15. Tony Carty, 'The Origins of the Doctrine of Deterrence', *Ethics and Deterrence: Power and Responsibility in the Nuclear Age*, ed. Howard Davis, Blackwell 1986, pp. 109–122.

16. Carty, 'The Origins of the Doctrine of Deterrence', pp. 122–128.

17. Robert Jungk, *Brighter than a Thousand Suns*, Penguin 1964, pp. 106–7.

18. Carty, 'The Origins of the Doctrine of Deterrence', p. 132.

19. Denis de Rougemont, *Passion and Society*, trans. Montgomery Belgion, Faber and Faber, second edition 1956.

20. Irving Singer, *The Nature of Love*, vol.2: *Courtly and Romantic*, Chicago: University of Chicago Press 1984, pp. x–xi, 28, 135; Roger Boase *The Origin and Meaning of Courtly Love*, Manchester University Press 1977, pp. 37–40.

21. de Rougemont, *Passion and Society* p. 259.

22. Albert Camus, *The Rebel*, Penguin, 1962, p. 82.

23. de Rougemont, *Passion and Society*, p. 260.

24. For a detailed application of this thesis to German history, see Hans Kohn *The Mind of Germany: The Education of a Nation*, Macmillan 1961.

25. Kohn, *The Mind of Germany*, pp. 65, 67, 72; Leonard Krieger, *The German Idea of Freedom*, Chicago, University of Chicago Press, pp. 174–215.

26. Johann G. Fichte, *Discours a la Nation Allemande*, Paris, Librairie Delgrave 1895, Discours IX.

27. Georg W.F. Hegel, *Lectures on the Philosophy of History*, New York, Dover 1956, pp. 16, 38.

28. *Hegel's Philosophy of Right*, trans. S.W. Dyde, G. Bell and Sons 1896, pp. 244–7.

29. Albert Camus, *The Rebel*, Penguin 1962, p. 78.

30. Ibid., p. 148.

31. Ibid., p. 149. Camus' judgment is borne out by recent studies: see Roger Woods, *Ernst Jünger and the Nature of Political Committment*, Stuttgarter Arbeiter fur Germanistik no. 116, Stuttgart: Akademischer Verlag Hans-Dieter Heinz 1982, chs 5, 6. Jeffrey Herf *Reactionary Modernism: Technology, culture and politics in Weimar and the Third Reich*, Cambridge University Press 1984, ch.4. Note also Joseph P. Stern, *Ernst Jünger: A Writer of Our Time*, Bowes and Bowes 1953, p. 45.

32. Jünger, 'Nationalismus und modernes Leben', *Arminius* VII (1927) pp. 4–6, cited in Herf, *Reactionary Modernism*, p. 83.

33. Jünger, 'Nation und Luftfahrt', *Vormarsch* I (1927–8), pp. 314–7, cited in Herf, *Reactionary Modernism*, p. 85.

34. Ministry of Defence, *Statement on the Defence Estimates, 1981*, Cmnd. 8212–I, HMSO 1981, pp. 13–14.

35. Ministry of Defence, *Statement on the Defence Estimates*, Cm. 101–I, HMSO 1987, pp. 4–7.

36. I am indebted in the following to the analysis of Ignaz Maybaum, especially in *Creation and Guilt: A Theological Assessment of Freud's Father-Son Conflict*, Vallentine Mitchell 1969.

7.   *Styles of Documentary Engagement*

1. See Robin Gill, *Beyond Decline: A Challenge to the Churches*, SCM Press 1988, ch. 2.

2. A notable example of this is the processes in the Board for Social Responsibility and General Synod surrounding the report *The Church and the Bomb*, Hodder & Stoughton 1982.

3. Geneva, World Council of Churches 1983.

4. The reprint used here is found in *Catholics and Nuclear War: A Commentary on 'The Challenge of Peace': The US Catholic Bishops' Letter on War and Peace*, ed. Philip J. Murnion, Geoffrey Chapman 1983.

5. The Report should be read in conjunction with: General Synod, *The Church and the Bomb*, (GS 542), CIO Publishing 1983.

6. See also in this connection 'Violence, Nonviolence and the Struggle for Social Change: Exploring Strategies for Radical Social Change', *Study Encounter*, VII, (1971), pp. 1–8; David M. Gill, *A Survey of Reactions to the Report of the Cardiff Consultation on 'Violence, Nonviolence and the Struggle for Social Justice'*, mimeographed, World Council of Churches, Church and Society Working Committee, Geneva 1973.

7. *BITL.*, p. 3.

8. *BITL.*, p. 383.

9. *BITL.*, p. 4.

10. *BITL.*, p. 5.

11. *BITL.*, p. 5.

12. *Public Policy and the Expert*, The Council on Religion and International Affairs, New York 1971, p. 69.

13. *Public Policy*, p. 70.

14. *Public Policy*, p. 108.

15. *BITL.*, p. 384.

16. James F. Dougherty, *The Bishops and Nuclear Weapons: The Catholic Pastoral Letter on War and Peace*, Archon Books, Hamden CT 1984, p. 119.

17. Dougherty, *The Bishops*, pp. 123f.
18. Murnion (ed.), *Catholics and Nuclear War*, p. ix.
19. Sandra M. Schneiders, in ibid., pp. 91–105.
20. *TCOP*, para. 55.
21. *TCOP*, Summary.
22. *TCOP*, para. 19.
23. J. Bryan Hehir, in *Catholics and Nuclear War*, p. 79.
24. Ibid., p. 80.
25. Dougherty, op. cit., p. 127.
26. *The Churches Survey their Task: The Report of the Conference at Oxford, July 1937, on Church, Community and State*, Allen & Unwin 1937, pp. 179–181.
27. Hollenbach, in *Catholics and Nuclear War*, p. 8.
28. Dougherty, op. cit., p. 135.
29. For this section see also *Report of Proceedings*, General Synod February Group of Sessions, Vol. 14, No. 1, CIO Publishing 1983, pp. 237–306.
30. *TCATB*, p. vii.
31. Ibid.
32. GS 414, Church Information Office 1979.
33. *TCATB*, p. vii.
34. *TCATB*, p. 73.
35. *TCOP*, para 258.
36. *TCATB*, p. 143.
37. See R. H. Preston, *Explorations in Theology 9*, SCM Press 1981, Ch. 3; Dennis P. McCann, in Thomas W. Ogletree (ed.), *The Annual of the Society of Christian Ethics, 1981*, Dallas 1981, pp. 73–96; Duncan B. Forrester, in Michael H. Taylor (ed.), *Christians and the Future of Social Democracy*, C. W. & A. Hesketh 1982, pp. 33–45.
38. Preston, op. cit., p. 40.
39. R. Deem, *Schooling for Women's Work*, Routledge & Kegan Paul 1980, p. 2.
40. *TCATB*, p. 125 (my italics). Cf., 'our concern is to find God's will in this given situation – the will of a God of whom it may not be said that He does certain things in general, but nothing in particular', in *The British Nuclear Deterrent*, SCM Press 1963, p. 12.
41. *VANV*, p. 1.
42. *VANV*, p. 3.
43. *VANV*, p. 23.
44. *VANV*, p. 25.
45. Appendix B, in 'The Preservation, Promotion and Renewal of Peace: A Memorandum of the Evangelical Church in Germany', *EKD Bulletin*, [1981].
46. Nancy Harstock, 'The Barracks Community in Western Political Thought: Prolegomena to a Feminist Critique of War and Politics', *Women's Studies International Forum*, vol. 5, 1982, p. 283.
47. Ibid., p. 286.
48. Jean Bethke Elshtain, 'Reflections on War and Political Discourse: Realism, Just War, and Feminism in a Nuclear Age', *Political Theory*, 13, 1985, p. 44.
49. Ibid., p. 45.
50. Ibid., p. 45.
51. Ibid., p. 45.
52. Ibid., pp. 45f.
53. Ibid., p. 48.

54. See note 5 above.
55. G. Weigel, *Tranquillitas Ordinis*, Oxford University Press 1987.
56. Ibid., p. 285.
57. Ibid., p. 284.
58. Ibid., pp. 280f.

8. Reflections on Love, Power and Justice

1. *The Challenge of Peace*, Catholic Truth Society and SPCK, 1983.
2. *Ethics and Defence*, Blackwell 1986.
3. The difficulties in the English language, which has only one word, love, to cover several Greek words, including *agape*, *philia*, and *eros*, is not relevant to the present discussion.
4. Job 31. 31ff; Ezek. 36.26f.
5. Matt. 18.21ff.
6. Phil. 2.11.
7. A good, modern, revisionist, treatment from a Lutheran background of the Two Kingdoms doctrine is K. H. Hertz (ed.), *Two Kingdoms and One World*, Augsburg 1976.
8. Jer. 2.8; 23.10.
9. E.g. Jer. 27.6; Isa. 45.1.
10. This understanding of God and his relation to human history is not, as already mentioned, argued in the Bible but is its most characteristic presupposition. It differs in some respects from a widely prevalent Christian doctrine of God arrived at when this biblical tradition met Greek metaphysics; and from some modern expressions of the doctrine influenced by process thought or analytical philosophy. All have their difficulties which are studied by philosophical theology. In the compass of this chapter I have remained within the first because (1) it is most characteristic of the biblical tradition and most characteristically reflected in Christian worship; (2) it underlies most recent Christian discussions of the theme; (3) it is in my view the least inadequate doctrine of God.
11. See, for example, the examination of the New Testament data in two recent Church of England reports, *Marriage, Divorce and the Church*, SPCK 1974, Appendix 1, and *Marriage and the Church's Task*, Church Information Office Publishing 1978, Appendix 2.
12. Col. 3. 18–24; Eph. 5.12–6.9; I Peter 2.11–3.12; and 5.1–5; Titus 2.1–3.2; I Tim. 2.1–6.19; I Clement 21.
13. See Geoffrey Nuttall, *Christian Pacifism in History*, Blackwell 1958.
14. The middle level is often referred to by the misleading term 'middle axioms'; I have examined their nature and status in *Church and Society in the Late Twentieth Century: The Economic and Political Task*, SCM Press 1983, Appendix 2.
15. The best treatment is still that of Emil Brunner in his *Das Gebot und die Ordnungen* 1932 (ET *The Divine Imperative* 1937). The concept goes back to pre-Reformation scholastic concepts of an hierarchy of sex and the family, economics and politics, but it was expressed in this way at the Reformation. Like all traditional Christian concepts it has been given a socially conservative interpretation. But this is a distortion. Other terms for the concept in this century have been orders of Objective Obligation (Troeltsch), Preservation (Künneth and at first in Bonhoeffer), Divine Patience (Thielicke), Provines

(Barth), and Mandates (later Bonhoeffer). On this theme see the chapter by Keith Clements.

16. Tillich, *Love, Power and Justice*, Oxford University Press 1954, p. 12.

17. *Summa Theologiae* 2a, 2ae, q. 40, arts 1–3.

18. Among many expositions of the just war doctrines, their history and current relevance, are Joan D. Tooke, *The Just War in Aquinas and Grotius*, SPCK 1965, and Paul Ramsey, *The Just War: Force and Political Responsibility*, Scribner's NY 1968. Its roots go back to Greek philosophy, and to the *lex talionis* in the Old Testament which was designed to set limits to the use of force.

19. Contrast the opinions of Rowan Williams (quoting Santoni) and Geoffrey Price in this volume.

20. Sydney Bailey takes a different view. In a letter to me he refers to the delayed radiation released by the explosion of a small nuclear bomb. 'The heat, blast and *prompt* radiation from a nuclear explosion are distributed in a rough circle, so that it is possible to direct them to a military target without harm to non-combatants. The *delayed* radiation, representing about ten per cent of the total yield, is dispersed in an elliptical pattern down wind from the point of explosion, and then sucked into the upper atmosphere and slowly descends again as fall-out. Although there are differences of scientific judgment about the precise effects of radiation, I think that all reputable scientists agree that it is always harmful even in small quantities. I have taken the line that there is no way that nuclear weapons can actually be used without violating Just War principles.' It is not quite clear to me that in all cases principles of discrimination and proportion will be violated.

21. Here I differ from Simon Maimela.

9. *Defence, Deterrence and the Taking of Life*

1. This chapter draws extensively on material previously published in 'Defence Policy, the Just War and the Intention to Deter', *Defense Analysis*, Vol. 3, 1987.

2. G. Berkeley, *A New Theory of Vision and Other Writings*, Dent 1960, p. 163, n. 1: 'One may make a great progress in *school ethics*, without ever being the wiser or better man for it, or knowing how to behave himself, in the affairs of life, more to the advantage of himself, or his neighbour, than he did before.'

3. See J. Finnis, *Fundamentals of Ethics*, Clarendon Press 1983; G. Grisez, *The Way of the Lord Jesus, I: Christian Moral Principles*, Franciscan Herald Press 1984; and G. J. Hughes, *Authority in Morals*, Sheed & Ward 1983. Two further names should be mentioned here: those of Elizabeth Anscombe and Peter Geach who have been influential in the development of analytical naturalist ethics and of first-order moral philosophy; see G. E. M. Anscombe, *Ethics, Religion and Politics: Collected Philosophical Papers, Vol. III*, Blackwell 1981; and P. Geach, *The Virtues*, Cambridge University Press 1977.

4. See G. J. Hughes, 'The Intention to Deter', in F. Bridger (ed.), *The Cross and the Bomb*, Mowbrays 1983; and J. Finnis, J. M. Boyle, Jr., and G. Grisez, *Nuclear Deterrence, Morality and Realism*, Clarendon Press 1987. The latter is to my knowledge the best, most comprehensive, extended treatment of the issues so far published. For an interesting discussion of it see G. J. Hughes 'Nuclear Deterrence, Morality and Realism', *The Heythrop Journal*, Vol. 29, 1988.

5. In the area of medical ethics, for example. See J. Haldane, 'Medical Ethics – An Alternative Approach', *Journal of Medical Ethics*, Vol. 12, No. 3, 1986.

6. Conditions 1–3 correspond to those elaborated by Aquinas in *Summa Theologiae*, 2a, 2ae, q. 40, art 1. The others also originate in scholastic moral theology. For a useful discussion of the tradition of the just war see J. Teichman, *Pacifism and the Just War*, Blackwell 1986. This includes extracts from several historically influential texts.

7. This said, any use of nuclear weapons may put non-combatant lives at risk either by prompting retaliatory countervalue attacks, or by virtue of the collateral effects of even counterforce exchanges. The dangers of escalation are authoritatively discussed by M. Bundy, G. Kennan, R. McNamara and G. Smith, 'Nuclear Weapons and the Atlantic Alliance', *Foreign Affairs*, Vol. 60, No. 4, 1982. On the various effects of nuclear attacks see *The Effects of Nuclear War*, Washington DC: Office of Technology Assessment 1979; and C. Sagan 'Nuclear War and Climate Catastrophe: Some Policy Implications', *Foreign Affairs*, Vol. 62, No. 2, 1983. These matters are interestingly examined and set within a moral context by J. Child, *Nuclear War: The Moral Dimension*, Transaction Books & Social Philosophy and Policy Center 1986. This latter is a clear, well-informed and well argued defence of deterrence as a legitimate policy option.

8. For further discussion of this see J. Haldane, 'Ethics and Biological Warfare', *Arms Control*, Vol. 8, No. 1, 1987.

9. In his contribution to the present volume ('What if Deterrence Fails?') General Sir Hugh Beach focusses on the issue of proportionality, i.e. the requirement that the costs of war (of individual operations and of the whole campaign) be proportionate to the goods achieved by it. But this focus gives insufficient attention to other essential factors. Considering the prospect of a strategic interchange involving an allied retaliatory strike on Minsk, the effects of which are 'many times worse' than those suffered by Birmingham in the initial Soviet attack, he comments: 'Most people would have no difficulty in determining the moral propriety of this action. The allied nuclear strike though undoubtedly indiscriminate is redeemed by being proportionate both in the sense of tit for tat but in the much more important sense that the good achieved (of stopping the war) far exceeds the damage inflicted horrifying though that is', see below, pp. 208f.

Setting aside questions about the greater violence of the retaliation and about 'tit for tat' justification, it is important to note that failure to satisfy one condition of *Jus de bello* is not something that can be 'redeemed' by satisfying another. Satisfaction of each requirement is individually necessary and only *jointly* sufficient for just war. Thus, the admission that a prospective attack is 'undoubtedly indiscriminate' is enough to condemn it. The matter is perhaps obscured by confusing a scenario of the type depicted with one familiar from the last war in which an attack directed upon a military target causes non-combatant deaths. Since the latter are foreseen but not intended one might justify such an attack by appeal to the principle of double effect (see Section V below). Here proportionality is relevant as it serves to restrict the scope of the principle. Collateral damage must be proportionate to the good secured. In the envisaged strategic interchange, however, both Soviet and Allied strikes are directed against non-combatants and thus are knowingly and intentionally indiscriminate. This renders them immoral. The contrary verdict, which Sir Hugh considers would be the judgment of most people and which he endorses, employs the idea of proportionality in a consequentialist fashion alien to its role in just war theory.

10. For an examination of Western retaliatory threats see Finnis et al., *Nuclear Deterrence, Morality and Realism*, op. cit., Part One, and for an interesting discussion of the British dimension see L. Freedman, 'British Nuclear Targetting', *Defense Analysis*, Vol. 1, No. 2, 1985.

11. John 18. 12–15.

12. Rom. 3. 5–21.

13. The problem touched on here is an ancient one which has greatly exercised both philosophers and theologians – none less so than those, such as the scholastics of the middle ages, who have belonged to both camps. For an account of the problem and of some mediaeval attempts to resolve it see J. Haldane. 'Voluntarism and Realism in Mediaeval Ethics', *Journal of Medical Ethics*, Vol. 15, No. 1, 1989.

14. This thought is as ancient as Aristotle, as is the general framework of action theory employed in this section. In the *Nicomachean Ethics*, 1107a 10–25, Aristotle wirtes: '[some actions and passions] imply by their names that they are themselves bad . . . It is not possible, then, ever to be right with regard to them: one must always be wrong.'

15. See General Sir Hugh Beach, 'What if Deterrence Fails?' below pp. 197f for a clear elaboration of this point.

16. The question of the possession of nuclear weapons in circumstances where the power to which they belong disavows any intention of ever using them – even in retaliation – raises a number of interesting and important issues. The idea that the mere retention of weapons may be morally justified if it is accompanied by the active pursuit of multilateral disarmament, in which process the weapons are discarded only as and when others also disarm, has found favour among philosophers and theologians who are otherwise opposed to nuclear defence policies on grounds similar to those presented above. See, for example, Anthony Kenny, 'The Logic and Ethics of Nuclear Deterrence', in A. Ellis (ed.), *Ethics and International Relations*, Manchester University Press in association with the Fulbright Commission 1986 pp. 92–105 – for responses to Kenny by Sir Arthur Hockaday and others see the following pages 105–112. Support for similar positions has been voiced by several Roman Catholic Church leaders including Pope John Paul II in his message to the Second Session of the UN General Assembly Devoted to Disarmament (1982), Cardinal Basil Hume 'Towards a Nuclear Morality', *The Times*, 17 November 1983, and Cardinal John Krol in his testimony to the Senate Foreign Relations Committee on behalf of the US Catholic Conference, *Origins* 1979, pp. 195–9.

So far as concerns the morality of 'possession without intention' it is liable to objection on grounds additional to the broadly consequentialist ones indicated above. The advocate of mere retention hopes to evade the charge of immorality by disavowing even conditional intentions of use while still securing the deterrent benefits of possession. For potential aggressors are likely to continue to be dissuaded from risking an attack since, notwithstanding all one's declarations and sincere intentions, it remains a possibility that the weapons may yet be used – either because of a change of heart, or because of a change of leadership.

Certainly, weapons retained after public disavowals of intentions of use may continue to deter but this casts doubts upon the scope of such declarations. To remain an effective threat a nuclear arsenal needs to be maintained and updated. Instruction in its possible use must also continue. Thus, to preserve the threat by which deterrence is secured, a power must go on threatening potential aggressors by continuing to operate a system designed to destroy centres of population. Given this, countenancing anything but the very briefest period of retention following disavowal undermines the claim to have abandoned completely any intention of ever using the system and thereby renders a practitioner of this policy liable to the charge of persisting in his murderous intent.

17. An excellent presentation of this line of argument is given by G. J. Hughes in 'The Intention to Deter', op. cit. For a short discussion of this and of a recent attempt to defend the possibility of deterrence by mere bluff see J. Haldane, 'The Morality of Deterrence', *The Heythrop Journal*, Vol. 26, No. 1, 1985. My criticisms of the latter are themselves challenged in J. Thomas, 'A Comment on Dr John J. Haldane's Article', same issue of *The Heythrop Journal*. On the ethics of intention with regard to defence see G. Kavka, *Moral Paradoxes of Nuclear Deterrence* Cambridge University Press 1988, especially Chs. 1 and 2.

18. See G. J. Hughes, 'The Intention to Deter', pp. 32–34.

10.   Risk Decisions and Moral Values

1. Nicholas A. Simms (ed.), *Explorations in Ethics and International Relations*, Croom Helm 1981, p. 97.

2. Cf. Harry Otway, 'The Perception of Technological Risks: a Psychological Perspective', in M. Dierkes, S. Edwards and R. Coppock (eds.), *Technological Risk*, Oelgeschaler, Gunn and Hann, Massachusetts 1980, pp. 35–44.

3. For a critical discussion of this see, W. D. Hudson, *Modern Moral Philosophy*, second edition, Macmillan 1983, pp. 266–277.

4. I. Kant, *Groundwork of the Metaphysic of Morals*, trans. H. J. Paton, Harper Torchbooks 1964, p. 83.

5. Thomas Aquinas, *Summa Theologiae*, 2. 2. q. 47, art 3.

6. Ibid.

7. Ibid., art 4.

8. H. McCabe, 'Aquinas on Good Sense', *New Blackfriars*, October 1986, p. 431.

9. A. MacIntyre, *After Virtue*, Duckworth 1981, pp. 49–59.

10. Ian Clark, *Limited Nuclear War*, Martin Robertson 1982, p. 239.

11. Nicholas Rescher, *Risk*, University Press of America 1983, p. 73.

12. Baruch Fischoff, et al. (eds.), *Acceptable Risk*, Cambridge University Press 1981, p. 37.

13. It may also jeopardize 'extended deterrence'; i.e. its linkage between US and European security.

14. Rob Coppock, 'A Synopsis of Discussion and Suggestions for Further Action', in M. Dierkes, S. Edwards and R. Coppock (eds.), *Technological Risk*, p. 134.

15. Roger E. Kasperson and Murdo Morrison, 'A Proposal for International Risk Management Research', in C. Hohenemser, and J. X. Kasperson (eds.), *Risk in Technological Society*, Westview Press 1982, pp. 303–331.

11.   The Ethics of SDI

1. The relevant parts of the text are printed in Robert M. Bowman, *Star Wars. A Defense Expert's Case Against the Strategic Defense Initiative*, Los Angeles 1986, pp. 131–133. This is a most valuable book, by a supporter of some aspects of classical deterrence doctrine, and I am much indebted to it. For discussion of political, strategic and technical problems with SDI, see also E. P. Thompson (ed.), *Star Wars*, Penguin Books 1985. I also gratefully acknowledge the profit I have had from the discussion of some of the issues here touched on with my colleague Oliver O'Donovan, and from unpublished lectures of his on the ethics of deterrence.

2. Bowman, op. cit., p. 133.

3. Article II of the Treaty; text in Bowman, op. cit., p. 119.

4. Bowman, op. cit., p. 8; cf. pp. 10–11.

5. Ibid., p. 73.

6. Ibid., p. 82.

7. Ibid., p. 31.

8. Freeman Dyson, *Weapons and Hope*, New York, 1984, p. 70.

9. Bowman, op. cit., Ch. 2.

10. Ibid., p. 132.

11. Paul Abrecht and Ninan Koshy (eds.), *Before It's Too Late. The Challenge of Nuclear Disarmament* (the record of the WCC Hearing), Geneva 1983, p. 124. Calogero's submission (pp. 120–128) is entitled 'Advanced Weapons Technology and the Obsolescence of Military Strategy'.

12. Ronald E. Santoni, '"Just War" and Nuclear Reality', *Philosophy Today*, Fall 1985 (pp. 175–190), p. 190, n. 9, on the area of devastation (1000 sq. miles) from one megaton bomb. This essay is an important challenge to the idea that *any* form of just war theory is applicable in the nuclear age to international conflict.

13. Ibid., p. 186.

14. Abrecht and Koshy (above, n. 11), p. 109. Ruina is Professor of Electrical Engineering and Computer Science at MIT and a former director of weapons research for the US Department of Defence; his paper is on 'Military Research and Development in the Arms Race' (pp. 103–111).

15. Ibid., pp. 106–7.

16. Dietrich Ritschl, 'Zur Logik der Friedenssicherung. Eine Theologische Position' (a lecture given to general audiences in Mainz and Heidelberg in 1984), *Konzepte. Ökumene, Medizin, Ethik: Gesammelte Aufsätze*, Munich 1986 (pp. 334–351), p. 347.

17. Laurence Martin, *Minimum Deterrence* (Faraday Discussion Paper No. 8), Council for Arms Control 1987, p. 3.

18. Quoted in Peter Walker (Bishop of Ely), *Power Unlimited and Exclusive. Nuclear Arms and the Vision of George Bell*, Cambridge, Christian CND, p. 11.

19. Bowman, op. cit., pp. 90–93.

20. *Weapons and Hope*, Chs 6 and 7.

21. On the technical problems of such a system operated by the US against the USSR, see Bowman, ch. 2, esp. pp. 18–23.

22. Barrie Paskins, 'Prohibitions, Restraints and Scientists', in Nicholas A. Simms (ed.), *Explorations in Ethics and International Relations*, Croom Helm 1981, (pp. 68–83) p. 79.

23. *Weapons and Hope*, p. 84.

24. *Weapons and Hope*, p. 55.

12.   *International Society, International Law and the Common Good*

1. *North-South: A Programme for Survival*, Pan Books 1980, and *Common Crisis – North-South: Cooperation for World Recovery*, Pan Books 1983; *Common Security: A Programme for Disarmament*, Pan Books 1982.
2. Cf. the intercession in the service of Holy Communion: 'that men may honour one another and seek the common good'.
3. Clements, above p. 70.
4. F. L. Schuman, *International Politics*, 4th ed. 1948, p. vii.
5. Paraphrased by G. Schwarzenberger, *The Frontiers of International Law*, Stevens 1962, p. 10, citing also Spinoza: 'the natural right of every individual is only determined by his power', *Tractatus Theologico – Politicus* (1670), ch. 16.
6. Schwarzenberger, op. cit., p. 11.
7. Ch. de Visscher, *Theory and Reality in Public International Law*, originally published in French, 1953. English trans. by P. E. Corbett, Princeton University Press 1957, p. 71.
8. Ibid., p. 74.
9. Ibid.
10. G. Schwarzenberger, *Power Politics: A Study of World Society* (hereinafter *Power Politics*) Stevens, 3rd ed. 1964, p. 500.
11. See *inter alia* J. Schell, *The Abolition*, Picador 1984, p. 104, and J. L. Gaddis, *The Long Peace: Inquiries into the History of the Cold War*, (hereinafter *The Long Peace*) Oxford University Press 1987, p. 237ff.
12. *Power Politics*, p. 553.
13. USSR and United States: Treaty on the Elimination of Their Intermediate Range and Shorter-Range Missiles, signed at Washington, 8 December 1987; text in 27 *International Legal Materials* (1988) p. 90, together with Protocol on Elimination (p. 183) and Protocol on Inspection (p. 190). The same issue of *International Legal Materials* contains the text of the US-USSR Agreement on the establishment of Nuclear Risk Reduction Centers (p. 78) which builds upon the 1971 Agreement on Measures to Reduce the Risk of Outbreak of Nuclear War between the two countries.
14. HMSO, HC 280 (1987–88); *The Times*, 5 August 1988. FCO reply, Cd. 476(1987).
15. See R. Higgins, *Conflict of Interests: International Law in a Divided World*, Bodley Head 1965, for earlier examples, including 'Relations between Christian and Non-Christian States' pp. 9–45.
16. UN Charter, Arts. 2(1), 2(3) and 2(4).
17. *Case Concerning Military and Paramilitary Activities In and Against Nicaragua* (Nicaragua v United States of America), Merits, *ICJ Reports 1986* pp. 94, 102–106, 119–122. Cf. the views of Judge Schwebel, Dissenting Opinion, pp. 347–348, 352–377, and Judge Sir Robert Jennings, Dissenting Opinion, pp. 530–531, 542–546. Judge Schwebel is a US national and Judge Jennings is British.
18. See *inter alia* G. Schwarzenberger, *The Legality of Nuclear Weapons*, Stevens 1958; Tony Carty, Chs 6 and 7 in *Ethics and Defence: Power and Responsibility in the Nuclear Age*, ed. Howard Davis, Blackwell 1986, and B. A. Wortley, 'Observations on the Revision of the 1949 Geneva "Red Cross" Conventions', 54 *British Year Book of Internationa 1 Law* (1983) p. 143, pp. 154–162.
19. For the contrary argument, made in full terms from the natural law

standpoint see, above all, E. B. F. Midgeley, *The Natural Law Tradition and the Theory of International Relations*, P. Elek 1975, especially pp. 393–426.

20. G. Schwarzenberger, *The Dynamics of International Law*, Professional Books 1976, pp. 68–71, 74.

21. Gen. Ass. Resolution 2625 (XXV), Declaration on Principles of International Law concerning Friendly Relations and Co-operation Among States in Accordance with the Charter of the United Nations, principle of sovereign equality of States, element (f): 'Each State has the duty to comply fully and in good faith with its international obligations and to live in peace with other states.'

22. See in particular the Helsinki Final Act 1975 adopted at the Conference on Security and Cooperation in Europe (CSCE). Text in Cmnd. 6932 and in 14 *International Legal Materials* (1975) p. 1293. See G. White, 'East-West Détente and International Law: Language and Substance'. 2, *Manchester Memoirs* (1981–82) New Series (Manchester Literary and Philosophical Society), pp. 5–23.

There have been several follow-up meetings of the CSCE; the third such Conference began in Vienna in Nov. 1986 and continues at this writing. See *Keesing's Record of World Events*, Vol. XXXIV, 1988, p. 35737.

23. Theodore Meron 'Teaching Human Rights', *Human Rights in International Law: Legal and Policy Issues*, ed. Meron, Clarendon Press, Oxford 1985, p. 17.

24. *The Times*, 24 May 1988. In a recent review of K. Grzybowski's *Soviet International Law and the World Economic Order* (Duke University Press 1987) Dominik Lasok reminds us that 'despite the adherence to the Helsinki Agreement no international control over the administration of human rights is acceptable to Soviet legislation or jurisprudence', 37, *International and Comparative Law Quarterly*, 1988, p. 734.

25. Esther R. Cohen, *Human Rights in the Israeli-occupied Territories 1967–1982*, Manchester University Press 1986, pp. xvi–xvii, 284–289.

26. See G. I. Tunkin, *Theory of International Law*, trans. William E. Butler, Allen & Unwin 1974, passim but particularly pp. 49–86, 246–248.

27. In his recent analysis, *The Soviet Study of International Relations*, Cambridge University Press 1987, A. Lynch observes that a major factor producing uncertainty for the Soviet leaders is the evolution of China 'from ally to ideological, political and ultimately security threat "to the general growth of the might and influence of the socialist community".' (p. 100). He concludes that Soviet denials that China can be considered a superpower and that the global military balance remains bipolar, 'though plausible, hardly conceal Soviet anxiety about the prospect of Sino-American politico-strategic collaboration'. Ibid.

On China's approach to international law see Jerome A. Cohen, *China's Practice of International Law: Some Case Studies*, Harvard University Press 1972; Cohen and Hungdah Chiu, *People's China and International Law: A Documentary Study*, Princeton University Press 1974, and Jeanette Greenfield, *China and the Law of the Sea, Air and Environment*, Sijthoff and Noordhoff 1979.

28. Texts of all the 1972 Agreement reprinted in 11 *International Legal Materials*, 1972, pp. 756, 784, 791 and 796. See Julie Dahlitz, *Nuclear Arms Control*, Allen & Unwin 1983, pp. 20–21, 29–31, 148–151 and Palme Report (1982) pp. 120–126, 134–137.

29. Unhappily, the permanent members were unable or unwilling (which often are indistinguishable) to take any action to prevent the terrible war

between Iraq and Iran which began in 1980 and may at last be coming to a negotiated end. The five states are taking public credit for their unanimity in adopting S C res. 598 in July 1987, which to some extent has paved the way for the ceasefire taking effect at the time of this writing.

30. Although there are corresponding bilateral agreements between the UK and the USSR, at least on 'hot line' and on measures to prevent incidents on and over the high seas. The US/Soviet 'high seas incidents' agreement 1972 is reprinted in 11, *International Legal Materials* 1972, p. 778. The corresponding agreement with the UK is Cm. 57 UKTS No. 5 (1987).

31. 27 *International Legal Materials*, 1988, p. 76.

32. 'High seas incidents' agreement, see note 30 above. The 'notification' agreement is the Agreement on Measures to Reduce the Risk of Outbreak of Nuclear War, 10 *International Legal Materials*, 1971, p. 1173.

33. As well as the full text 27 *International Legal Materials* 1988, includes an article-by-article analysis by the US Department of State, p. 199.

34. J. Dahlitz, op. cit., n. 28 above, opines that these clauses 'can be attributed to a realistic appraisal of the difficulties involved in attempting to coerce a State to adhere to a treaty after a decision has been made by it to withdraw' (p. 17).

35. Six months notice is required. Art. XV (2).

36. See Arts. XI-XIII in particular and US Department of State analysis, 27 *International Legal Materials*, 1988, pp. 95–97, 218–222.

37. Verification of previous bilateral agreements on nuclear arms limitation has been by 'national technical means', principally satellite observation. See J. Dahlitz op. cit., pp. 21, 164–165, 187–191.

38. See e.g. references to work by S. Bastid (France) and M. Bartos (Yugoslavia) in G. I. Tunkin, op. cit., n. 26 above, p. 74.

39. Raymond Aron, *The Great Debate*, Anchor Books 1965, p. 7.

40. Gaddis, op. cit., n. 11 above, p. 238.

41. E.g. in particular Paul Keal, *Unspoken Rules and Superpower Dominance*, Macmillan 1983 on spheres of influence, A. Lynch, op. cit., n. 27 above, passim, M. P. Gehlen, *The Politics of Coexistence: Soviet Methods and Motives*, Indiana University Press 1967.

42. Gaddis, op. cit., p. 238.

43. Res. 1962 (XVIII).

44. W. A. McDougall, *The Heavens and the Earth: A Political History of the Space Age*, Basic Books 1985, p. 274.

45. R. A. Falk, 'The interplay of Westphalia and Charter conceptions of international legal order', *The Future of the International Legal Order*, vol. 1, ed. R. A. Falk and C. E. Black, Princeton University Press 1969, p. 34. Falk's argument, contained in several writings, is summarized by Keal, op. cit., n. 41 above, pp. 190–191.

46. *Power Politics*, (1964), p. 507.

47. Ibid., p. 535.

48. W. E. Butler, 'Anglo-American Research on Soviet Approaches to Public   International Law', *International Law in Comparative Perspective*, ed. W. E. Butler, Sijthoff and Noordhoff 1980, p. 178.

49. Ibid.

50. Trevor Huddleston, *The True and Living God*, Fontana 1964, p. 50.

13. *International Humanitarian Law and the Nürenberg Principles*

1. Pierre Boissier, *From Solferino to Tsushima*, Geneva, Henri Dunant Institut 1985, pp. 58, 74, 80.

2. Ibid., pp. 353–5.

3. G. P. Gooch and H. Temperley, *British Documents on the Origins of the War, 1898–1914*, HMSO vol. 1, 1927, p. 226.

4. F. W. Holls, *The Peace Conference at the Hague and its bearing on international law and policy*, Macmillan 1900, p. 143.

5. *Trial of the Major War Criminals before the International Military Tribunal, Nürnberg*, International Military Tribunal Secretariat 1947, vol. I, pp. 253–4.

6. International Court of Justice Reports, 1986, para. 218.

7. Article 26 of the Regulations annexed to the Hague Conventions.

8. *International Law – The Conduct of Armed Conflict and Air Operations*, Washington DC, Department of the Air Force 1976 (pamphlet 110–31), para. 15–3.

9. General Assembly resolution 95(I), 11 December 1946.

10. General Assembly Official Records, 5th session, Supplement no. 12, A/1316, para. 99.

11. Convention I (wounded and sick on land), Arts. 49–54; Convention II (wounded, sick, and shipwrecked at sea), Arts. 50–3; Convention III (POWs), Arts. 129–32; Convention IV (civilians under occupation), Arts. 146–9; Protocol I (international conflicts), Arts. 85–91.

12. Art. 85(5).

13. Art. 87.

14. Pakistan eventually requested the Court to discontinue the proceedings.

15. General Assembly Official Records, 4th session, Supplement no. 10, A/925, para, 18.

16. General Assembly resolution 489(V), 12 Dec. 1950.

17. General Assembly resolution 3314(XXIX), 14 Dec. 1974.

18. General Assembly resolution 36/106, 10 Dec. 1981.

19. General Assembly resolution 177(II), 21 Nov. 1947.

20. General Assembly Official Records, 9th session, Supplement no. 9, A/2683, chapter III, para. 54.

21. UN docs. A/CN.4/364, A/CN.4/377 and Corr.1, A/CN.4/387, A/CN.4/398 and Corr.1–3.

22. General Assembly Official Records, 38th session, Supplement no. 10 (A/38/10), paras. 26–69; 29th session, Supplement no. 10 (A/39/10), paras. 10–65; 40th session, Supplement no. 10 (A/40/10), paras.11–101; 41st session, Supplement no. 10 (A/41/10), paras.66–185; 42nd session, Supplement no. 10 (A/42/10), paras. 471–667; 43rd session, Supplement no. 10 (A/43/10), paras. 192–280.

23. General Assembly resolution 1653(XVI), 24 Nov. 1961.

24. UN doc. A/39/644, 9 Nov. 1984.

25. FM27–10, 1956, para. 35.

26. Para. 113.

27. Frits Kalshoven, *Belligerent Reprisals*, Leyden, Sijthoff 1971, pp. 375, 377.

28. *The Red Cross as a Factor in World Peace*, Geneva, International Committee of the Red Cross, 1968, p. 9.

29. 'The Protocols additional to the Geneva Conventions: a quest for

universality', *International Review of the Red Cross*, no. 258, May–June 1987, p. 245.

14.   *What if Deterrence Fails?*

1. Leonard Cheshire, *The Light of Many Suns*, Methuen 1985, p. 32.
2. See above Chapter 9, page 134.
3. David Fisher, *Morality and the Bomb*, Croom Helm 1985, p. 90.
4. William V. O'Brien and John Langan SJ, *The Nuclear Dilemma and the Just War Tradition*, Lexington Books, D. C. Heath and Co. 1986, p. 165.
5. Herbert Butterfield, *Christianity and History*, Fontana Books 1949, pp. 178–9.
6. General Sir John Hackett, *The Third World War August 1985*, Sidgwick & Jackson 1978.
7. O'Brien and Langan, op. cit., p. 182.
8. *The Church and the Bomb, the general synod debate*, CIO Publishing 1983.
9. Message of His Holiness Pope John Paul II to the Second Session of the Un General Assembly, New York, 11 June 1982.

Bibliography

This is a bibliography of recent work, not on all aspects of the nuclear weapons debate, but specifically on the theological and ethical issues in the debate. Although some significant older works have been included, the emphasis is on literature published since 1982. It is hoped that this bibliography will prove useful for further research in this field.

Books

Abrecht, P. and Koshy, N. (eds.), *Before it's Too Late: the challenge of nuclear disarmament*, Geneva: World Council of Churches 1983.

Anders, G., *Die atomare Drohung*, Munich 1983.

Aukerman, D., *Darkening Valley: A Biblical Perspective on Nuclear War*, New York: Seabury Press 1981.

Barclay, O. R. (ed.), *Pacifism and War*, Inter-Varsity Press 1984.

Barrs, J., *Who are the Peacemakers? The Christian Case for Nuclear Deterrence*, Westchester, Illinois, Crossway Books 1983.

Blake, N. and Pole, K. (ed.), *Dangers of Deterrence: Philosophers on Nuclear Strategy*, Routledge & Kegan Paul 1983.

Bridger, F. (ed.), *The Cross and the Bomb*, Mowbray 1983.

British Council of Churches, *Christians and Atomic War*, BCC 1959.

British Council of Churches, *The British Nuclear Deterrent*, BCC 1963.

British Council of Churches, *The Valley of Decision: The Christian dilemma in the nuclear age*, BCC 1964.

Ceadal, M., *Thinking about Peace and War*, Oxford University Press 1987.

Chapman, G. Clarke, *Facing the Nuclear Heresy: A Call to Reformation*, Elgin, Illinois, Brethren Press 1986.

Chernus, I., *Dr Strangegod: On the Symbolic Meaning of Nuclear Weapons*, Columbia: South Carolina: University of South Carolina Press 1986.

Child, J., *Nuclear War: The Moral Dimension*, Transaction Books/Social Philosophy and Policy Centre 1986.

[Church of England] *Peacemaking in a Nuclear Age: A report of a Working Party of the Board for Social Responsibility of the General Synod of the Church of England*, Church House Publishing 1988.

[Church of England] *The Church and the Bomb: Nuclear Weapons and Christian Conscience*, Hodder & Stoughton/CIO Publishing 1982.

Curry, D. C. (ed.), *Evangelicals and the Bishops' Pastoral Letter*, Grand Rapids, Michigan: Eerdmans 1984.

Davies, D. R., *Theology and the Atomic Age*, London: Latimer House 1947.

Davis, H. (ed.), *Ethics and Defence: Power and Responsibility in the Nuclear Age*, Blackwell 1986.

Donaghy, J. (ed.), *To Proclaim Peace: Religious Communities Speak Out on the Arms Race*, Nyack, New York: Fellowship of Reconciliation 1983.

Ellis, A. (ed.), *Ethics and International Relations*, Manchester University Press 1986.

Fenton, I. (ed.), *The Psychology of Nuclear Conflict*, Coventure 1986.

Finnis, J., Boyle, J. M. and Grisez G., *Nuclear Deterrence, Morality and Realism*, Clarendon Press 1987.

Ford, H. and Winters, F. X. (eds.), *Ethics and Nuclear Strategy*, New York: Orbis 1972.

Garrison, J., *The Darkness of God: Theology after Hiroshima*, SCM Press 1982.

Gill, R., *The Cross Against the Bomb*, Epworth 1984.

Gladwin, J. (ed.), *Dropping the Bomb*, Hodder & Stoughton 1985.

Goodwin, G. (ed.), *Ethics and Nuclear Deterrence*, Croom Helm 1982.

Goudzwaard, B., *Idols of our Time*, Downers Grove, Illinois: Inter-Varsity Press 1984.

Grinspoon, L. (ed.), *The Long Darkness: Psychological and Moral Perspectives on Nuclear Winter*, Yale University Press 1986.

Harries, R. (ed.), *What Hope in an Armed World?* Pickering & Inglis 1982.

Hauerwas, S., *Should War Be Eliminated? Philosophical and Theological Investigations*, Milwaukee: Marquette University Press 1984.

Heyer, R. (ed.), *Nuclear Disarmament: Key Statements*, Ramsay, New Jersey: Paulist Press 1982.

Hollenbach, D., *Nuclear Ethics: A Christian Moral Argument*, New York: Paulist Press 1983.

Johnson, J. T., *The Quest for Peace: three moral traditions in Western cultural history*, Princeton University Press 1987.

Kaufman, G. D., *Theology for a Nuclear Age*, Manchester University Press 1985.

Kavka, G., *Moral Paradoxes of Nuclear Deterrence*, Cambridge University Press 1988.

Kenny, A., *The Logic of Deterrence*, Firethorn Press 1985.

Kirk, A. (ed.), *Handling Problems of Peace and War: An Evangelical Debate*, Marshall Pickering 1988.

Knox, R., *God and the Atom*, Sheed & Ward 1945.

Küng, H. and Moltmann, J. (eds.), *A Council for Peace*, T. & T. Clark 1988 (= *Concilium* 195).

Mackinnon, D. M., *Creon and Antigone: ethical problems of nuclear warfare*, Menard Press, 1982; reprinted as chapter 8 of *Themes in Theology: The Three-Fold Cord*, T. &. T. Clark 1987.

Macquarrie, J., *The Concept of Peace*, SCM Press 1973.

Martin, D. and Mullen P. (eds.), *Unholy Warfare*, Blackwell 1983.

Mills-Powell, D. (ed.), *Decide for Peace: Evangelicals and the Bomb*, Marshall Pickering 1986.

Mills-Powell, M., *Praying in the Shadow of the Bomb*, Grove Books 1984.

Murnion, P. J. (ed.), *Catholics and Nuclear War: A Commentary on 'The*

Challenge of Peace': The US Catholic Bishops' Pastoral Letter on War and Peace, Geoffrey Chapman 1983.

O'Mahony, P. J., *Swords and Ploughshares: Can man live and progress with a technology of death?,* Sheed & Ward 1986.

Paskins, B. and Dockrill, M., *Ethics of War,* Duckworth 1979.

Phipps, J. F., *Time and the Bomb,* Oxford: Pica Press 1982.

Race, A. (ed.), *Theology against the Nuclear Horizon,* SCM Press 1988.

Rowe, D., *Living with the Bomb,* Routledge & Kegan Paul 1985.

Ruston, R., *Nuclear Deterrence – Right or Wrong?,* Catholic Information Services 1981.

Schell, J., *The Fate of the Earth,* Pan 1982.

Senior, D. and Pawlikowski, J. (eds.), *The Way to Peace: Theological and Biblical Reflections on the Bishops' Pastoral on Nuclear War and Peace,* Wilmington, Delaware: Michael Glazier 1984.

Shannon, T. A. (ed.), *War or Peace? The Search for New Answers,* Maryknoll, New York: Orbis 1980.

Sider, R. and Taylor, R., *Nuclear Holocaust and Christian Hope,* Hodder & Stoughton 1982.

Solms, F. and Reuver, M., *Churches as Peacemakers?,* Rome: IDOC International 1985.

Sterba, J. (ed.), *The Ethics of War and Nuclear Deterrence,* Belmont, California: Wadsworth 1985.

Stein, W. (ed.), *Nuclear Weapons and Christian Conscience,* Merlin Press 1961.

Stein, W. (ed.), *Peace on Earth: The Way Ahead,* Sheed & Ward 1966.

Teichman, J., *Pacifism and the Just War,* Blackwell 1986.

Thompson, C. S., *Morals and Missiles,* James Clarke 1959.

US Catholic Bishops, *The Challenge of Peace: God's Promise and Our Response,* CTS/SPCK 1983.

Vincent, J. J., *Christ in a Nuclear World,* Manchester: Crux 1961.

Vogel, H., *Um die Zukunft des Menschen im atomaren Zeitalter,* Berlin: Lettner 1960.

Wallis, J. (ed.), *Waging Peace,* New York: Harper & Row 1982.

Walzer, M., *Just and Unjust Wars: A Moral Argument with Historical Illustrations,* Allen Lane 1978, Penguin 1980.

Weart, S. R., *Nuclear Fear: A history of images,* Harvard University Press 1988.

Williams, R. D., *The Truce of God,* Collins (Fount) 1983.

Wyshogrod, E., *Spirit in Ashes: Hegel, Heidegger, and Man-Made Mass Death,* Yale University Press 1985.

Articles

Aagaard, A. M., 'Apocalypse Now' – Spirituality in the 80s', *Studia Theologica* 35, 1981, pp. 145–155.

Bailey, S., 'Nuclear Deterrence: A Reply to Michael Quinlan', *Modern Churchman* 27/3, 1985, pp. 22–28.

Baker, J. A., 'Theology and Nuclear Weapons', *King's Theological Review* 6, 1983, pp. 1–4 (with reply by U. Simon: ibid., 7, 1984, pp. 21–22).

Bauckham, R. J., 'The Genesis Flood and the Nuclear Holocaust', *Churchman* 99, 1985, pp. 146–155.

Bauckham, R. J., 'Theology after Hiroshima', *Scottish Journal of Theology* 38, 1986, pp. 583–601.

Chapman, G. Clarke, 'American Theology in the Shadow of the Bomb', *Union Seminary Quarterly Review* 41, 1987, pp. 25–38.

Chapman, G. Clarke, 'Amerikanische Theologie im Schatten der Bombe', *Evangelische Theologie* 47, 1987, pp. 32–49. (German version of the preceding item)

Chapman, G. Clarke, 'Approaching Nuclearism as a Heresy: Four Paradigms', *Union Seminary Quarterly Review* 39, 1984, pp. 255–268.

Chapman, G. Clarke, 'The Ideology of Deterrence and Nuclearism', *Concilium* 195 (1/1988) = *A Council for Peace*, ed. H. Küng and J. Moltmann, T. & T. Clark 1988, pp. 89–94.

Chernus, I., 'Mythologies of Nuclear War', *Journal of the American Academy of Religion* 50, 1982, pp. 255–273.

Chernus, I., 'Paul Tillich: Depth Dimension of the Nuclear Age', *Union Seminary Quarterly Review* 41, 1987, pp. 1–24.

Chernus, I., 'War and Myth: "The Show Must Go On",' *Journal of the American Academy of Religion* 53, 1985, pp. 449–464.

Clifford, M., 'Narcissism, "Nuclearism," and "Inner Infanticide": Psychoanalytic Perspectives on the Idea of the Child in the Nuclear Age', *Union Seminary Quarterly Review* 38, 1983, pp. 35–73.

Connolly, J. R., 'The Morality of Nuclear Deterrence: Conditional or Unconditional?', *Irish Theological Quarterly* 54, 1988, pp. 1–20.

Downey, M., 'Worship between the Holocausts', *Theology Today* 43, 1986, pp. 75–87.

Dwyer, J. A., 'Catholic Thought on Nuclear Weapons: A Review of the Literature', *Religious Studies Review* 10, 1984, pp. 103–106.

Eaton, J. E., 'Moral Apologetics and the Nuclear Dilemma', *Union Seminary Quarterly Review* 41, 1987, pp. 33–44.

Good, R. M., 'Just War in Ancient Israel', *Journal of Biblical Literature* 104, 1985, pp. 385–400.

Haldane, J. J., 'The Morality of Deterrence', *Heythrop Journal* 26, 1985, pp. 41–46 (with J. Thomas, 'A Comment . . . ' pp. 46–47).

Hanna, M., 'From Civil Religion to Prophetic Church: American Bishops and the Bomb', *Humanities in Society* 6, 1983, pp. 41–51.

Harcourt-Norton, C., 'Theology under the Mushroom Cloud', *Colloquium* 17, 1985, pp. 55–61.

Hauerwas, S., 'An eschatological perspective on nuclear disarmament', in *Against the Nations: War and Survival in a Liberal Society*, Minneapolis, Minnesota: Seabury Press 1985, pp. 160–168.

Hauerwas, S., 'The nonresistant Church: the theological ethics of John

Howard Yoder', in *Vision and Virtue: Essays in critical ethical reflection*, Notre Dame: Fides 1974, pp. 197–221.

Hellwig, M. K., 'Soteriology in the Nuclear Age', *Thomist* 48, 1984, pp. 634–644.

Herzog, K., 'Die friedfertige Frau? Theologische Perspektiven zum Thema Frauen, Krieg und Frieden', *Evangelische Theologie* 47, 1987, pp. 60–82.

Higgins, J., 'Moral Aspects of Nuclear Deterrence, II', *Downside Review* 103, 1985, pp. 299–317.

Hoekema, D. A., 'Protestant Statements on Nuclear Disarmament', *Religious Studies Review* 10, 1984, pp. 97 ff.

Hollenbach, D., 'War and Peace in American Catholic Thought: A Heritage Abandoned?', *Theological Studies* 48, 1987, pp. 711–726.

Honecker, M., 'Die Diskussion um den Frieden 1981–83', *Theologische Rundschau* 49, 1984, pp. 372 ff.

Hordern, R. P., 'The Gospel of Peace: Theological Reflections in the Nuclear Age', *Union Seminary Quarterly Review* 39, 1984, pp. 115–128.

Hughes, G. J., 'Nuclear Deterrence, Morality and Realism', *Heythrop Journal* 29, 1988.

Jewett, R., 'Coming to terms with the doom boom', *Quarterly Review* 4, 1984, pp. 9–22.

Johnson, J. T., 'Historical Tradition and Moral Judgment: The Case of Just War Tradition', *Journal of Religion* 64, 1984, pp. 299–317.

Jung, L. S., 'Nuclear Eschatology', *Theology Today* 40, 1983, pp. 184–194.

Kaufman, G. D., 'Nuclear Eschatology and the Study of Religion', *Journal of the American Academy of Religion* 51, 1983, pp. 3–14.

Kibble, D. G., 'A Theology for the Nuclear Debate', *Churchman* 99, 1985, pp. 41–50.

Lakeland, P., 'God in the Nuclear Age', *Month* 17, April 1984, pp. 119–23.

Langan, J., 'The American Hierarchy and Nuclear Weapons', *Theological Studies* 43, 1982, pp. 447–467.

Lewis, H. D., 'The Sword of Damocles or Christ?', *Theology* 87, 1984, pp. 3–6.

McDonald, J. I. H., 'Towards a Theology of Peace', in *Theology and Practice* ed. D. Forrester, Ormskirk and Northridge: Hesketh 1986.

McGray, J. W., 'Nuclear Deterrence: Is the War-and-Peace Pastoral Inconsistent?', *Theological Studies* 46, 1985, pp. 700–710.

McKim, R., 'An Examination of a Moral Argument against Nuclear Deterrence', *Journal of Religious Ethics* 13, 1985, pp. 279–297.

Melchin, K. R., 'Just War, Pacifism and the Ethics of Nuclear Policy', *Église et théologie* 17, 1986, pp. 41–55.

Mieth, D., 'Zum Stand der Friedensdiskussion in der katholischen Kirche', *Evangelische Theologie* 47, 1987, pp. 22–32 (includes a considerable German bibliography).

Miles, M., 'Pilgrimage as Metaphor in a Nuclear Age', *Theology Today* 45, 1988, pp. 166–179.

Miller, R. B., 'Christian Pacifism and Just-War Tenets: How Do They Diverge?', *Theological Studies* 47, 1986, pp. 448–472.

Miller, R. B., 'Tradition and Modernity in the Nuclear Age', *Journal of Religion* 65, 1985, pp. 258–270.

Moltmann, J., 'Die atomare Katastrophe: wo bleibt Gott?', *Evangelische Theologie* 47, 1987, pp. 50–60.

Moltmann, J., 'The Possible Nuclear Catastrophe and Where is God?', *Scottish Journal of Religious Studies* 9, 1988, pp. 71–83. (English version of preceding item).

Moltmann, J., 'Discipleship of Christ in an Age of Nuclear War', in *On Human Dignity*, SCM Press 1984, pp. 113–131.

Nickelsburg, G. W. E., 'The God of the Bible in a Nuclear Age', *Currents in Theology and Mission* 11, 1984, pp. 213–224.

O'Brien, W. V., 'Counterterror Deterrence/Defense and Just-War Doctrine', *Theological Studies* 48, 1987, pp. 647–676.

O'Donovan, O., 'Hope for a MAD world?', *Third Way* 9/8, August 1986, pp. 10–13; 9/9, September 1986, pp. 22–24.

Ormrod, D. and Race, A., 'Building a Theology of Disarmament in the USSR', *Theology* 88, 1985, pp. 189–199.

Paskins, B., 'Bibliography: The Ethics of Nuclear Deterrence', *Modern Churchman* 26, 1984, pp. 35–39.

Price, G. L., 'The Nuclear Issue and the Human Sciences', in *Religion and Culture: Essays in Honor of Bernard Lonergan S.J.*, ed. T. P. Fallon and P. B. Riley, State University of New York Press 1987, pp. 277–292.

Quinlan, M., 'Can the Possession of Nuclear Weapons be Morally Justifiable?', *Modern Churchman* 27/2, 1985, pp. 22–27.

Quinlan, M., 'The Ethics of Nuclear Deterrence: A Critical Comment on the Pastoral Letter of the US Catholic Bishops', *Theological Studies* 48, 1987, pp. 3–24.

Risse-Kappen, T., 'The Double Face of Deterrence: Politico-Scientific Observations on the Ecclesiastical Controversies surrounding Nuclear Deterrence and the Conduct of War', in *Politik und Ethik der Abschreckung: Theologische und sozialwissenschaftliche Bieträge zur Herausforderung der Nuklearwaffen*, ed. F. Böckle and G. Krell, Mainz: Mathias Grünewald/Munich: Chr. Kaiser 1984.

Roth, G., 'Max Weber's Ethics and the Peace Movement Today', *Theory and Society* 13, 1984, pp. 491–511.

Ruston, R., 'Apocalyptic and the Peace Movement', *New Blackfriars* 67, May 1986, pp. 204–215.

Schall, J. V., 'Apocalypse as a Secular Enterprise', *Scottish Journal of Theology* 9, 1976, pp. 357–373.

Selby, P., 'Apocalyptic – Christian and Nuclear', *Modern Churchman* 26, 1984, pp. 3–10.

Sine, T., 'Bringing down the final curtain: doomsday predictions and the God of history', *Sojourners* 13, 1984, pp. 10–14.

Taylor, M. K., 'Theology's new fact', *Theology Today* 42, 1985, pp. 78–83.

Thaidigsmann, E., 'Vermittlung oder Entscheidung: Bermerkungen zur

Friedens-Denkschrift der EKD und zur Erklärung des Moderamens des Reformierten Bundes zur Friedesverantwortung der Kirche', *Evangelische Theologie* 47, 1987, pp. 3–21.

Towner, W. Sibley, 'Tribulation and Peace: The Fate of Shalom in Jewish Apocalyptic', *Horizons in Biblical Theology* 6, 1984, pp. 1–26.

Vernant, J., 'L'Apocalypse et le nucléaire', in *Apocalypses et Voyages dans l'Au-delà*, ed. C. Kappler, Paris: Cerf 1987, pp. 449–465.

Wagar, W., 'World's end: secular eschatologies in modern fiction', in *The Secular Mind: transformations of faith in modern Europe*, ed. W. Wagar, New York: Holmes & Meier 1982, pp. 239–264.

Walters, G. J., 'Karl Jaspers on the Role of "Conversion" in the Nuclear Age', *Journal of the American Academy of Religion* 56, 1988, pp. 229–256.

Warren, M., 'Young People and the Nuclear Threat', *Concilium* 181 (5/1985) = *Youth without a future?*, ed. J. Coleman and G. Baum, T. & T. Clark 1985, pp. 83–94.

Weigart, A. J., 'Christian Eschatological Identities and the Nuclear Context', *Journal for the Scientific Study of Religion* 27, 1988, pp. 175–191.

Welch, S. D., 'A Genealogy of the Logic of Deterrence: Habermas, Foucault and a Feminist Ethic of Risk', *Union Seminary Quarterly Review* 41, 1987, pp. 13–32.

Williams, R. E., 'Christian Realism and "The Bomb": Reinhold Niebuhr on the Dilemmas of the Nuclear Age', *Journal of Church and State* 28, 1986, pp. 289–304.

Winters, F. X., 'After Tension, Détente: A Continuing Chronicle of European Episcopal Views on Nuclear Deterrence', *Theological Studies* 45, 1984, pp. 343–351.

Winters, F. X., 'Nuclear Deterrence and Morality: Atlantic Community Bishops in Tension', *Theological Studies* 43, 1982, 343–351.

Wolff, H. W., 'Use of the Bible in Theology: A Case Study', *Evangelical Review of Theology* 11, 1987, pp. 37–52.

Wren, B., 'Not Quite Damocles . . . ', *Theology* 87, 1984, pp. 276–283.

Wyschogrod, E., 'Man-Made Mass Death: Challenging Paradigms of Selfhood', *Union Seminary Quarterly Review* 38, 1983, pp. 15–28.

Yoder, J. H., 'Armaments and Eschatology', *Studies in Christian Ethics* 1, 1988.

Index of Names

Index of Subjects